D0933921

The
Presidents
and the
Prime Ministers

LAWRENCE MARTIN

The Presidents and the Prime Ministers

Washington and Ottawa Face to Face:
The Myth of Bilateral Bliss
1867-1982

1982
DOUBLEDAY CANADA LIMITED
Toronto, Ontario
DOUBLEDAY & COMPANY, INC.
Garden City, New York

Library of Congress Catalog Card Number: 82-45259

Copyright © 1982 by Lawrence Martin
All Rights Reserved
First Edition
Second Printing

Designed by Robert Burgess Garbutt
Jacket Designed by David Wyman
Printed and Bound in Canada by T. H. Best Printing Company Ltd.
Typeset by ART-U Graphics Ltd.

Canadian Cataloguing in Publication Data

Martin, Lawrence
 The presidents and the prime ministers

ISBN 0-385-17981-2

1. Canada—Relations—United States. 2. United
States—Relations—Canada. 3. Prime ministers—
Canada. 4. Presidents—United States. I. Title.

FC249.M37   327.71'073   C82-094925-6
F1029.5.U6M37

For David Martin (1944-1972)

CONTENTS

1 / 'A Little More than Kin and Less than Kind'   *1*

2 / The First Findings: John A. Macdonald and Ulysses S. Grant   *22*

3 / Games Presidents Play: Grant, Hayes, Arthur, Cleveland, and Harrison   *33*

4 / "I'm going to be ugly": Tempestuous Teddy and Wilfrid Laurier   *51*

5 / The Missing Tact of President Taft   *68*

6 / Borden and the Fight for Recognition   *82*

7 / The Last Voyage of Warren Harding   *93*

8 / Hoover Wagons, Bennett Buggies   *101*

9 / The Best Bilateral Years: Franklin Roosevelt and Mackenzie King   *113*

10 / Life with Harry   *147*

11 / Country Cousins: Ike and Uncle Louis   *166*

12 / The Diefenbaker-Kennedy Schism   *181*

13 / 'Burlesque Circus': LBJ and Lester Pearson   *212*

14 / Nixon and Trudeau: Ending Something Special   *236*

15 / Jimmy Carter and Shattered Expectations   *262*

16 / Moving Backward   *277*

Notes   *286*

Index   *293*

AUTHOR'S NOTE

The Presidents and the Prime Ministers was born one Washington night when sleep wouldn't come and thoughts stirred as to how to make the important subject of Canada-U.S. relations interesting to the general reader. The result was a decision to tell the story in the context of the leaders of the countries, thereby bringing some flesh and blood to a subject which can be intimidatingly dry. Because the focus is frequently more on the personalities than the issues, the book should not be viewed as a comprehensive study of bilateral relations. Since 115 years of history are covered in a relatively short space, the treatment in some areas is necessarily general and sweeping. Any resulting errors in interpretation or detail are the sole responsibility of the author. In keeping with the general-interest nature of the work, the number of footnotes have been limited. Frequently sources are indicated in the text itself. In important cases where they aren't, footnotes are used, provided that the people interviewed did not object to being cited.

The book is a product of the assistance and thoughtfulness of many. Special gratitude is owed to Richard Doyle, editor-in-chief of the *Globe and Mail*. Mr. Doyle made the work possible in two ways, first by having the faith in my ability to appoint me Washington correspondent of the paper, second by granting a year's leave of absence to complete the book. No one is more important in the making of a book than one's editor and at Doubleday I had a gem in Janet Turnbull. Too wise to be so young, Miss Turnbull's intelligence, judgment, considerateness, and insight make one feel very secure about the future of Canadian publishing.

The Canada Council helped make the venture financially feasible and is due many thanks. Roger Swanson provided helpful advice and his work, *Canadian-American Summit Diplomacy, 1923-1973*, is an indispensable collection of speeches and notes to anyone doing work on the subject. In the summer of 1981, Marshall Auerback, now a law student at Oxford, did some diligent research in the Canadian Public Archives. My thanks to him and to the helpful staff at the Archives, particularly Ian McClymont. The staff at the Canadian Embassy Library in Washington was most cooperative as were the people at every presidential library in the United States and at the Library of Congress in Washington. Thanks also to those who read the manuscript in advance and offered comments, to the many who granted their time for long interviews, to Washington colleagues Jean Pelletier and John Honderich, to Rick Archbold, to Anthony Westell, to the many at the *Globe and Mail* who offered advice and support, to the Cronkhite gang at Harvard who offered companionship and comic relief, and to Dermot Nolan and William Crandall for their good counsel, for their unwavering friendship, and, in keeping with the spirit of the Rogues, for their abiding dedication to the banishment of boredom. Finally my gratitude to the closest people: my parents, always with me, my brothers, especially Ian Martin who along with his wife Sandy proofread the manuscript, my sister, my precious daughter Katie, and Maureen Cussion Martin who, in the early days, with a force of conviction which only she can muster, rescued the book from oblivion.

Cambridge, Massachusetts
June 20, 1982

THE PRESIDENTS
AND THE PRIME MINISTERS
(1867-1982)

Andrew Johnson   1865-1869
Ulysses Grant   1869-1877
Rutherford Hayes   1877-1881
James Garfield   1881
Chester Arthur   1881-1885
Grover Cleveland   1885-1889
Benjamin Harrison   1889-1893
Grover Cleveland   1893-1897
William McKinley   1897-1901
Theodore Roosevelt   1901-1909
William Taft   1909-1913
Woodrow Wilson   1913-1921
Warren Harding   1921-1923
Calvin Coolidge   1923-1929
Herbert Hoover   1929-1933
Franklin Roosevelt   1933-1945
Harry Truman   1945-1953
Dwight Eisenhower   1953-1961
John Kennedy   1961-1963
Lyndon Johnson   1963-1969
Richard Nixon   1969-1974
Gerald Ford   1974-1977
Jimmy Carter   1977-1981
Ronald Reagan   1981-

John A. Macdonald   1867-1873
Alexander Mackenzie   1873-1878
John A. Macdonald   1878-1891
John Abbott   1891-1892
John Thompson   1892-1894
Mackenzie Bowell   1894-1896
Charles Tupper   1896
Wilfrid Laurier   1896-1911
Robert Borden   1911-1920
Arthur Meighen   1920-1921
Mackenzie King   1921-1926
Arthur Meighen   1926
Mackenzie King   1926-1930
R.B. Bennett   1930-1935
Mackenzie King   1935-1948
Louis St. Laurent   1948-1957
John Diefenbaker   1957-1963
Lester Pearson   1963-1968
Pierre Trudeau   1968-1979
Joe Clark   1979-1980
Pierre Trudeau   1980-

The
Presidents
and the
Prime Ministers

CHAPTER ONE

'A Little More than Kin and Less than Kind'

PRESIDENT LYNDON JOHNSON failed to appear at the helicopter landing area for Lester Pearson's arrival at Camp David. Like pall-bearers, two advisers, who showed up in his place, escorted the uneasy Canadian prime minister to their master's cabin. Johnson greeted Pearson civilly there, but unmasked a truer disposition at the sound of newsmen's cameras clicking behind him. He turned to press secretary George Reedy. "Get those bastards out of here!"

At the lunch table, silence dominated. The president drank one bloody mary instead of his usual two or three. Distant, glowering, he ordered a telephone to his side and called bureaucrats to discuss matters of no urgency. Pearson picked gingerly at his food and, for lack of more engaging enterprise, talked to Lady Bird about his helicopter flight. He knew the reason for his host's foul nature. In a speech in Philadelphia the previous evening, April 2, 1965, Pearson had denounced Johnson's decision to begin Operation Rolling Thunder—the bombing of North Vietnam. Coming from a friend and ally like Pearson, the dissent angered Johnson. Coming in the United States, "my own backyard," it enraged him.

As the luncheon dragged mercilessly on, Pearson finally chose to throw the raw meat on the table. "Well," he offered daintily, "what did you think of my speech?" LBJ's growl was audible. "Awwwful." He stretched his large hand across the table, clutched the prime minister by the upper arm, and led him on to the terrace where there was room for wrath. Striding the porch, his arms sawing the air, his sulphurous vocabulary contaminating it, Johnson ripped into Pearson full-voltage. The prime minister had betrayed the president. He had joined the ranks of ignorant liberals, "those know-nothing do-gooders," like "Walter Lippmann."

"Okay, you don't want us there [Vietnam], we can clear out, really clear out and then see what happens." Johnson was livid at the insinuation of Pearson and others that he was hawkish. The Pentagon, he stormed, had been advising him for weeks to fry the enemy area with nuclear weapons. But he had resisted. "Not bad for a warmonger!"

Inside, the houseguests minced uncomfortably around the dining-room table, not catching all the defamation, but guaranteed a resounding "Horseshit!" from the president about every three minutes.

For more than an hour he tore on until ultimately, in a piece of bilateral diplomacy knowing no equal, he moved beyond the realm of words. Having pinned the much smaller Pearson against the railing, the president of the United States grabbed him by the shirt collar, twisted it and lifted the shaken prime minister by the neck. The verbal abuse continued in a venomous torrent. "You pissed on my rug!" he thundered.

Charles Ritchie, the distinguished Canadian ambassador, was looking through the window, aghast. Jack Valenti, a Johnson aide, assured him that the president would soon calm down, and at last the noise abated. The two leaders moved inside where Pearson, having rearranged himself, was able to move the discussion topic away from his Vietnam speech and thus restore LBJ's decibel range to human levels.[1]

Then it was time to meet the press, time to let the world in on the developments of the day. First up was President Johnson. "We had a general discussion," he said. "A friendly one." Pearson was next: "I haven't much to say except that it has been a very pleasant couple of hours and I am grateful to the President for giving me the chance to come to Camp David."

The newsmen, not entirely oblivious to the smoke billowing from each man's head, were suspicious. They chased spokesmen for more details but, particularly in the Canadian case, were less than successful. Among the many papers which were misled was the *Globe and Mail*.

The headline for its half-page feature story declared: "Lester and Lyndon: A Unique Friendship." The subtitle read: "Nowhere Else are There Two Leaders Who Enjoy Such an Easy Relationship." Bruce Macdonald, the paper's Washington correspondent, was the reporter victimized by Lester Pearson and his flacks. "There appears to have been a complete absence of rancor," Macdonald waxed. "According to Canadian authorities this latest round of talks with the President was the most effective and rewarding they have undertaken.... The two men get along extremely well together."

Canadians went to bed that night satisfied, as usual, that all was well with the president and the prime minister, and that all was well with the Canada-U.S. relationship. In the prime minister's office there was relief and not a wholesale rush to amend the mistaken media reports. It was absolutely mandatory that the real story not get out. If it did, if Canadians discovered that the president had physically manhandled their prime minister, if they found out that their prime minister had been treated like the leader of one of the Soviet Union's eastern satellites, the damage to the bilateral bliss would be enormous. Irreparable.

The Ottawa press gallery was in repose, but soon Dick O'Hagan, Pearson's press secretary, was edgy. In the other capital, reports were suggesting that Camp David had not been a "very pleasant couple of hours." White House officials, to O'Hagan's regret, hadn't remained fully silent. On the same day of the flogging the president himself had met an Israeli diplomat and boastfully provided a graphic account. The diplomat, outfitted with choice Oval Office gossip, told others and the word spread.

The White House reporters hadn't uncovered the most vivid details — the fact that the president had picked up the prime minister by the scruff of the neck. They might have, had they shown more interest. But in this respect, O'Hagan had history on his side. In Washington, Canada was usually about as hot a news topic as Borneo. By 1980, the *Wall Street Journal* could still report that Canada had twelve provinces, two more than uncovered in the previous Canadian census. But on the Camp David story the American reporters did reveal that Johnson had strongly reprimanded Pearson for his Vietnam speech and this was enough to stir Canadian newspapermen. Having seen the U.S. reports, they came after O'Hagan. Macdonald, an accomplished professional, was burning. George Bain, also of the

Globe and Mail, and Arch Mackenzie of the Canadian Press, smelled a double cross.

O'Hagan, a consummate public relations man who would earn a top reputation, threw up a time-buying barricade and embarked on a campaign to refute the Washington stories. His misinformation effort was made easier in that Pearson hadn't given him all the details. O'Hagan knew it had been a profanity-infested clash but even he didn't know it had reached physical proportions.[2] It was also made easier by the availability of someone he considered an easy target among Canadian newsmen — Bruce Phillips, who was later to become one of Canada's best TV reporters. O'Hagan felt Phillips was a sucker for anti-American bait. He threw out the line, Phillips jumped like O'Hagan hoped he would, and the press secretary gloated. In a 2,500-word memorandum to Pearson he outlined his manipulation efforts:

"I also called Bruce Phillips and gave him a run-down from our standpoint. I did this because of his tendency to take an anti-U.S. position on the slightest justification and I wanted, if at all possible, to forestall what appeared to me to be a developing American propaganda line." In brackets, he added, "I was successful in this, rather to his [Phillips'] subsequent chagrin."

O'Hagan put the squeeze on Arch Mackenzie: "The next major development of note, was the publication of the Evans-Novak column. I then undertook to beat down the effects of that, and again I met with some success. You will recall that External Affairs was aroused because of the dispatch of a story from Washington from a Canadian correspondent there — Arch Mackenzie. There were a number of relatively minor facts in error which gave me an excuse to telephone Mackenzie. I talked to the ambassador about this and advocated he see Mackenzie.... At any rate Mackenzie was clearly disturbed, not knowing who to believe."

But O'Hagan didn't like the cover-up business, the idea that the reporters and the public were being geared. Showing a measure of integrity not prevalent in his business, he informed the prime minister in the same extraordinary memo that he should have been apprised of all the Camp David details, that he wanted more candour from Pearson, and that reporters deserved more candour. "I don't think we can indulge in any semantic footwork in a matter as serious as this; in other words I think I should be in a position to say something clearly to a man like Bain, even if it is to be an interpretation of something that may have been said...I think we now have to face the reality that Mackenzie, Macdonald and all the others who were professionally implicated in this affair would subscribe to Bain's proposition that consciously or not what I and other Canadian spokesmen said had the effect of playing down the idea of a disagreement and that it amounted to a 'steer in the opposite direction.'"[3]

The real Camp David story reached only some Liberal caucus members and senior public servants, among them Ed Ritchie, number two in command at External Affairs (no relation to Charles). Today the memory of Johnson's actions still rankles. "If I'd have been there I think I would have cuffed him," said Ritchie.[4] He and his colleagues couldn't imagine Johnson doing the same to Charles de Gaulle—nor to any other foreign leader.

For the rest of the Canadian population, a decade would pass until some of the particulars of the story began to emerge. O'Hagan's steer in the opposite direction, whatever his regrets, worked. It produced a steered Canadian public. In the context of the relationships between the presidents and the prime ministers, and in the context of bilateral relations generally, it produced, in other words, something not terribly unique.

The U.S. presidents and the Canadian prime ministers would meet more than eighty times, more times than the presidents would meet with any other foreign leaders, with the possible exception of the British. Virtually all of the meetings, according to the public pronouncements, would be splendid successes. The two leaders would smile after their pleasant couple of hours and expound on the accomplishments. Sometimes a "new era of consultation" would be born and it would be followed in the near future by another "new era of consultation." During each era, the Canada-U.S. discussions would always be "open and frank," and if they had that open and frank quality, there would be an excellent chance that a "great rapport" would be established. The great rapport in turn would often lead to another "historic agreement," serving to keep the "undefended border" undefended.

In the words of Prime Minister Pierre Trudeau and many other observers, the Canada-U.S. relationship would come to be "the standard for enlightened international relations." It would be the yardstick by which all other countries were to measure their relations and their behaviour with other countries. Because of this, because of the exalted image of the Canada-U.S. "special relationship," it became very important that the image be upheld, even in the trying times when the president was having the prime minister's shirt for dessert. It became so important that in the same year as Pearson's visit to Camp David a report on the bilateral relationship was released recommending that Canada-U.S. disputes be kept out of the public eye, that in effect, they be covered up. Authored by Livingston Merchant and Arnold Heeney, former ambassadors to Ottawa and Washington respectively, the report spawned considerable incredulity, being viewed as an underhanded way of preserving the "special relationship" — even if one didn't exist. That it was written by two esteemed diplomats, the calibre of Merchant and Heeney, was double cause for consternation.

But Merchant and Heeney had just experienced John Diefenbaker and John Kennedy. They knew what the relations between the presidents and the prime ministers were sometimes like. They knew that in order to help maintain harmony on the continent, in order to maintain the lustrous world image of the Canada-U.S. relationship, such a formula was probably needed.

In early 1963, the Kennedy administration had issued a press release, that did to Diefenbaker on paper what Johnson did to Pearson on the porch. It brazenly contradicted the prime minister's declarations on Canadian defence issues and on the question of nuclear weapons for NATO allies. To Arthur Krock of the New York *Times,* the press release was "one of the most hamhanded, ill-conceived and undiplomatic employments in the record of U.S. diplomacy." To the Diefenbaker government, it was calamitous. Shortly after its release, the Tories lost a non-confidence motion based largely on bungled U.S. relations and, with Diefenbaker alleging a White House plot to sack him, were tossed out in the ensuing election.

A controversy followed as to the exact role the Kennedy White House, in its "special relationship" with Canada, had played in the outcome, a Quebec lawyer named Pierre Trudeau siding with Diefenbaker's views of American interference. One of the key figures in the press release drama was McGeorge Bundy, a national security adviser to both Kennedy and Johnson. Bundy, one of the men who escorted Pearson to Johnson at Camp David, gave White House authorization for the press release. He had done it hurriedly because, as usual, there were always more important matters to see to than Canada. But after viewing its ramifications, he felt somewhat guilty. The feeling persisted into the Johnson administration, and one day he wrote a memorandum to the president which contained a suggestion that it would perhaps be a good idea to be nicer to Canadians. His memo would have interested Diefenbaker in particular. Had he seen it before he died, the stormy Tory might have felt a little better, just a little more vindicated about his accusations in the early 1960s regarding White House interference.

"I might add," Bundy wrote Johnson, "that I myself have been sensitive to the need for being extra polite to Canadians ever since George Ball and I knocked over the Diefenbaker Government by one incautious press release."[5]

The knocking over of Diefenbaker and the knocking over of Pearson, although among the low points in the history of the presidents and the prime ministers, were not entirely unrepresentative. Much of the Canada-U.S. imagery presented to the rest of the world has been little more than imagery, little more than a reflection of the candy-coating called for in the Merchant-Heeney report, and embodied in the LBJ-Pearson press conference.

Beyond the facade of the world's greatest country-to-country relationship, are preoccupied presidents who don't know about Canada, who don't have the time or inclination to care about Canada, and who presume that Canada is on the leash forever. Beyond the facade are prime ministers who, reflecting a nationalistic need of their people to 'jeer at the man across the border' have been obstreperous and sometimes peevish in their dealings with the White House; prime ministers who became exasperated with Oval Office oversight and satellite treatment and ultimately began looking for somewhere else to turn.

Most important, beyond the facade of the "special relationship" are two countries bound by geographic and economic necessity but losing the tie that really binds—the tie of spirit. The spirit of the continental relationship is primarily the responsibility of the presidents and the prime ministers. They set the guiding tone, the leading temperament. If there is genuine warmth and harmony between them, there is usually the same between the countries.

In the bilateral context the responsibility falls somewhat heavily on the president, for he is the player who carries the weight. He is the leader who, much more than the prime minister, can make things happen.

Following his stint as U.S. ambassador to Canada in the late 1970s

Kenneth Curtis, a former governor of Maine, said somewhat sadly that, to his knowledge, no American president had ever taken time to work on the Canadian relationship.[6] In fairness to the chief executives, he was slightly incorrect. Since Canadian confederation there have been twenty-three presidents and twenty-two have not worked to any appreciable degree on the Canadian relationship. The one exception was Franklin Delano Roosevelt. He and Prime Minister William Lyon Mackenzie King fashioned the one period in Canada-U.S. history when the relationship was truly shining: 1935 to 1945. In the other years, in the other 105 years since the birth of Canada, the relationship has hardly been special. There have been some good years, notably the fifteen following FDR, and there have been flashes of promise for great years. But no other president could sustain an interest in the country like Roosevelt.

FDR was a gem for Canada. He loved the land. His family owned a summer home at Campobello, New Brunswick, and young Franklin spent his summers there fishing, boating, golfing, and learning about the country and its people. It was in the waters beside his Canadian cottage that he contracted polio. The disease crippled him at the age of thirty-nine, in the prime of his life, and the memory of that tragedy would keep him away from his beloved island for more than a decade. But the memory wouldn't stain his regard for the northern country whose vastness and potential captivated him. In office, he visited Canada more times than any other president, he had the prime ministers to Washington more than any other, and he kept the prime ministers more informed of major developments. He accorded Canada and its leader the treatment of a major power. He came to know Canadians and Canadian issues. Roosevelt could name members of Canadian cabinets, a feat unheard of for presidents. He had a lasting concern for the Quebec problem, and while World War II raged, he sat down one day and wrote a long letter to Mackenzie King on his conceptions of it, giving the prime minister advice on how the French could be more easily assimilated.

The skeptics would suggest that Roosevelt was seeking to use King and Canada to his own selfish ends. There is likely some truth in what they say as there is likely some truth in ascribing selfish motivations to the actions of any world leader. But whatever his purpose, the end result was that the Roosevelt-King years were the ones when the bilateral clichés took on real meaning, when milestone trade and defence agreements helped get the countries healthily through the war, and when Canada and the United States did set the "standard for enlightened international relations." During this period, Franklin Roosevelt, sensing it all, would write King and say it himself: "Sometimes I indulge in the thoroughly sanctimonious and pharisaical thought, which I hope that you are occasionally guilty of, that it is a grand and glorious thing for Canada and the United States to have the team of Mackenzie and Roosevelt at the helm in days like these."

Because of its impressive performance in World War II and in the organization of NATO and the United Nations, and because so many other countries were war-ravaged, Canada became a more powerful world force in the post-Roosevelt period. But the ingredients in FDR's success with Canada—knowledge, interest, respect—were not to be found to the same degree or even close to the same degree in the succeeding presidents. The perception took hold again among Canadians that White House deliberations in respect to their country were made while the presidents were sleepwalking. Pearson was most struck by the ignorance of Dwight Eisenhower about Canada. After one trip to the White House, he came out shaking his head, stunned that Ike, the golfing president, hadn't heard of a particular Canadian concern: "You'd think his caddy would have mentioned it to him."

Canadian officials have two favourite phrases to describe the Washington attitude to their country: "taken for granted," and "benign neglect." Most U.S. officials grant there is some truth to both. Generally Americans see Canada as a powerless, fifty-first-state type of neighbour, a thin band of cities and towns stretching along the edge of the border, hugging the United States in suitably satellite style.

There is no recognition in the White House or among Americans generally that Canada, as Pearson and Livingston Merchant argued, has become the most important country to the United States in the noncommunist world. Economically there is no argument as no other nation is in the same league as Canada in significance. By a vast margin it is the United States' largest trading partner. In terms of strategic value, the other most important criteria, the United States could less afford to lose Canada as an ally than any other country. West Germany and Britain make far more important military contributions to NATO than Canada, but their strategic locations do not equal in importance for the Americans the giant land mass that separates the United States from the USSR.

Most of the presidents have either been unaware of Canada's

importance, as when Richard Nixon said that Japan was his largest trading partner, or have chosen to ignore it. Franklin Roosevelt's concern and understanding have been displaced in large part by disinterest and ignorance. Not disinterest and ignorance with respect to the bilateral issues, but in areas somewhat more basic to the relationship. With the presidents and their relations with the prime ministers it is first necessary to start with what has been among the highest of the hurdles—knowing the prime ministers' names.

From the overall perspective, it should be understood initially that it has not been the American way to achieve erudition in other ways besides the American way. Essentially an isolationist country from its birth in 1776 until 1940, there was never as compelling a need for Americans to address international questions as there was for other countries. This deficiency, on occasion, has had a way of manifesting itself. At Harvard University, a story is told about an opinion sampling taken in Cincinnati, Ohio. The respondents were asked in a multiple choice format to identify names by circling the appropriate corresponding word or phrase. In identifying U Thant, secretary general of the United Nations, there was some difficulty. Many Americans chose "submarine."

As for the presidents themselves, they were late arrivals internationally. The first twenty-four presidents never set foot outside of the United States. Teddy Roosevelt finally broke the tradition, travelling to Panama in 1906, and Woodrow Wilson became the first president to travel overseas, going to the Paris Peace Conference after World War I—142 years into the country's history. But in itself, the history of detachment can hardly explain the difficulties the chief executives have encountered with some of the more rudimentary aspects of the Canadian scene.

President Harry Truman called a press conference in January 1949 to announce, among other things, that he had a visitor coming from Canada. He delivered a short two-paragraph statement in which he alluded to the prime minister of Canada five times without mentioning his name. Finally Tony Vaccaro, an Associated Press reporter, interrupted. "For bulletin purposes, sir," he said half-jokingly, "what's his name?" "I was very carefully trying to avoid it," said Truman, "because I don't know how to pronounce it." Then he tried: "Louis St. Laurent—L-a-u-r-e-n-t. I don't know how to pronounce it. That's a French pronunciation. I wouldn't attempt to pronounce it. Tony, you put me on the spot." "I was myself on the spot," said Vaccaro.

Given the state of the post-war world, St. Laurent's Canada was the world's fourth largest power. A dignified gentleman, he did not fancy his name being so obscure. Soon he received a letter from one William Wilson of a Philadelphia radio station:

"Dear Mr. Prime Minister...I think there is no one better acquainted with how your name should be pronounced than you. Will you be kind enough to break your name down syllabically, displaying the proper accent. In order to facilitate the interpretation please think of some English name or word which rhymes with your name....Thank you very much for your attention. You may enter your outline in the spaces provided below."

Pearson's suspicions about Eisenhower were borne out during a visit in 1960 by Diefenbaker to the White House. "Every member of this company," said the president, "feels a very definite sense of honor and distinction in the privilege of having with us tonight the Prime Minister of the Great Republic of Canada." Having their country referred to as a Republic was disillusioning to the Canadian guests, but if any of the White House officials noticed the gaffe, they didn't tell Ike. He did it again on the same visit.

Diefenbaker had served three years as prime minister by the time John Kennedy became president yet Kennedy still had not heard the prime minister's name enough to be able to pronounce it properly. To avoid a Truman-style embarrassment, he asked Secretary of State Dean Rusk to check it out. Rusk took the problem to a department official of German origin and reported promptly that the correct pronunciation was "Diefenbawker." The president told a press conference that he would be delighted to be welcoming Prime Minister "Diefenbawker" to the White House. Diefenbaker, burdened by the incredible size of his ego throughout his tempestuous tenure, was astounded. The Kennedy slip marked a frightful beginning to a disastrous relationship. It was also a sorry start to the Kennedy-Rusk relationship. Recalled Rusk, "Kennedy was furious with me."[7]

When President Johnson wasn't blaspheming Pearson with names, he was getting his name wrong. Welcoming the Nobel Prize-winning prime minister to his Texas home before a cluster of TV cameras, Johnson announced that it was great to have "Mr. Wilson" there and that he was about to take Wilson on a tour of the ranch.

Johnson's brass extended to his bodyguards. On a visit to Canada in 1967, the Johnson entourage moved *en masse* into Pearson's cottage residence at Harrington Lake. After the talks broke off one evening,

Pearson started toward his washroom and was confronted by a broad-shouldered Johnson guard standing in the hallway. "Who are you and where are you going?" he demanded. Pearson looked up at his chin. "I'm the Prime Minister of Canada, I live here and I'm about to go and have a leak."

Richard Nixon's difficulty wasn't so much in remembering the name Trudeau as it was in the adjectives he sometimes selected to bestow on it, one being "asshole."

Although presidents addressed the Canadian Parliament as early as FDR's day, Trudeau was the first Canadian prime minister to speak before the Congress. He was quickly baptized into the world of congressional enlightenment that day when, after his oration, congressman Clement Zablocki of Wisconsin appraised it: "Some members of Congress didn't think a Canadian could speak such good English."

The isolated occurrences, though not a fair reflection of the overall treatment, indicate some of the effrontery Canadians have endured at the hands of Americans. Ulysses Grant began the Canada-U.S. relationship rather inauspiciously when, shortly after Confederation, he started vying to absorb the new Canada. He wanted it in time for his re-election bid in 1872. His plan was to work out a deal with the British, who owed the United States compensation for damages inflicted by the *Alabama*, a boat built in British yards for use by the south in the Civil War. Grant's pitch? Press the British to cede Canada in exchange for the damages caused by the boat.[8] It was an early-day American example of linkage.

Rutherford B. Hayes bubbled with the prospect of gaining Canada, Grover Cleveland ordered a boycott against all goods from the country, and Teddy Roosevelt considered it a shame that Canada wasn't part of the Union—a shame for Canadians more than for Americans. Particularly enchanted with the Canadian west, he wrote that it "should lie wholly within our limits...less for our sake than for the sake of the men who lie along their banks." As Americans, these people "would hold positions incomparably more important, grander and more dignified than they can ever hope to reach."

As Roosevelt's successor, William Taft discovered in an embarrassing way that, despite Teddy's magnanimity, Canadians preferred to lie along their own banks, however shabby. Taft pushed for a free-trade agreement with Canada, publicly proclaiming that it was not a step toward annexation, while privately writing that it could be. Canadians, ever suspicious of the intent of presidents, sided with his private view, defeating the proposal and dealing a president one of the most costly blows ever rendered by Canada.

The Taft presidency closed the first of four distinguishable periods in the Oval Office-Ottawa relationship. The first, from 1867 to 1911, was the period of the annexationist presidents and the powerless prime ministers. The ten presidents of the period, eight of whom were Republicans, were not blatantly bent on taking over Canada, but it was the privately expressed wish of most and the policy of a few. Not until a pressured Taft formally renounced northern territorial ambitions could Canadians—those who didn't want to be annexed—cast off such fears. Canadian foreign policy through this period was ultimately controlled by London, a source of acute aggravation for the prime ministers in dealing with the White House.

The second period, from 1911 to 1932, was the age of aloof and indifferent presidents. Although Canada threw off its British bondage in this time, and although it gained control of its foreign policy in Washington, and gained world respect as a separate entity with its war performance, the presidents showed less interest in Canada in this era than in the first, when the prospect of annexation had danced in their dreams.

Calvin Coolidge typified for Canada the sleepwalker breed of president in these two decades. "Cool Cal" once made the remark: "When people are out of work, unemployment results." On Canada he held views of comparable depth. One of his few statements on the country in his files showed him wondering, though born in the border state of Vermont, whether Toronto was near a lake.

Woodrow Wilson and Herbert Hoover were only slightly more interested. But an exception in this period was Warren Harding, the Ohio Republican who became the first sitting president to visit Canada officially when he stopped off in Vancouver, British Columbia on his way back from Alaska in 1923. The Canadian reception was glorious, and surprisingly emotional, matching that usually accorded a member of the royal family. Harding, a handsome president, his voice sonorous and comforting, responded with what still ranks as the most beautiful of speeches made by presidents in Canada. But the splendour of his day blackened as his hidden health problems chose Vancouver to unveil themselves. He fell ill while playing golf with his

Canadian hosts, cut short his round, and returned to his hotel suite for rest. Doing his best to camouflage exhaustion, doing his best to thank a city that had displayed deep admiration, he completed his public duties for the day. Then he sailed out of a dark Vancouver harbour, never to make it back to Washington alive.

With the Harding visit a trend indicating the "who's who" of the relationship began. Canadian prime ministers would visit the presidents close to four times for every once the presidents would reciprocate. The U.S. leaders' appearances in Canada would usually come when they were nearing, or in, election campaigns, Canada being considered a good publicity trip.

The "special relationship" was such that the first visit by a prime minister to Washington was in 1871, and the first visit by a president to the Canadian capital of Ottawa was seventy-two years later, in 1943. Franklin Roosevelt was the guest. Shattering the tradition of detachment, he saw King on nineteen separate occasions, leaving his wife, Eleanor, to puzzle over what interested him in the Canadian she considered boring. Roosevelt ushered in the good-neighbour era of Canada-U.S. relations, a period which, though declining with his successors, lasted roughly from 1933 to 1959. Following FDR's death in 1945, there was ominous speculation in Ottawa over his replacement, the governor-general telling Prime Minister King that Harry Truman was a "crook." But King warmed to Truman, and the Truman administration warmed to King, so much so that it pushed for a free-trade plan that revived annexationist fears in the prime minister.

In 1952, following two decades of Democrats, Eisenhower brought the Republicans back to the White House. The Republicans were the party of least favour in Canada and would remain so. The party and its presidents had been more annexationist than the Democrats. They introduced high protective tariffs which shut out Canadian manufacturers. They were élitist, big business, and considered more condescending toward Canada. Particularly in the post-1950 period, the Grand Old Party was the one which chose to fight inflation instead of unemployment as its top priority. War on inflation usually resulted in recession, and recession in the United States normally meant recession in Canada. The coolness of Canadians to the right side of the political spectrum, the Republican side, was demonstrated by the country's election results. For sixty of the twentieth century's first eighty-two years, Liberal governments were in power. If Canadians had been selecting the presidents, the Democrats would have been the big winners—all the way up to Jimmy Carter winning over Ronald Reagan.

Eisenhower, however, came in as a most popular Republican in Canadian eyes. He had commanded Canadian armies in the war and had been accorded a hero's welcome on a post-war visit to Ottawa. His attitude toward Canada was avuncular, benign, and more platitudinous than pointed. As Pearson's problem with him suggested, he never let knowledge of the country get in the way of his dealings with it. The detail work was left to Secretary of State John Foster Dulles, and although Canadian officials respected his ability, they also found him a pompous boor. Canadian ambassador Arnold Heeney, who had the pleasure of hosting the Dulles' for dinner, reflected on the experience: "Our dinner for the Dulles' was good except for the Dulles'."[9] To Heeney he was a "strange, almost gauche creature... lacking or spurning any social graces." To other Canadian officials like George Glazebrook, he was the prototype American power-pusher that Canadians disliked most, a bull-headed autocrat who, in Kremlinesque fashion, would haul in the wayward client state's representative and issue orders, blowtorch style, to obey or pay the consequences.

Initially, it was because of this kind of thing, because of the Canadian perception of being pushed around, that the good-neighbour era died and the unending era of distance and doubt was born.

The feeling of being bullied by U.S. presidents was not a new one in Canada. It was in place in 1867, and continued in varying degrees throughout history. In the early post-Confederation period, the feeling was sharp because the prime ministers, who would sometimes go to Washington for extended periods to negotiate Canada-U.S. matters as part of British commissions, were always beaten at the bargaining table. They were pitted not only against the American presidents, whose power even in those pre-super-status periods was many times greater, but also the desires of the British, whose final say on the Canadian position was often more pliant than Ottawa's. The repeated losses of the prime ministers, engendering strong anti-American strains, triggered demands for foreign policy independence in Washington which Britain granted in the 1920s. The prime ministers were then in a position to back up their noise with decision, but they also faced the prospect of negotiating with Washington without having the power of the British as leverage. They were on their own. They were the little men against the giants and the perception endured and still endures today that they were browbeaten, domineered, and that like Pearson on Johnson's porch, they wilted under the pressure.

But as much as conventional wisdom suggests it is true, as much as self-flagellating Canadians might like to think it is true, the prime ministers have not been afraid to stand up to the presidents. Although always sensitive to the disproportionate power of the neighbour to the south, the prime ministers, in most cases, have demonstrated a stubbornness and fiery pride which, although insufficient for Canadian nationalists who crave a Tito of the West, repudiates any cowering stereotypes.

John A. Macdonald would alienate all of Washington with displays of contempt for the presidents and their men. When the Cleveland administration called for a boycott of Canada, it would witness the brave albeit slightly ludicrous spectacle of Macdonald and his Defence minister threatening to take up arms and redo 1812. Wilfrid Laurier, visiting President McKinley in Chicago, would speak to an audience entirely in French and tell complaining Americans that if they didn't like it, it was too bad. Robert Borden would line up the Dominions against the wishes of Woodrow Wilson at the Paris Peace Conference. R. B. Bennett would hand the unpopular Herbert Hoover the ultimate snub by refusing to be seen with him. After Ottawa and Washington had put together a free-trade package in the late 1940s, King would tell the Truman administration to forget it, just like Canadians had told Taft to forget his plan in 1911. St. Laurent would inform a stalling Truman that Canada had waited long enough and was going ahead on plans for the development of the St. Lawrence Seaway by itself. Compelled to attend an Eisenhower election year publicity junket in West Virginia, St. Laurent would put in the most disdainful of performances, embarrassing even his Canadian colleagues. Diefenbaker would treat Kennedy with contempt. Pearson, though battered at Camp David, would have the courage to go into the United States and criticize the Vietnam war in the first place, something other foreign leaders wouldn't do. And Trudeau, indomitable on the international stage, not about to be pushed anywhere by anyone, would tell the presidents that Canada wanted to do some looking— elsewhere.

If the performances of the prime ministers are a reflection of the character of their countrymen, there is some grit and determination there.

But there is a streak of masochism in the Canadian view of the White House which makes Canadians reluctant to accept the notion that their prime ministers have been firm in the face of presidential abuse. Such a notion is a threat to many Canadians' deeply imbedded poor-us psyche, which requires that the presidents subjugate the prime ministers. Teddy Roosevelt noticed as early as the turn of the century, and Pearson and Dean Rusk noticed later, that anti-Americanism is a Canadian necessity.

"Canadians," said the first Roosevelt, "like to indulge themselves as a harmless luxury in a feeling of hostility to the United States. Practically this does not operate at all. Practically Canada will take an American, Van Horne, to run its railway system and America will take a Canadian, Hill, to run its.... But the average Canadian likes to feel patriotic by jeering at the man across the border, just as to a lesser degree the average Scotchman for similar reasons adopts a similar attitude toward England."

Pearson, who in the United States is considered Canada's greatest statesman, took the thought a step further, asserting: "worry about the Americans and their friendly pressures is still probably the strongest unifying Canadian force. At a time when some of us are in doubt about the nature or even the reality of a separate Canadian identity... we can stand shoulder to shoulder, one thin but unbroken red line facing Washington and proclaim: 'No surrender.'"

The Canadian attitude was a factor which exacerbated the strains. Predisposed to the suspicion of Oval Office subjugation, Canadians would tend to find neglectful treatment by the presidents on occasions when it wasn't there. Sometimes they might have done well to question the behaviour of their own prime ministers toward the White House. "Sometimes," said Jack Pickersgill, a cabinet member and adviser to prime ministers for three decades, "I thought they treated us like adults and we often acted like adolescents."

Rusk, secretary of state for Kennedy and Johnson, grew distressed in his Canadian diplomatic ventures, finding in the Ottawa officials a "knee-jerk disposition to disagree—just to demonstrate independence." Finally, at a NATO foreign ministers' meeting, he decided he'd taken enough, and when Paul Martin, External Affairs minister, asked him his position on a certain issue, he used a new tact. "My friend," said Rusk, "you speak first because if you speak first I might be able to agree with you. But if I speak first, you would be compelled to disagree."[10]

In 1960, the turning point year, the year when the strong Canada-U.S. spirit built by Roosevelt and King began to crumble, the Canadian disposition to disagree would be provided with the ingredients of unprecedented growth. The presidents of 1960 and beyond would sag to new depths of carelessness and neglect in their treatment of Canada. Foremost among the offenders would be John Kennedy who, in his period with Diefenbaker, acted as though he thought he could control Canada as if it were one of his limbs. The prime ministers of 1960 and beyond would be more anti-American in their approach than their predecessors. Foremost among the new breed was Diefenbaker, who was less willing to buckle under presidential power than any other prime minister. The personal relationship between the leaders from 1960 on would be either dreadful, distant, or disappointing. Finally the Canadian condition from 1960 on would be more nationalist than in any period since Theodore Roosevelt.

All the signals were ominous. Even before Kennedy came to power, Diefenbaker's mail—and mail was so important to his perception of the public will—was telling him Canadians felt they were being pushed around on economic and defence issues. But Diefenbaker liked Eisenhower too much to confront him personally on the problem. He had a rapport, a friendship with this president, and it was important to him. He would tell friends he could get Ike any time just by picking up the phone at his elbow. The disputes could await the election of a president for whom he had no respect. On that president's arrival, the Canada-U.S. good-will era would explode.

Observers would saddle Diefenbaker with the burden of blame. But the seeds of his personal feud with Kennedy and therefore the seeds of the era of hostility were planted as much by the young president as by Diefenbaker. In the nascent stages of their relationship, the vital stages, it was Diefenbaker who would show some good will, and Kennedy a haughty disregard. It was Kennedy who publicly ridiculed Diefenbaker's ability to speak French. It was Kennedy who, to the prime minister's face, mocked one of Diefenbaker's chief sources of pride — his ability to fish. It was Kennedy who couldn't pronounce his name properly. It was Kennedy who, after being told privately by Diefenbaker that Canada was not interested in joining the Organization of American States, went over the head of the prime minister with a call to the Canadian public to join anyway. It was Kennedy who left behind a memorandum in Ottawa which did not, as legacy has it, refer to Diefenbaker as an S.O.B., but which was imperious and insulting in tone.

The Kennedy posture toward Diefenbaker's Canada was that of a president stretching his legs across the Canadian border and demanding a shoeshine. With Pearson, a person Kennedy could admire, the border links were slightly rebuilt, but the president's death came too soon, and his replacement Johnson was as incompatible with Pearson as Kennedy was with Diefenbaker. After the prime minister's Vietnam speech and Camp David, a constructive relationship was impossible — the loss of bilateral respect illustrated one night when Rusk spotted ambassador Ed Ritchie at a reception. The usually urbane Rusk cornered the ambassador, demanded a meeting to set him straight on some issues and, setting the time and place, snapped, "And you better wear your asbestos shorts cause I'm going to burn your ass."[11]

Ill fortune became a significant contributor to the ill will. The string of opposite personalities in the seats of power continued. In Pierre Trudeau and Richard Nixon, the personality mix alone was a recipe for disaster. With economic nationalism a booming business in Canada, with the United States locked in a war as unpopular north of the border as anywhere else, with America losing more respect in Canada as a result of assassinations, racial riots and economic misery, opportunity was a missing word in the purview of bilateral relations.

Nixon revealed his regard for Canada in August 1971 when, as part of an American balance of payments overhaul, he announced the imposition of a ten percent surcharge on imports. Canada, traditionally exempted or at least informed well in advance of such far-reaching trade measures, was neither exempted nor informed well in advance and Trudeau began to wonder about what Mr. Nixon was up to. "Has America stopped loving us?" the prime minister asked. He met with Nixon in Ottawa in April of 1972 and it was one of those occasions in which the atmospherics were in harmony with the intent.

Snow was still on the ground and, imagining that Canadian demonstrators might wish to throw snowballs at President Nixon, government officials exercised considerable foresight. They called in a platoon of hosers from the Public Works Department and the men hosed down the snow with steaming hot water until it disappeared.

At the prime minister's office, Bob Haldeman's advance men arrived and quickly won no friends. They didn't like the tan colour of Mr. Trudeau's furniture because it wouldn't provide a suitable backdrop for the president on television. They attempted, failingly, to have it changed to blue. There was a problem with the Canadian arrangements to have the president stay at Government House, the home of the governor-general. The president didn't want to stay there. He would stay at his ambassador's residence, they suggested. And about the grand gala at the National Arts Centre—the president would have other business to look after, they said. He could only afford a few token minutes at the gala.

Henry Kissinger, a bachelor at this time, needed a date. The prime minister's office lined up Charlotte Gobeil, an attractive local television personality. Miss Gobeil was escorted by Kissinger to the entertainment gala, where one unknown troupe from one unknown corner of the north country followed another unknown troupe from another unknown corner, until the oozing Canadiana was such that a squirming Kissinger turned to Gobeil. "My God," he grumbled. "When is this going to end? How many more acts?"[12]

There were other problems at the gala. Flower boxes on the first tier dripped water on the people below. A queasy, courtly matron rumbled through the rows toward the ladies' salon but didn't make it. Having forgotten his security pass, cabinet member Jean Marchand was escorted back out onto Wellington Street, shouting, "Don't you know who I am?" Haldeman was furious at not being able to get Nixon out of the Arts Centre immediately after the performance and chose to parade his anger in front of everyone.

There were problems after the gala. It had been kind of an uneven evening for Mr. Kissinger and Miss Gobeil, the latter taking advantage of the occasion to attack his war strategy. "Your Vietnamization policy? It's a flop, isn't it?" The secretary of state had no intention of escorting her home. But when Miss Gobeil grabbed him by the arm in the parking lot in front of many dignitaries and clamoured that she was his date and the very least he could do was drop her off, Kissinger didn't have much choice. "You're absolutely right," he said. "You're absolutely right."

But the timing was bad. Miss Gobeil invited Kissinger in for a drink and Kissinger, though Nixon wanted him for an important meeting on Vietnam, obliged. Inside, she was about to get some wine when she heard the shower running. It was located next to her bedroom and she walked there, with Kissinger, to her disappointment, following. At the doorway they looked in to see a male companion of Miss Gobeil's climbing out of the shower, naked. Kissinger flinched, was introduced to designer Bob Smith, and quickly repaired to the living room.[13] When Smith, who had thought he was seeing an oversized *Time* magazine cover coming through the door, was presentable, the three had a quick drink, Miss Gobeil noticing that Kissinger "had kind of lost interest." On the way out, several Kissinger security guards, not having seen Smith enter, accosted him, and the secretary of state had to come to his rescue, explaining that he was a friend. Relieved to be free of Miss Gobeil, Kissinger returned to Government House where, with Nixon, he made an important decision on the Vietnam war.

The visit, not entirely saturated with good will, turned out to be an appropriate one for Nixon to make a major statement, a statement of telling significance, on the Canada-U.S. relationship.

The past speeches of the presidents and the prime ministers, he explained in addressing Parliament, tended to be cliché-ridden exercises that camouflaged the "real problems" between the countries. "They have tended to create the false impression that our countries are essentially alike."

Now, Nixon said, "It is time for Canadians and Americans to move beyond the sentimental rhetoric of the past. It is time for us to recognize that we have very separate identities; that we have significant differences; and that nobody's interests are furthered when these realities are obscured."

Nixon, in effect, was declaring an end to the special relationship between the two countries. It was time, he was saying, to recognize a new reality on the continent. Trudeau was looking on happily. He had known what Nixon was going to say and he had wanted him to say it.[14] Like Nixon, he thought the special relationship unworkable and undesirable. He was intrigued by the prospect of finding something to replace it. After more than one hundred years in which the countries had moved closer together, the president and the prime minister had decided for many reasons that it would be best if they started moving apart.

CHAPTER TWO

The First Findings: John A. Macdonald and Ulysses S. Grant

IT WAS DECEMBER 8, 1870, and in the opinion of John A. Macdonald it would be "a century" before Canada would be "strong enough to walk alone." Ulysses S. Grant, on this day, was issuing one of the only State of the Union addresses in which Canada would merit mention. The Republican president, as yet unscarred by the scandals which would shadow his stewardship, called the three-year-old country an "irresponsible agent." It was "vexatious…unfriendly…unneighbourly." Citing harsh acts by Ottawa against American fishermen, he asked Congress for special authority: "I recommend you to confer upon the Executive the power to suspend by proclamation the operation of the laws authorizing the transit of goods, wares and merchandise across the territory of the United States to Canada." Further, "to suspend the operation of any laws whereby the vessels of the Dominion of Canada are permitted to enter the waters of the United States."

On Prime Minister Macdonald's orders Canadian authorities had seized hundreds of U.S. fishing vessels in maritime waters. The Americans had allegedly violated an ambiguous fifty-year-old treaty setting the boundary on the east coast. Grant, outraged at Macdonald's nerve, was requesting special retaliatory powers so that he could teach the Canadian some manners if the abuse continued.

The eighteenth president had great difficulty with Canada. Its very existence bothered him. Since his first days in office one of his goals was to make it part of the United States. Annexation of Canada would more than double the U.S. land mass. It would remove a potential source of conflict from the continent. It would satisfy the demands of Manifest Destiny. It would be a nice plus for Grant's re-election campaign. It would look good on his resumé.

His first idea was to slay the infant country softly. Induce England to allow a referendum in Canada on total independence from the motherland. Canada would vote yes, the young president assumed, and then it would be a simple matter for the Americans to walk in and absorb. No British guns would offer protection. Grant, who guided the Union forces to victory in the Civil War, would hardly have to draw on his experience.

Secretary of State Hamilton Fish, one of the best at the job the United States would produce, thought Grant was overly optimistic. The goal was laudable, he noted in his diary, but the timetable formidable. On Grant's request he saw Sir Edward Thornton, the British ambassador to Washington, and in as much as Ottawa had no control over its foreign policy, the Canadian ambassador as well. Not a chance, said Thornton. He didn't care about the Dominion, and London wasn't fussy either. But the Canadians didn't want total independence. Macdonald would set up a howl. He and his government knew that it would be tantamount to U.S. annexation, Thornton said. They wouldn't agree to a referendum.

Grant had another idea—have Britain cede Canada to him in exchange for damages rendered on the Union forces by the British-built warship, the *Alabama*. A straight-up, uncomplicated deal. For two years, he pushed the proposal but London was unwilling to relinquish a country that was adamant about not being relinquished. "The Canadians," Thornton told Fish, "find great fault with me for saying as openly as I do that we are ready to let them go whenever they shall wish."

Fish believed that Canadian opinion favoured independence and perhaps annexation. "I referred to the number of Canadians now resident in the United States, the influx of French Canadians into the States, the number of mechanics and laborers who come here for the greater part of the year." With the exception of the Canadian élite, he said, there is "a very large preponderance of sentiment in favor of separation from Great Britain."[1]

But the Gladstone government held firm and now Grant, another annexation plan thwarted, his resentment pricked by a brash prime minister's escapades in the maritimes, was getting testy. The Ohio-born West Point graduate had several weaknesses as president: an inability to choose responsible advisers, an affair with the bottle, an appalling lack of class, and like several occupants of the Oval Office in his time, an ignorance of foreign affairs. But one thing Grant did have was grit. No one questioned that. He had rebounded from every career crash. On the battlefield he had sprung back from desperate circumstance. On his death bed, contesting the agony of cancer, he would complete his memoirs two days before passing away. "I can't spare this man," Lincoln once said as pressures to dismiss Grant climbed. "He fights."

Ottawa was at least a little fearful that the president would do something rash, like take up arms. It would not be out of character for him. Nor, at this stage of its history, would it be out of character for his country.

It was America's "Manifest Destiny," John O'Sullivan, editor of the *Democratic Review*, wrote in 1844, "to overspread the continent allotted by Providence for the free development of our multiplying millions." One of history's more turgid pronouncements, the Manifest Destiny philosophy meant it was not only in the United States' interest to expand on the continent but its duty. Room was needed for the population to spread, for the superior political system to spread, for the natural dynamism to flex. The doctrine would be used to support the purchase of Alaska, the annexation of Hawaii, and the U.S. entry into the Spanish-American war.

Andrew Johnson, Grant's hapless predecessor and the first president Canada faced, was among the many who thought the doctrine should apply to Canada. For the Dominion, whose birth in 1867 he neglected to acknowledge by congratulatory telegram or any means, Johnson had what he termed a "national policy." Upon the acquisition of Alaska in 1868, he said that "comprehensive national policy would seem to sanction the acquisition and incorporation into our federal union of the several adjacent continental and insular communities." But Johnson's presidency was plagued by adversity. Much of the first half was spent trying to dispel the belief that he was a drunkard. On the day he was inaugurated vice-president, he drank too much in trying to curb a cold, turned in a teetering performance, and was forever saddled with the image. Much of the second half was spent trying to fight off impeachment. There was no time for his national policy.

In 1870, with his annexation strategies failing, with the fisheries quarrel continuing, President Grant came to a cabinet meeting in a Manifest Destiny kind of mood. He had studied the boundary treaty and was convinced Macdonald was in error. He looked over his unspectacular cabinet group, went into a harangue over the fisheries, and lit up all faces with a declaration that he was ready to "take Canada and wipe out her commerce...."[2] He would ask Congress to declare war, he said, but for the fact that there was a large debt. Hamilton Fish shook his head discouragingly. Treasury Secretary George Boutwell urged patience, at least until Congress voted funds. "Oh yes," said Grant. "But really I am tired of all this arrogance and assumption."

Atlantic coast fisheries jurisdiction was an issue that had plagued relations between the North American neighbours since 1776. It was an issue that would plague bilateral relations all the way into the Pierre Trudeau-Ronald Reagan era. It would take its place along with four other issues at the top of the Canada-U.S. disputes list: continental defence, free trade and investment, boundaries, the environment.

The fisheries were the richest in the world. As American colonies prior to the revolution, the American states enjoyed the same rights to the waters as the northern colonies. The Treaty of Paris, which ended the revolution, changed little, but the War of 1812 led the British to withdraw many of the American privileges. U.S. fishermen were given access to offshore areas but, to the more rich waters inside the three-mile coastal zones, they were allowed entry only for shelter and other non-fishing purposes, and only upon purchase of licences. These conditions remained until 1854 when another agreement appeared to satisfy everyone. Inshore rights were given to the Americans in return for a free-trade pact with the Dominion on natural products. However, alleged British and Canadian support for the south in the Civil War, along with the suspicion that the Canadians were getting the better of the 1854 deal, prompted Washington to cancel the trade concessions. The treaty was thereby abrogated, the rules of 1818 came back into effect, and an angry Macdonald began ordering the boat seizures.

The fisheries were of overwhelming importance to the economies of the New England states and the Canadian provinces. Macdonald described them as "our Alsace and Lorraine." He was well aware of the hostility festering in Mr. Grant, and of the president's wish to annex Canada. He knew also of Grant's support for the Fenian raids. The Fenians, a hysterically anti-British group of Irish-Americans, were willing to do anything to enrage London, and the takeover of Canada was thought to be appropriate—for the Fenians and for the presidents. President Johnson had countenanced the first invasions a few years earlier saying he would recognize the establishment of a Fenian Republic in Canada. At that time the incursions were repelled, but, in August of 1870, the Fenians were massing for another attack and the always upright Mr. Fish asked Mr. Grant if it would perhaps be wise to seize their arms to prevent the aggression. Grant said no, let them attack. They did, the Fenians were repelled again, and yet another piece of presidential scheming against the Dominion was dashed.

Finally, faced with an empty war chest, faced with the prospect that a conflict with Canada would bring in Britain, and faced with pressure from his secretary of state, President Grant agreed to attempt a negotiated settlement on the fisheries, along with other Canadian issues, and the *Alabama* claims. The British, bogged down with European difficulties, would be anxious for an easy settlement, Grant was advised. More important was the Canadian angle. Britain would be doing the negotiating for Canada and Britain didn't even desire the Dominion any more. Thornton had told the White House as much. It was only because Canadians wanted the connection that the connection remained. To suspect that London would put up a hard-bargaining front for a country it barely cared about while risking good relations with Washington was unreasonable.

John A. Macdonald had many reasons to be depressed in 1870 and, as he nursed his bad health, his sick child, and his endless bottles of port, the thought of being pushed into an unjust fisheries settlement by Grant and Thornton pained him constantly. As a sop to the Dominion, the British had decided that one Canadian could sit on its five-member commission undertaking the negotiations. But it was made abundantly clear that the Canadian would not be a splinter third force but an integral, submissive part of the British group. The prime minister had to accept the conditions and the decision to be made was whether or not he should be the Canadian to sit on the commission.

It would meet for two and half months. It would meet in Washington. He would face only adversaries. He was not yet recovered from a severe attack of gallstones which nearly killed him several months earlier. He was heartsick over the physical abnormality of his eighteen-month-old daughter Mary, who had been born with an oversized head. He faced little but political peril in the negotiating venture. There would be minimal acclaim in the unlikely prospect that he gained a favourable settlement. There would be a hurricane of criticism in the probable prospect of failure. But Macdonald's fear that other parties would "play the devil" with Canadian interests overshadowed all these concerns. The first Canadian prime minister decided it was time for his first visit to Washington. It would not be long before he would write back home: "I stand alone, fighting the battle of Canada."[3]

Macdonald first arrived in New York where he read about himself in a New York *Herald* article datelined Prescott, Ontario. "Now I had met or seen nobody at Prescott," he wrote Charles Tupper. "In the course of the day I was interviewed at New York by another New York *Herald* man who has published an equally fallacious account. Among other things he says that I told him that my views had been correctly stated in the account of the long and interesting interview I had with the *Herald* correspondent the day before at Prescott."[4]

At the Washington train station where, to his relief, there were no *Herald* reporters to greet him, Macdonald searched longingly for someone else. These were not the days when prime ministers merited nineteen-gun salutes. Naturally, President Grant wasn't there. But nor was Fish or a single American official. The Canadian representative in the capital, Thornton, didn't even bother to show. Thornton sent his carriage and an attaché, the Honourable Mr. Trench, who was accorded the distinction of greeting the first prime minister to visit Washington and who promptly took him to a hotel across the river in Arlington, Virginia.

Few of note stayed overnight in Washington because it was judged not fit to stay in. While Ottawa was a coarse lumber town in the mid- to late-nineteenth century, it compared favourably to the languid village on the Potomac. In 1791 when George Washington beheld a few acres between Georgetown, Maryland, and Alexandria, Virginia and anointed it the future U.S. capital, there was nothing there but field and swamp and cows and huts. Three glorious white edifices were soon interspersed in the bog: the Congress building, the White House, and the Supreme Court. They were physically separated by considerable distance to symbolize the separation of powers called for in the Constitution. But the mile's journey from the White House to the Congress was more like picking one's way through jungle so that the separation came to be regarded as far more than symbolic.

The ruling elite of Washington was supposed to quickly attract wealth, people, and growth to the city but through Grant's time it hadn't yet happened. A "class of swaggering sycophants" — the confidence men, soup-seeking vagabonds, petitioning Indians — were the ones who came early and the ones who tended to remain. [5]

Politicians were viewed with even greater skepticism than in modern times. Rather than attract people to the city they were more apt to deter them. As a result the underdeveloped District of Columbia, so mocked for its philistine ways by British and French diplomats, had become an uninviting area which, oddly enough, was what some of the planners initially had in mind. Prior to 1800, fractious mobs kept forcing the government of the new republic to shift from town to town, so that a priority for the creators of Washington became a somewhat isolated location far from the madding crowd. To that purpose they made a stipulation for the district that has remained, with controversy, through time: no participation by the Washington citizenry in state or local government; no senators elected from the district; no representatives.

On his first full day in the city, Macdonald, who was not to be introduced to the president for a week, was taken with the other British commissioners on a tour of Congress where he met some annexationist senators, heard some impressive speeches, and learned of the amusing antics of legislators who couldn't read or write. To impress their constituents they chose to purchase speeches from freelance literates and have them inserted in the Congressional record of the day under their own name. But the writers would sometimes sell the same speech to several members leaving constituents to discover that by stunning coincidence their Congressman had uttered exactly the same speech in the House as many others. [6]

Prime Minister Macdonald was fast into the Washington social scene. Not a politician to confine himself to tea, he turned out to be about the only Canadian leader who could imbibe glass for glass with the presidents. (Later Mackenzie King would toss about in bed at night frightened that he had offended FDR by not sharing a drink with him. Truman would have to bring his own branch water to Ottawa. Brandy and cigars with Kennedy after dinner was disagreeable to Diefenbaker, and Lester Pearson was offended when Lyndon Johnson tried to get him smashed on bourbons before sunset.)

One of the Washington entertainments was the Potomac yacht party and, at one of the many he attended, Macdonald fell into conversation with a senator's wife who was not aware that she was speaking to the prime minister of Canada. It was terrible, she said, that Canadians were governed by that "perfect rascal," Macdonald. "Yes," said the prime minister, "he is a perfect rascal." "Why," she came back, "do they keep such a man in power?" "Well," said Macdonald, "they can't seem to get on without him." The lady's husband strolled into the conversation and introduced Mr. Macdonald to his incredulous spouse. "Don't apologize," said the prime minister. "All you've said is perfectly true and well known at home."[7]

The Macdonald position in the negotiations provided that if maritime inshore fishing rights were to be returned to the Americans, a wide ranging free-trade arrangement, like the one agreed to in 1854, would have to be granted in return. Secretary of State Fish, who headed up the American commission, wasn't interested in trade concessions. Meeting daily with the president on strategy, he came forward with a straight cash proposal of one million dollars for fishing rights in perpetuity. Macdonald was outraged. Well prepared, he tabled figures showing that the American catch from Canadian shores in one year alone was worth six million dollars. "Utterly inadmissable," he declared. Grant and Fish tried a compromise: a cash sum plus free trade in a small number of items — coal, fish, and firewood. Macdonald found the list, particularly firewood, insultingly inconsequential. The other British commissioners thought it was appropriate. They were beginning to wonder about this Canadian upstart and their anxiety turned instantly to anger when, in a daring diplomatic stroke, Macdonald went above everyone's head via cable to the Gladstone government in London and was successful. He won a statement that the Canadian fishing rights should not be given up for money and that all matters in the prospective treaty relating to Canada would have to be ratified by the Parliament in Ottawa.[8]

Among the Macdonald adversaries now was the press. "The New York papers are beginning to pitch into me as being 'the nigger on the fence.' I am rather glad of it as it will do me no harm in Canada." Fish was becoming increasingly distressed by the Canadian's obstinacy. The former governor of New York, cultured, wise, wealthy, was the Grant cabinet's calibre person. Compared to the others, the San Francisco *Chronicle* would write, he "stood alone like a purifying eucalyptus tree in a malarial swamp. His presence saved the name of the American Government from utter disgrace."

Grant was an aloof president who deigned to see the prime minister only twice during his eleven-week stay. Once to be introduced, once to say goodbye. Contact and often judgment was deferred to Fish and it didn't take long before the secretary was taking Lord De Grey, the head of the British Commission, aside and pressuring him to bring Macdonald into line. "I shall take the opportunity of letting Macdonald understand," De Grey assured him, "that he is here not as a representative of the Canadian but of the British Government."

Fish and his colleagues couldn't understand that the Canadian Parliament could possibly have any real power of ratification. "They pooh pooh it altogether," wrote Macdonald. "They think that when the treaty is once made the ultimate ratification of it by the Canadian parliament is a mere matter of form."

His opinion of Grant and company was less than flattering. "The present government here is as weak as water and they have not the pluck to resist the pressure from their friends in the Senate in the slightest degree.... The absurd attempts of the U.S. commissioners to depreciate the value of our Fisheries would be ridiculous if they were not so annoying." As for the British he said that "they seem to have one thing on their minds. That is to go home to England with a treaty in their pockets, settling everything, no matter at what cost to Canada." As for himself: "I have been in many responsible and many disagreeable positions. But in both respects my present position exceeds everything I have previously undertaken.... The sooner I am out of it, the better."9

Macdonald had rejected many American compromise proposals and now, pushing his fortunes further, he turned down yet another — a straight trade offer with an enlarged list of goods in the free-entry category. Again his British co-commissioners were incensed. Again the American commissioners were incensed. And again the prime minister contacted London. Gladstone, in another surprise, backed him. The commission was cabled. They were informed that the Dominion would not have to accept the latest offer.

But the end was near. Grant and Fish now decided they had tolerated enough. They decided not only against any further trade concessions but, arguing that no trade package could get through the protectionist Congress, decided to withdraw all trade concessions. They offered only a cash settlement to be determined by international arbitration. Later, as an afterthought, they decided they would throw in the free entry of Canadian fish.

Macdonald was predictably furious. He predictably turned down the offer. He predictably wired London for help, but his wrath was becoming redundant. The negotiations were dragging and all parties were becoming restless. Other issues had been settled, and only the nagging Canadian fisheries problem remained. This time De Grey cabled London. "If you don't back us up against Macdonald he will be quite unmanageable and I see no chance of coming to an arrangement." As a favour to the Dominion the British decided they would pay Ottawa compensation for the Fenian raids, something Macdonald had been chasing Washington to do. This done, Gladstone felt that the prime minister should accept the latest American proposal. His word was final, and with Macdonald having nowhere else to turn, the agreement with the Americans was made.

The signing day for the Treaty of Washington was May 8, 1871. It was a splendid day in the capital, the sunlight rushing through the mellow spring air, exhilarating almost everything it touched. The signing parties assembled in the State Department with a merriment that matched the weather. For Grant, the settlement of the British and Canadian disputes would greatly enhance his re-election efforts. For the British, a strengthened friendship with Washington was a most positive development. The only person who wasn't grinning was John A. Macdonald. There were to be no phoney airs from the Canadian prime minister. He had asked that his objections be recorded in the text of the treaty. He had been refused this but in the intrepid manner which marked the lonely stand of the brandy-nosed leader of the child-country against the Americans, Macdonald had at least won the right to have his condemnation officially recorded in letters to all the commissioners.

Now Hamilton Fish, sporting a triumphant glow, circulated in the treaty room and Lord De Grey took his hand. "This is the proudest day of my life," De Grey gushed. "It is a great result," said Fish. While the congratulations poured forth and the papers were readied for signing, the flush of enthusiasm was momentarily interrupted when a commissioner accidentally knocked burning sealing wax on a clerk's hands. Horrendous pain brought a look of strangulation to the poor man's face. He tried valiantly, given the dignity and joy of the occasion, to suppress his anguish. But finally he buckled over in tears and cries of pain.

Macdonald felt like doing the same thing. The documents were moved to him and he readied to sign. But he could not resist the temptation to register his discontent. He looked up at the secretary of state. "Here go the fisheries," he said. "You get a good equivalent for them," Hamilton Fish responded. "No," said Macdonald as the hushed gathering looked on. "We give them away."

He signed his name and rose from the table. "They are gone," he said.[10]

CHAPTER THREE

Games Presidents Play: Grant, Hayes, Arthur, Cleveland, and Harrison

WITH A CONDESCENSION that characterized much of official America's attitude toward the new Dominion, The New York *Star* pontificated on the results of the Washington Treaty: "Never before were people more doomed to disappointment than these ever sanguine Canadians.... Here are a people who in consequence of having acquired a sort of quasi-independence put on all the airs of a great power." But have pity on them, the newspaper said. "These luckless vassals of royalty are entitled to some commiseration. They went to the federal capital for wool and came back shorn."

It wouldn't be long before the luckless vassals would be back in Washington for wool again only to come back shorn again. A pattern of familiarity developed in the relationships between the men at the top in the early decades. It involved passionately stubborn Canadian prime ministers or cabinet members or diplomats throwing themselves into the pit against Americans of twice the power and, with rare exception, meeting the predictable oblivion. But what mattered most, it seemed, was the fight, the will to stand alone. There was a lot of that in the Canadians. They had a nation to build.

Alexander Mackenzie, the stern, highly principled prime minister who interrupted Macdonald's reign, dearly wanted a new trade treaty and would be disappointed when the prospects for his negotiator, George Brown, turned gloomy. But what would console him would be the effort, the fight. "Whether we obtain a treaty or not," he wrote Brown's wife Anne, "we have found this great advantage; That the Yankees know now that the Canadians are able to do their own negotiating effectively and that the days of English diplomatic buffoonery and blundering are over on this continent." He concluded: "After this we will at least be respected and can respect ourselves."

Mackenzie, who swept into power and also into one of Canada's worst depressions on the heels of the Conservatives' railway scandal, was insulted by the Washington Treaty and the arrogance of Mr. Fish. "It looks as if he considered us as a sort of political beggar looking with longing eyes to him for the crumbs the Republic might drop to us." But Mackenzie's wracked economy could use crumbs. It badly needed a stripping away of American trade barriers. The Liberal government's program called for such: looser ties with Britain, and greater economic integration on the continent.

An opportunity arrived immediately as a result of two factors. The newly elected Congress was more oriented toward free trade. The international tribunal set up by the Washington Treaty to determine the price of American privileges in Canadian waters hadn't yet convened. Now there were suggestions that rather than pay a high price, Washington might consider the alternative of trade concessions. Mackenzie sent Senator Brown, the cocky, truculent editor of the Toronto *Globe* to the capital on a scouting mission. Never short on optimism, Brown reported that there was a distinctly receptive mood. Later he would predict that a deal could be worked out which will make Canada "a great country ere many years to come."

Prime Minister Mackenzie was not about to confront the hopeless negotiating odds that faced Macdonald. Through hard bargaining he secured a negotiating commission in which Ottawa had equal status with Britain. Brown was named one co-commissioner and ambassador Thornton, the other.

The Brown performance featured tireless, unorthodox and, for the Americans, exceptionally aggravating diplomacy. It was not the custom and it would never be the custom for foreign diplomats to lobby legislators on Capitol Hill. Negotiation is supposed to be restricted to the White House and the executive departments. Throughout history this limitation would hinder Canadian efforts. On more than a dozen occasions negotiators would arrange pacts with the administration only to have them turned down by an unconvinced Congress.

George Brown paid no attention to such protocol. His strategy was to furiously work the Hill, obtain its support, and have President Grant feel the pressure. He rode about the muddy, still unfinished capital in a cherry-satined coach with "a portly, dignified colored gentleman on the dickey in full blazing livery and buttons that would fairly have stolen the heart of Ginney [daughter]." He mixed continuously with senators, men "entirely ignorant of the facts," and reported home that "we were soon as thick as thieves." He started a campaign with the nation's leading newspapers, visiting them one by one, explaining the Canadian position and eliciting such favourable press that Fish was soon complaining about his behaviour. As temperatures soared in the Washington spring of 1874, the Canadian became overwhelmingly confident. "Nothing but bad management can now prevent a really satisfactory agreement from being obtained."[1]

Whether the Yankees, as Prime Minister Mackenzie called them, were as impressed with Brown's performance as was Brown was another question. He had marshalled some support in Congress for a trade package but the president and his men were hardly stirred. Grant, trying to cope with assorted kickback scandals and other more important matters, was largely indifferent to Brown's hard sell and Fish, lead negotiator for the Americans, was moving slowly. While Brown was wiring most positive news to Mackenzie, Fish was dispassionately noting in his diary that the prospects were grim.

Congress would be adjourning for the summer on June 22, 1874. At the start of the month, Brown and Fish still had nothing to put to it. Brown was becoming suspicious of Fish, who he suspected was deliberately stalling until the recess date when the issue would die. But, "at his time of life, to go into so elaborate a cheat without any gain seems incredible." After an Ottawa visit by Brown to get further instructions from Mackenzie, after days of haggling over fine points, an agreement was finally reached—one week before adjournment.

Then the British government demanded that the entire text of the treaty be wired for approval to London. It took valuable time and Brown was furious. "Three precious days lost."

On June 18 he got an opportunity to meet with Grant. The president held the fate of the treaty in his hands. If he sent it to Congress with a ringing personal endorsement, it would likely be taken up in the dying days and passed. If he sent it over without fanfare, it would have little chance. Brown, in the White House for a reception, hung around until almost everyone had left, waited for the opportune moment, approached Grant and began to plug the treaty. The president gave him great news. In Brown's words, he "broke out enthusiastically" for the pact. "He congratulated me on the great success that I had accomplished and assured me that he would take every measure to have the Senate endorse it."

But Brown didn't know Ulysses Grant. The president, a few hours before the reception, had met with Secretary of State Fish. The treaty was on the president's desk. Fish asked him how it should be forwarded to the Senate. "Without recommendation," Grant said.[2]

It was over. Without the push from the president, the Senate did not take up the treaty before the session closed. Grant had told Brown one thing, while doing the opposite. George Brown wired the prime minister. "Had he sent it down honestly as a Government measure it would have been sustained." Relentless, as Macdonald had been, Brown travelled to Washington when Congress reopened in December to hustle the treaty again. Fish told him immediately that his cause was hopeless. It was. All Brown got from the trip were some introductions to visiting dignitaries such as the King of the Canary Islands. "I saw King Kalalua today.... He is a fine looking savage — tall, robust and quite able to digest a reasonably sized baby at a meal."

Ottawa had been thwarted again. Another treaty-making effort had been spurned. Ulysses Grant, unable to achieve his annexation wish, could not have been expected to do the Dominion any favours and he didn't. The tariffs would remain high. The Canadian economy would suffer. But there may have been a little irony in it all. In treating his neighbour so callously, Grant may have played a crucial role in saving it. His protectionist policies became a major motivating factor in sustaining John A. Macdonald's national policy. The high American tariffs helped forge a realization in the new country that the United States could not be relied on for economic help; that Canada would have to become more self-sufficient; that a trans-Canada railway was necessary to tie the country together economically as well as physically; that Canada had to prepare itself to go it alone on the continent; that the national policy was needed.

Following Grant's exit in 1876, the trade issue and the fisheries dispute continued to haunt the early decades of the bilateral relationship, driving a wedge between the presidents and the prime ministers and their countries. President Grover Cleveland would regret the day he got entangled in the disputes and suffer badly at the polls as a result of them. Wilfrid Laurier would drop two elections because of his free-trade fetish. William Howard Taft would be dealt a harsh political setback by the Canadian electorate on reciprocity.

Rutherford B. Hayes, Grant's successor, was viewed with promise in the Canadian capital. Lord Dufferin, the governor-general, had visited Hayes at the White House and Hayes had shocked him by returning the visit, stopping by at his hotel. "Such a proceeding," Dufferin wrote Mackenzie, "is very unusual as President Grant did not even return Prince Alfred's visit." It is, he said, "to be taken as a proof of the anxiety of this government to evince the friendly spirit with which it regards Canada." Make sure the newspapers know about this "exceptional act of courtesy," he advised the prime minister. "After cudgelling my brains it occurred to me that I might gratify him by asking his son... to return with me to Ottawa."

In narrowly electing the Republican Hayes, Americans chose an honest, pious man to follow a scandal-tarred administration, just as one hundred years later they chose an honest and pious man in Jimmy Carter to follow a scandal-tarred administration. But although Hayes, a former Union army general and Ohio governor, displayed a surface kindness toward Canada, there was little doubt as to his real motivation.

On May 25, 1879, the president made a one-paragraph entry in his diary. Lord Dufferin would have found it interesting. "The annexation to the U.S.," wrote Hayes, "of the adjacent parts of the continent both north and south seems to be, according to the phrase of 1844, our 'manifest destiny.' I am not in favor of artificial stimulants to this tendency. But I think I see plainly that it is now for the interests of both Canada and the United States that properly and in order and with due regard to the feelings of Great Britain, the two countries should come under one government. If it were known that we would probably pay the whole or part of the Canadian debts, or would assume to pay them, would it not stimulate the feeling in favor of annexation in Canada?"

William Henry, a friend, visited Hayes at the White House and wrote: "I find that the President is full of the question of annexation and would like to bring it about during his own Administration. He is doing everything that is proper to have the question fairly considered by the thoughtful men of the two countries and is keeping up a pretty active correspondence."

Hayes had a special motive in the possible addition of Canada. He saw Canadians as a distinctly conservative breed who would vote Republican.

His thoughts on the possible acquisition of Canada were summed up by Henry: "His plan is for the United States to assume the debt and for our people to push into the Red River country and thus Americanize that portion of the country from Lake Superior to the Pacific. This is being done rapidly, and whether in time for this Administration or of the next, it is soon to be."

Henry advised the president that Macdonald, back in power in Ottawa, was making an added push to keep Manitobans loyal through the use of the press. Hayes planned to open negotiations with the British for Canada when the conditions were right. But such conditions never arrived. London wasn't overly keen, Canada was certainly opposed, and while opinion in Washington favoured absorption, the climate wasn't hot enough to command action. William Evarts, Hayes' secretary of state and formerly counsel for the United States on the Treaty of Washington, was surprisingly lukewarm.

The Hayes presidency was otherwise uneventful from a Canadian point of view, but when he stepped aside in 1880, Macdonald had high cause for concern. James Garfield became president and his secretary of state, James G. Blaine, was an American whose appetite for the continent was more voracious than most. But Macdonald did not have to worry for long. As Garfield and Blaine stood in the Washington railway station just four months after inauguration, a member of the Stalwarts, the conservative wing of the Republican party, shouted, "I am a Stalwart and now Arthur is President." He fired two shots, one grazing Garfield's arm, the other burying in his back. Garfield died four months later and then Vice President Arthur was president and Blaine no longer the secretary of state.

Chester Arthur, the Vermont-born lawyer who disappointed many of his followers by refusing to ladle out patronage in conveyor-belt fashion, distinguished himself in Canadian annals by bringing back the fish war. Following Brown's unsuccessful venture, an international commission meeting in Halifax set a price of $5,500,000 for American use of the Atlantic fisheries over a twelve-year period. Even though Ottawa had vehemently opposed the idea of a cash settlement, the

Halifax outcome was viewed as somewhat of a victory. "The first Canadian diplomatic triumph," Prime Minister Mackenzie called it. "It will justify me in insisting that we know our neighbours and our own business better than any Englishman." The high price disgusted official Washington and Hayes and Evarts came close to demanding a new hearing.

Bitterness built in the ensuing years, and complaints arose against not only the exorbitant price tag, but also the part of the treaty allowing the free entry of Canadian fish. At the close of his term, President Arthur, supporting a move in Congress, reneged on the Washington Treaty. Washington had abrogated the treaty of 1854 and won a new deal in 1871. Now it was abrogating the treaty of 1871 and demanding another new deal. "Mr. Arthur is now engaged in the amiable work of embarrassing his successor," Macdonald wrote with prescience on Christmas Day in 1884. Observing closely, as he always did, the American political scene, the prime minister feared even worse problems. With Arthur stepping down, he witnessed the nomination by the Republicans of his number one foe. "I am awfully disappointed at Blaine's nomination. If he is elected we may look out for continental trouble.... His nomination however will disgust the respectable Republicans and if the Democratic Convention shortly to be held has the sense to nominate a candidate of high character... he would have a very fair chance of election." To the delight of Macdonald, the Democrats nominated Grover Cleveland of Buffalo, and in a general election, which may have saved Macdonald's Dominion from an annexation bid, Cleveland defeated Blaine.

But the corpulent Cleveland, who won despite the scandalous campaign revelation that he had sired a bastard child, was not the president that Macdonald hoped he would be. The exigencies of politics, so powerful a force in the unravelling of the affairs of the continent, played tricks with the good will of this dedicated and diligent chief executive, pushing him to levels of belligerence that had Canadians on the verge of taking up arms.

The latest American treaty abrogation again remitted fisheries jurisdiction to the treaty of 1818, meaning that Americans could only enter inshore waters for non-fishing purposes and required licences to do even that. Provoked by Washington's latest breach of faith, Macdonald had American boats seized for the most trivial of infractions. When the *David J. Adams* was taken, the ensuing uproar in the New

England states prompted the Cleveland administration to lodge a complaint in London that Canada did not have the right to enforce the articles of a U.S. treaty made originally with Great Britain. An indignant Canadian Parliament responded by passing a fisheries bill with clauses almost identical to the pact of 1818. Seizures continued at an evocative pace. At a Prince Edward Island port, an unlicenced American boat docked and its crew purchased potatoes. Canadian authorities boarded the boat, seized the potatoes, and, hearing that the captain had eaten some, administered an emetic to him, and disembarked with his emissions. They were making sure that even the eaten spuds didn't make it out of port.

With pressure from the White House and London, Macdonald sent Finance minister Charles Tupper to the U.S. capital for consultations. "Well Sir Charles," said Secretary of State Thomas Bayard to the surprised visitor, "the Confederation of Canada and the construction of the Canadian Pacific Railway have brought us face to face with a nation and we may as well discuss public questions from that point of view." It was not the point of view that the Dominion's diplomats were used to hearing. But Cleveland, who worked late nights studying the history of the fisheries problem, and the gracious Bayard were alarmed by the trend in bilateral relations and wanted a settlement.

"A full and clear survey of the situation," Bayard said in a letter to businessmen, "causes me to recognize that a crisis in the affairs of this continent is probably at hand. The nature of the policies now to be determined upon in our relations with the Dominion of Canada is most important to the welfare of this and succeeding generations."

To Tupper, Bayard wrote with equal apprehension: "The gravity of the present affairs between our two countries demands entire frankness. I feel we stand at the parting of the ways. In one direction I can see a well assured, steady, healthful relationship, devoid of petty jealousies, and filled with the fruits of a prosperity arising out of a friendship cemented by mutual interests.... On the other a career of embittered rivalry, staining our long frontier with the hues of hostility, in which victory means the destruction of an adjacent prosperity without gain to the prevalent party. A mutual, physical and moral deterioration which ought to be abhorrent to patriots on both sides."[3]

The Democrat Cleveland had broken a run of six straight Republican presidents, but the Senate, which must ratify all treaties, was still dominated by Republicans, and they didn't want consultation with Canada. They wanted retaliation. "Whenever the American flag on an American fishing smack is touched by a foreigner," cried congressman Henry Cabot Lodge in reacting to a flag-burning episode in the disputed zones, "the American heart is touched." The Congress passed legislation in February 1887 authorizing the president to exclude Canadian vessels from U.S. waters and stop the importation of Canadian fish. Cleveland signed it, but had no intention of putting it into effect. He regarded the bill as a product of the regional interests of New England and if any action was to be taken, he said, it would have to be in the national interest.

Finally, with an interim arrangement in force to keep the maritime waters calm, yet another joint high commission was appointed to look at the fisheries and other trade matters. Each side named three commissioners, and as was the case in 1871, the Canadian side consisted of mainly non-Canadians. Queen Victoria selected the distinguished Joseph Chamberlain, and the undistinguished Sir Lionel Sackville-West, the British ambassador in Washington. Bayard described him as a "postage stamp." His only vocal contribution in three months of hearings was to ask that a certain window be closed. Tupper was the sole Canadian representative, but was nevertheless able to exercise a steering influence over the commission. His presence led Bayard to complain that the control of the negotiations had been yielded to a man who subjected all questions to "the demands of Canadian politics."

But in keeping with what was becoming a familiar pattern, the Yankees frustrated and infuriated the Dominion side. Having originally agreed that the commission would deal with the entire question of commercial relations, Bayard announced, on the first day, that negotiations would be limited to the fisheries. Then, having conceded that the Americans were only interested in finding a better arrangement for buying supplies in Canadian ports, and after moving to within a notch of a final agreement on that basis, Bayard suddenly declared that the United States now wanted fishing privileges. Canadian Justice Minister John Thompson, a future prime minister who was assisting Tupper, was prompted to write home: "These yankee politicians are the lowest race of thieves in existence....Nothing will come of our mission but the board bills." Chamberlain, the host of spectacular dinner parties during the hearings, exploded, calling the

American side "a bunch of dishonest tricksters." Prime Minister Macdonald had warned Tupper that "there is no fair dealing to be expected from them." Now he wrote: "I think the Americans are bargaining like costermongers."

With some sessions so ill-tempered that commissioners asked their contents to be struck from the official record, an agreement, which excited neither side, was reached. The Canadian government would have full jurisdiction over most estuaries and bays. American boats were given free navigation of the Strait of Canso and their fishermen guaranteed the right to purchase supplies on homeward voyages. A further mixed commission would decide details.

But a presidential election was nearing. The Republican Senate could not let a Democratic president head into the campaign taking credit for settling such an important, bitter dispute. The GOP solution? Label it a pro-Canadian, pro-British agreement signed by a pro-Canadian, pro-British president. Sell the citizenry on the idea that its government had been out-negotiated by the Canucks. Reject the treaty.

The plan was carried out. Posters were put up: "Cleveland runs well in England." The Senate defeated the treaty by a vote of thirty to twenty-seven. Ottawa was dealt yet another blow by the United States.

But the story was far from complete. The loss of the just-negotiated treaty was minor compared to what happened next. Neither the Canadian prime minister nor the Republican party had calculated the political animal in the person of Grover Cleveland. Comparatively speaking, the president had been rather favourably disposed to the north country. There was little, if any, absorption sentiment in the man. He had not overreacted to the boat seizures by Macdonald. He had shown a keen interest in understanding the complexities of bilateral relations and the feelings of Canadians. Only Franklin Roosevelt would be more interested, and only Jimmy Carter would know more details. There was no expectation that now, at the end of his first term, a president with the integrity of Cleveland would resort to shock treatment.

But at four o'clock on August 23, 1888, two days after the Senate rejected the treaty, a message from President Cleveland was read in Congress. A reporter from the New York *Times* was there. "The Republicans sat stupefied," he would write. "Lightning would not have stunned them more completely." James G. Blaine was there. "I must say," he would assert, "that considering all circumstances it is the most extraordinary document that ever was sent from the White House to the Capitol."

"Our citizens engaged in fishing enterprises in waters adjacent to Canada have been subjected to numerous vexatious interferences and annoyances," Cleveland's message said. "Their vessels have been seized upon the pretexts which appeared to be entirely inadmissable and they have otherwise been treated by the Canadian authorities and officials in a manner inexcusably harsh and oppressive...."

Then to the heart of his proclamation — an embargo of Canada. "I recommend immediate legislative action conferring upon the Executive the power to suspend by proclamation the operation of all laws and regulations permitting the transit of goods, wares and merchandise in bond across or over the territory of the United States to and from Canada.

"I am not unmindful of the gravity of the responsibility assumed in adopting the line of conduct nor do I fail in the least to appreciate its serious consequences. It will be impossible to injure our Canadian neighbours by retaliatory measures without inflicting some damage upon our own citizens."

The question was, why now? Why so late? The answer was politics. "It looks," said Republican senator Fassett, "rather late in the day for President Cleveland to pose as an aggressive American. I am afraid that some people will be mean enough to say that he does it for purely campaign purposes." A New York paper said the President has recommended "a course of action which, in his own conscience, he must regard as utterly barbarous."

Reporters caught up to Prime Minister Macdonald in Sydney, Nova Scotia. "It seems to me that the American people would look better in the eyes of the world if instead of retaliating they should make laws for the good of their country," he said. The recommended embargo, he said, "illustrates to my mind more forcibly than ever before the wonderful and monstrous pitfalls which American politics will load a man into. It is nothing more or less than an exigency arising from... the peculiar conditions of the two political parties."

Days later he asserted that Canadians need not worry for they are "as independent as any people under the sun." While Congress deliberates "we can afford to wait in calm, dignity and self respect for the action of our neighbours. If they shut the doors we can remain outside. If they keep them open we can remain as at present."

The rest of the country and the rest of Macdonald's cabinet were hot. In Nicolet, Quebec on September 5, 1888, Adolph Caron, federal minister of the militia, fired the passions of the French Canadians. "They [Americans] are jealous and envious of our great progress and transcontinental railroads. We are the fifth maritime power in the world and in the event of trouble, the fishermen of the Gulf of St. Lawrence would in the moment of danger rush as one man to the defense of our rights. We do not want to fight with our neighbours or with anyone else," he said. "But would we sacrifice our rights for the sake of peace?" The audience was worked up. "No!" they screamed. "No! Never!"

"No," said Caron. "I know you too well to think such a thing."

The Washington *Post*, which was not to deem Canada important enough to set up a bureau in the country, had a reporter in Nicolet for this occasion. "Sir Adolph was very excited during the speech and the Frenchmen waved their hats and cheered until they were hoarse over the patriotic sentiments uttered," he wrote.

He was amused by the Quebeckers. "It is actually the impression in this part of Quebec among the ignorant French Canadians that the United States and Canada are on the brink of a bloody war and that Sir Adolph would need very little urging to call out the militia and drive all the yankees into the gulf."

Americans greeted any prospect of war with Canada with a combination of ridicule and scorn. When Macdonald himself began sounding belligerent, a Baltimore paper reported that "he looked and talked fight." But "Sir John need not trouble himself to fight any battles before war is declared nor to violate the requirements of courtesy by swashbuckling...Sir John is simply guilty of very bad manners but his truculent tricklings alarm no one on this side of the line. We are respectful of the rights of our neighbours but if Canada should provoke war, the militia of the state of New York alone could whip her into the Gulf of St. Lawrence and send her blubbering for help to the home government."

The Brooklyn *Citizen* was insulting: "In the Dominion there is gnashing of teeth and abusive language. If the Canucks had the power, as they have the inclination, they would forthwith send an army over the border and whip us into subjection without delay.

Luckily for the peace of the American continent the Canadians are such small fry in every way that their wild talk meets with no response from this side and only excites ridicule and disgust in Great Britain... England is in no mood for getting into a quarrel with this country on the account of such an obstreperous and ungrateful child as the 21-year-old Dominion has proven to be."

But the American attitude was perhaps best displayed in a Washington *Post* editorial on the crisis: "We believe that the United States and Canada will eventually become one country and this belief grows out of the necessities of the situation. The Canadians are too intelligent and too much addicted to the habit of looking out for their own interests to continue much longer denying themselves the manifest and substantial advantages that would result from Union. They need the change much more than we do."

Cleveland's embargo Canada bill passed the House of Representatives on September 8, 1888 and went to the Senate for a vote on final approval. The president had the Republican senators in a deep quandary. Nominally, his bill had been aimed at Canada, but as Macdonald wisely noted in a letter to Governor-General Lansdowne, its real intent was to throw chaos into the Republican ranks. How could the president be accused of cuddling Canada and Britain when he was calling for such severe action? "Cleveland, I fancy," said the prime minister, "had ascertained that the Irish vote would carry New York against him and so, in desperation, took an extra twist at the tail of the British lion." Canada was being used purely for political ends. Republicans could vote against the bill, but they would be voting against harsh action the likes of which they had been advocating. They could vote for it, but that would put them into the embarrassing position of handing the president an election-eve victory on the campaign's most controversial issue.

The least damaging course, the Grand Old Party decided, was rejection. As rationale they claimed that the American economy would suffer just as much by the Cleveland measure as the Canadian. Detroit businessmen were bitterly complaining that they would face financial hardship. Buffalo was worried about the effect on import trade. New England railways carrying Canadian freight were raising a storm. Thus, the Republicans voted down the measure and Canadians, particularly the Quebeckers, were able to relax.

But John A. Macdonald, now in his seventy-fourth year, could not.

Running under the Republican banner against Cleveland was the dour Benjamin Harrison. Harrison was a strong admirer of James G. Blaine. If Harrison won, Blaine would be secretary of state and this, said Macdonald, "means continual discomfort for Canada not only for four years but Blaine will work steadily for the Presidentship for the following term and will therefore throw himself into the arms of the Irish Americans."

Cleveland's campaign looked promising in the early weeks. His embargo bill had stripped strength from the Republican effort to portray him as London's lackey. But none other than the nonentity named Sackville-West ignited the issue again, sending the Cleveland campaign tumbling. The British ambassador was victimized by the dirty tricks of an early-day replica of Richard Nixon's Donald Segretti. A Republican agent, masquerading as a naturalized Englishman named Murchison, wrote a letter to Sackville-West asking advice on how he should vote. When the ambassador wrote back saying that Cleveland still had the most favourable leanings to Britain and Canada, so vote for him, it was all the Republicans needed. They gleefully disseminated copies of the letter all over the country and particularly in New York where the heavy Irish vote would be crucial. The letter became a campaign sensation. Cleveland had Sackville-West dismissed with what a supporter termed "his biggest boot of best leather." But the situation wasn't saved. Harrison, with the help of Republican vote-buying, lost the popular vote by 96,000 but won the election in the electoral college, his win in New York deciding the outcome.

The likeable, hard-working Cleveland, a man so overweight that when he tried to stand up his head would tilt, a man whose last living words were, "I have tried so hard to do right," lumbered sadly from the centre stage, a victim of cruel circumstance. On entering office he had been determined to avoid foreign squabbles but the ramifications of the one and only such issue he was dragged in on had sealed his demise. But those who felt there was no justice would feel better in a few years. Cleveland would be back.

Benjamin Harrison, never burdened by a surfeit of charisma, was described by a young fellow Republican named Teddy Roosevelt as "a cold-blooded, narrow minded, obstinate, timid old psalm-singing politician." A humourless fifty-five-year-old lawyer from Indiana, he was embroiled in instant controversy when a story hit the American newspapers suggesting an all-too familiar theme to Canadian eyes—he wanted to take the country over. The story was based on statements Harrison made during the campaign and it led many scribes to his doorstep for reaction. "Well, you know, I have nothing to say upon matters of that sort. As yet I have not had time to give consideration to the Canadian question." But he denied suggesting annexation during the campaign: "I did, I believe, invade Canadian waters when I was at Middle Bass this summer and capture a few fish. But that is about as far as I have gone."

His disposition toward Canada was about as miserable as that of any of the presidents and Macdonald had been right in thinking that his secretary of state would be Blaine. Had the prime minister seen a memo lying around the State Department, he would have been even more distressed. The major tenet of foreign policy, the unsigned memorandum declared, was "to unite the continent, secure its independence and prevent the northern part of it from being turned into an outpost of European reaction." It added that union "would exclude war from the continent" and solve questions which, with an independent Canada, would be open to "an endless vista of dispute." The recommended strategy? "Union is likely to be promoted by everything which asserts the commercial autonomy of the continent and helps to make Canada feel that to enjoy her full measure of prosperity she must be economically a community of this hemisphere, not an outlying dependency of a European power."[4]

Initially, however, the Harrison administration went the opposite route. One of Harrison's top priorities being to appease the big business community, he brought in the highest tariff at that time in U.S. history. Sponsored by a future president, William McKinley, the legislation increased duties on imports so steeply that products from many foreign countries, including Canada, were effectively barred. Hit hardest were the Dominion's agricultural products, and coming as it did when the Canadian economy was already depressed, the tariff struck worry in Macdonald that the long reign of his Conservative government was over. In Canada, whose population was five million compared to sixty million in the United States, there were four factions: those favouring closer ties to Britain, those favouring the status quo, those favouring commercial reciprocity with the United States and, prompted by the plummeting condition of the Canadian economy, an increasing number favouring annexation. The prime minister thought the tariff was designed to starve Canada into union. "Sir Charles Tupper will tell you that every American statesman covets Canada," he wrote George Stephen, president of the Canadian Pacific Railway. "The greed for its acquisition is on the increase, and God knows where it will all end." The British ties still strong in him, the opposition Liberals gathering around a free-trade plank, Macdonald said: "We must face the fight at our next election and it is only the conviction that the battle will be better fought under my guidance than under another's that makes me undertake the task, handicapped as I am, with the infirmities of old age."

He had a fear, the same fear which was to grip John Diefenbaker, who would also run a campaign against the Americans, and whose idol was Macdonald. "If left to ourselves," Macdonald wrote, "I have no doubt of a decision in our favour, but I have serious apprehensions, which are shared by our friends here, that a large amount of Yankee money will be expended to corrupt our people."

Liberals, led by the elegant Wilfrid Laurier, had been holding meetings with Blaine and other American officials to find support for their unrestricted reciprocity plank. At the same time they were careful to emphasize that the closer commercial ties would not lead to annexation. As the 1891 campaign neared, Macdonald, anxious to have the electorate know that he was trying to do something about the McKinley tariff, leaked word that the Americans were willing to undertake formal negotiations, which would be aimed at Macdonald's goal of reduced tariffs on natural goods only—a moderate proposal compared to the Liberals. But Washington had not agreed to formal negotiations, preferring only informal introductory talks, and Blaine, anxious to help the Liberals, stung Macdonald with a vigourous denial of Ottawa's statements. "We have burned our boats," Macdonald said of the embarrassment, "and must now fight for our lives." Fight he did, as much against Washington as against the Liberals, because in this election, as they would be in the 1963 election involving Diefenbaker, they were both the enemy of the Conservative party.

Despite some American funding for the Grits, despite the attractive Laurier, despite the unhappy state of the Canadian economy, Macdonald won again. There was no mystery to the victory: "We worked the loyalty cry for all it was worth and it carried the country." But it couldn't have come any later: "The effect of the McKinley tariff is so disastrous," said Macdonald, "that if our election had been postponed until another harvest, we would have been swept out of existence."

The Conservative win distressed Blaine and Harrison because it removed all hopes of free trade and eventual annexation. The Ottawa-Washington relationship fell predictably into sustained acrimony, with President Harrison the lead player. When Ottawa's request for trade negotiations was finally granted, a team of Canadian negotiators boarded their train, steamed across the border, only to be informed shortly before they got to Washington that Harrison had changed his mind. Come back a few months later, the negotiators were told. A few months later they prepared to board a train again. But again, President Harrison made a last-minute cancellation. Finally even the antagonistic Mr. Blaine got to feeling bad about the situation and told the president that yet another postponement would be "considered a dodge if not a cheat and will injure us with our own people." In February of 1892, the negotiations were at last opened and then quickly closed. Ottawa wouldn't move from its demand for a limited reciprocity agreement like the one of 1854. Washington wouldn't move from its demand for a full one.

"Gentlemen," said Secretary of State Blaine, "there is only one satisfactory solution of this question. It is to let down the bars." After adjournment, President Harrison made a pointed summation to Congress. Every "thoughtful American" would agree, he said, that in a deal involving natural products only, benefits "would have inured almost wholly to Canada.... It is not for this government to argue against this announcement of Canadian official opinion. It must be accepted however, I think, as the statement of a condition which places an insuperable barrier in the way...of reciprocal trade which might otherwise be developed between the United States and the Dominion."

Harrison's adversarial attitude was mirrored in his treatment of Canada on the Bering Sea dispute. Americans slaughtered seals for pelts on the Pribilof Islands in the Bering. Canadian and British fishermen slaughtered them at sea before they got to the islands. In a move devoid of legal sustenance, the president made a declaration tantamount to declaring the Bering Sea closed to Canadian boats. When a commission was appointed to look into the issue, a dispute which would drag into the twentieth century, Harrison and Blaine jettisoned the by then established practice of allowing Canadians on the British negotiating team. Only a technical adviser from the Dominion was permitted.

By 1892 when Harrison was on his way to electoral defeat, and when Macdonald had finally been summoned by death's knell, twenty-five years had passed since Canadian Confederation and the relationship of the neighbours and of their leaders had moved from square one to nowhere. The grating fisheries and trade disputes still remained, the American annexationist sentiment still remained, the hostility among the leading personages still remained and through it all, the frustrations not only remained but had grown. And they were about to grow more.

CHAPTER FOUR

"I'm going to be ugly": Tempestuous Teddy and Wilfrid Laurier

"WHENEVER CANADA RAISES a bristle, Theodore Roosevelt roars like a Texas steer and romps around the ring screaming for instant war and ordering a million men to arms."

As the distinguished historian Henry Adams chose to note, Teddy Roosevelt and Canada were not intimate. The burly president, who fought bears in his spare moments, was sometimes driven to expend equal energies on his northern neighbour. The youngest of presidents, the most dynamic, the most colourful, the most prolific man to occupy the Oval Office, he bore no indigenous malice to Canada. But his convictions about his own country's greatness and his own greatness were so overpowering that his thoughts transcended hunks of geography as undistinguished as the Dominion. In the face of White House wishes, Canada, in Roosevelt's view, was not supposed to have knees.

Wilfrid Laurier, the Liberal prime minister who broke the Tory string in 1896, had a different view. Tall, graceful, white-gloved, he was more than just the physical opposite of the robust president. He was as fiercely Canadian as Roosevelt was fiercely American. In 1899 he visited President William McKinley, Roosevelt's predecessor, in Chicago and delivered a speech entirely in French. Dumbfounded Americans interrupted, demanding to know what he was doing. Pointedly, Laurier told them a little story. He had spoken to a U.S. Supreme Court justice recently, he said, and the judge told him about how superior the American system was to that of the Canadian and the British. Is it not one of the supposedly prime tenets of this supposedly superior American system, Laurier asked, that "freedom of speech prevails?" He would be speaking in English the next day if the man cared to come then, he said. To the lusty cheers of many in the audience who were his countrymen, he continued *en français.*[1]

The fervent patriotism of Wilfrid Laurier would crash into the same in Teddy Roosevelt. The consequence for the continent was one of the most bitter disputes in bilateral history. When gold was discovered in Alaska at the turn of the century, a long simmering wrangle over the location of the Canada-United States boundary exploded. It was decided that an international tribunal would fix the location of the line. But Roosevelt, outraged that his claim was contested in the first place, rigged the commission in his favour and just in case the decision didn't go exactly his way even while rigged, he had troops put in place to establish the American version of the line. The protests of Canadians were raucous, but futile at the time. But a few years later, in 1911, Canadians would be provided with an opportunity to register their views on the treatment by Presidents Grant, Harrison, Roosevelt, and the others in a more meaningful form. In that election year, Canadians would be asked how close a relationship they wanted with the United States.

The Alaska uproar may never have happened had Laurier taken a more flexible, less political approach in 1898 negotiations with the McKinley administration. An opportunity, a magnificent opportunity, existed then to clean the slate of all bilateral disputes by way of one super commission.

Following Harrison's 1892 defeat, which most Canadians welcomed, a relative calm enveloped affairs between the two countries until Laurier's 1896 triumph. Four successor Tory prime ministers to Macdonald—John Abbott, John Thompson (who had signed an annexation manifesto in Montreal in 1849), Mackenzie Bowell and Charles Tupper—shuffled in and out of office so quickly that sustained policy initiatives were rare. In Washington, Grover Cleveland was back in office and, given his previous experience, was reluctant to get involved in Canadian questions. Laurier, whose country was entering an economic boom period, was prepared to make an effort to overcome the differences. Soon after the Republican McKinley took office, the prime minister visited him, sparking widespread excitement in the

American press. At last there was a different political party in power in Ottawa, the reports said. A bargain could perhaps be struck drawing Canada away from Britain first commercially, and eventually politically.

McKinley and his cabinet secretaries led Laurier into the White House Blue Room. There, Laurier proposed the idea of an omnibus commission to settle every outstanding dispute. The president and his men agreed it was time to forge a better continental climate. They would gladly consider the idea.

The new prime minister was a hit. "Sir Wilfrid Laurier," a top U.S. official told the press, "has not only been received by the Government with great consideration but has made an excellent impression upon all the gentlemen with whom he has come in contact. As a staunch Canadian statesman he naturally demands concession for concession. At the same time he has shown a liberal spirit toward the plan of increasing the commercial intercourse of the two countries and if he meets the views of the United States halfway there is a very fair chance of removing from the present field of view the most important questions which have produced so much irritation between the countries."[2]

After some weeks McKinley agreed to a twelve-member commission in which the Dominion side would actually have Canadian representatives. Five of the six would be from the Dominion and, in another striking departure from the norm, one of the sessions would be held in neither Britain nor the U.S. but in Quebec City. Strangely, however, having pushed for the commission and having won favourable terms, Laurier, who headed up the Canadian team, was decidedly pessimistic. "I confess," he wrote a friend as the hearings opened on August 23, 1898, "that I have very serious doubts as to any practical results." It may have been because he didn't really want results. "If my judgment is worth anything to you," Clifford Sifton, his outstanding cabinet minister wrote him, "I feel that I ought to say it would be a frightful mistake for us to make any concessions to the United States in the proposed treaty for which we do not get ample returns.... I think it would be a serious blow to your popularity in the country and to the great confidence with which the people look to your control of the affairs of Government if any weakness were shown in this matter."

The commission came to swift agreement on many of the more minor issues: alien labour laws; control of inland fisheries; the boundary west of Lake Superior; conveyance of prisoners; and use of naval vessels by Americans in the Great Lakes. The latter was a follow-up to the Rush-Bagot agreement of 1817, which limited the number of ships in the lakes, and has come to be regarded by students of defence as one of the first meaningful disarmament agreements.

On tariffs Laurier suddenly turned away from his earlier free-trade policies and, to the disappointment of the Americans, went the John A. Macdonald national policy route. He wanted reduced barriers in some commodities, but a more economically prosperous Canada had relieved the need for wholesale changes. Sifton strongly favoured protection as did Canadian business. Laurier remembered that the same William McKinley who now wanted free trade had, less than a decade earlier, slapped a record tariff on Canadian goods.

But by linking one issue to another, it appeared that some overall solution to trade, the fisheries, and the Bering Sea dispute was retrievable, until the two sides clashed on the Alaska boundary. In 1825 a treaty between Great Britain and Russia had set the boundary line in the largely unexplored area in a loosely defined way. When the United States purchased Alaska from Russia in 1867 the ambiguous boundary with Canada remained. The Dominion's position was that the line gave Ottawa possession of the heads of the inlets along the jagged coastline and therefore control of the important access routes to the Yukon River and the gold fields. Washington claimed that this was nonsense and, to most observers, the bulk of the evidence seemed to support its case. The intent of the Russians in 1825 was to have the line exclude Britain from the navigable coastal waters. London argued but eventually acquiesced, unaware of the significance the area would come to have. In the 1888 negotiation with the Cleveland administration, the British-Canadian side put in a boundary claim which Washington found excessive. Now in 1898, the Canadians were putting forward an even larger demand, saying they should be entitled to a portion of the strategic Lynn Canal.

Laurier realized the strength of the American position. "I think myself that we should have the line drawn at the entrance of the Lynn Canal, but on the other hand, the Americans are in possession of it and as you know," he wrote to Governor-General Minto, "possession is nine points of the law." The Americans, he said, "have very many qualities but what they have, they keep and what they have not, they want."

A compromise was almost reached. The United States would have sovereignty over the Lynn Canal and Canada would be granted the use of an important harbour in it. But before the papers could be signed, details were leaked to the American press. On publication an uproar ensued, three states threatened to secede, and McKinley had little choice but to withdraw U.S. support for the proposal.

The commission had now moved to Washington where, like Macdonald, Prime Minister Laurier spent two and a half months out of his country, leaving colleagues in extended control. When no agreement seemed forthcoming on the boundary, it was decided that the best alternative would be to send the dispute to international arbitration. But this idea was scuttled when the Canadians would not agree to the proposed make-up of an arbitration body. The prime minister, feeling the Alaska issue to be paramount, then greatly annoyed McKinley by withdrawing all Canadian settlement proposals on the other issues. In effect, he was declaring the commission dead.

To Laurier, as he explained in a letter to Ontario Premier Hardy, there was "a question of dignity involved which must make it incumbent upon us to refuse to negotiate on anything else and this we will unless they give way [on Alaska]." The prime minister was fast joining the ranks of what was already becoming a Canadian tradition— heady, stubborn negotiators. On Alaska, he said, "the Americans are certainly in the wrong and I am not to be either bulldozed or bamboozled by them."

But it is far easier for a leader to be tough when playing to the politics of his home folk and Laurier's dealings with the McKinley administration were not without their political overhang. The prime minister was getting a lot of advice from the home front. Much of it was similar to this unabashed recommendation he received in a letter from the Ontario minister of Education, G. W. Ross:

"Nothing would please our people more than to be able to say that Sir Wilfrid Laurier and his colleagues contended with the Americans for four or five months for a fair treaty with Canada, and being unable to make such a treaty, they were content to trust the future of Canada to the self-reliance of its own people."

The possibility that Laurier could go home with nothing and still be a hero was not lost on the Americans. John Hay, former personal aide to Abraham Lincoln, was secretary of state to McKinley and would remain so for another four years with Teddy Roosevelt. He was fresh from orchestrating a U.S. victory in the Spanish-American war, a conflict which he dubbed "a splendid little war." He was quick to size up Laurier and other Dominion politicians.

"Their minds," Hay wrote, "are completely occupied with their own party and factional disputes and Sir Wilfrid Laurier is far more afraid of Sir Charles Tupper than he is of Lord Salisbury and McKinley combined." The failure of the commission was because "they preferred to stand before the Canadian Parliament in the attitude of stout defenders of Canadian rights and interests, rather than as signers of a treaty which would not meet the views of their advanced supporters." Hay, as indicated by several personal letters he wrote, was bitter, and his bitterness would be slow to leave him.

In Canada meanwhile, the advice of G. W. Ross was proving to be well-founded. With this failed commission, Canadians were not complaining. Their "dislike of the Yankees" was understandable, thought the Earl of Minto, the new governor-general. "What the Canadian sees and hears is constant Yankee bluff and swaggery and that eventually he means to possess Canada for himself."

"Personally," Laurier told Minto after the commission hearings, "I like the Americans." But, "I would like them much more if they were not so intensely selfish and grasping."[3]

The prime minister's visit to Chicago to see McKinley in 1899 came only seven months following the conclusion of the commission and it was apparent from the treatment McKinley accorded him that relations were cold. In celebrations marking Chicago Day — the order of parade carriages, the order of speeches, time with the president — Laurier was low priority, below that of Mexico's second in command, Vice President Don Ignacio Mariscal.

The prime minister had done little to ingratiate himself with McKinley with his intransigence in the recently concluded negotiations. On arrival in Illinois, Laurier compounded his difficulties by doing something that presidents and prime ministers never did — he made a partisan political comment on the other country's elections. Asked by reporters what he thought about William Jennings Bryan, McKinley's major Democratic party challenger, Laurier gave an honest reply, the second half of which did not amuse the McKinley White House. "Bryan's speech at the Chicago convention in 1896 was sophomoric," he said. "Since that time he has redeemed himself. I believe him to be a thinker and a philosopher."

Continuing his unrestrained behaviour, Laurier then made his all-French speech. Moving, as promised, to English the next day, Laurier called on both nations to desist from unrelenting partisanship. With the president and the Mexican looking on, Laurier was scraping in candour, conciliatory in tone, and by all accounts "electrifying."

"Mr. President," he began, "on the part of Canada and on the part of the United States, we are sometimes too prone to stand by the full conceptions of our rights and to exact all our rights to the last pound of flesh."

On introduction, Laurier had been embarrassed by the glow of the reception. The American master of ceremonies had called him "one of ours." But the prime minister was buoyed. "Shall I speak my mind?" he cried. "Yes, yes," the large crowd yelled. He continued: "May I be permitted to say here and now that we do not desire one inch of your land. But if I state however that we want to hold our own land, will that be an American sentiment, I want to know? I am here to say above all my fellow countrymen, that we want not to stand upon the extreme limits of our rights. We are ready to give and take. We can afford to be just. We can afford to be generous, because we are strong."

Relations, he said, were "not as good, as brotherly, as satisfactory as they ought to be. We are of the same stock. We spring from the same races on one side of the line as on the other. We speak the same language, we have the same literature and for more than a thousand years we have a common history.... When we go down to the bottom of our hearts we will find that there is between us a true, genuine friendship."[4]

There had been a few talks to small groups but the Laurier speech was the first formal address by a prime minister on bilateral relations in the United States. Its conciliatory tone was noteworthy because Laurier had recently been savaged by the State Department in a way which would make the Kennedy State Department's criticism of John Diefenbaker on nuclear policy pale by comparison.

On Saturday, July 22, 1899, Laurier had told the House of Commons that if compromise failed, only two ways were available to settle the Alaska boundary dispute. "One would be by arbitration, the other would be by war. I am sure no one would think of war." Taken out of context, reports in American papers made the statement sound like Laurier was threatening war. On Monday the State Department issued this blast: "Canada has acted badly.... It looks as if the Canadian premier actually prefers no settlement, even to the extent of a modus vivendi. Sir Wilfrid Laurier seems to be playing Dominion politics through these negotiations. Whenever the United States and the British Government have been at the point of making terms, the Canadian leader has upset the arrangement by some new condition. He has been so fertile and so fickle in his opposition to proposed terms of a modus, the conclusion is at last forced that he sees more for his partisan purposes in disagreement than in settlement. This Government will now let the matter rest and give Sir Wilfrid a period of uncertainty in which to play his Canadian politics. The remark of the Premier at Ottawa that the alternatives were arbitration or war need excite no uneasiness. It is a part of his local political program."

This abnormally undiplomatic and vivid swipe was only a sample of what the prime minister was to face when Vice President Roosevelt moved into the Oval Office following the assassination of McKinley in September 1901 in Buffalo. Roosevelt possessed superior descriptive powers and did not hesitate to use them. He once described Senator William Peffer as a "well-meaning, pin-headed, anarchistic crank of hirsute and slab-sided aspect." He harpooned a New York Supreme Court justice as an "amiable old fuzzy-wuzzy with sweetbread brains." Maurice Low, a reporter for the London *Morning Post* was "a circumcised skunk."

On the Alaska issue Roosevelt's posture was encapsulated in a comment to a British embassy official: "I'm going to be ugly." The new President, only forty-three, was irked by many aspects of the Dominion, beginning with the fact that it existed. He was disappointed that previous presidents missed annexation opportunities and he still clung to a fast-fading hope that the Phillipines, which the United States had acquired in the Spanish-American war, could be traded to Britain in exchange for Canada.

Roosevelt also felt that "the Canadians do not like the United States." He had been surprised by the gall of what he perceived to be a war threat in the Laurier speech. In no way could he comprehend the slightest case for Canada in the Alaska matter. He was as adamant on Alaska as on any issue and with Roosevelt, adamant meant adamant. Once the mind was made up, for Roosevelt, it was hunting time — and on the hunt this extraordinary man was ferocious. "I had an interesting and in a way eventful hunt, killing 12 cougars and 5 lynx," he wrote Arthur Hamilton Lee in the year he became president. "I shot 8 of the cougar with the rifle and killed 4 with the knife." With that introduction he moved to the Alaska question. "I have studied that question pretty thoroughly and I do not think the Canadians have a leg to stand on. We might just as well claim part of Newfoundland as to allow for one moment the Canadian claim."

In the first year of his administration there was no movement on the issue. The countries couldn't decide on the make-up of a commission and a pro tem arrangement for the boundary remained in force. But as news from Alaska suggested there were large deposits of gold in the region, the controversy took on a flaming edge. Laurier had feared all along it would happen. With great prescience he had written to Sifton in 1899 saying that he didn't want to leave Washington without an Alaska settlement. "The reason is obvious. There may be a discovery of gold in that section at any moment and probably there will be. Unless the boundary is settled here and now the most serious complications can arise."

As the speculation mounted, George Smalley, a London newspaper correspondent in Washington who sometimes acted as a go-between for the administration and Ottawa, told Roosevelt that new-found gold would likely trigger violence with the Canadians in the area. "What shall we do then?"

"I know very well what I shall do," the president replied. "I shall send up the engineers to run our boundary line as we assert it and I shall send troops to guard and hold it." But isn't that "very drastic?" said Smalley. Roosevelt regarded the journalist as "a copper-riveted idiot." He paused and exclaimed, "I mean it to be drastic."

The vital question of the make-up of an international tribunal to arbitrate the matter remained. In the summer, Laurier, who realized the Canadian case was not terribly strong, agreed to three members from each side. Previously he had objected, arguing that such an arrangement would only end in deadlock. Meanwhile, Roosevelt was vigorously opposed to the idea of any arbitration on the grounds that it would be a tacit admission on his part that the Canadians had a case in the first place. The only type of arbitration he was interested in was a rigged one. He wrote Secretary of State Hay, laying out the strategy: "It is difficult for me to make up my mind to any kind of arbitration in the matter. I will appoint three commissioners to meet three of their commissioners, if they so desire; but I think I shall instruct our three commissioners when appointed that they are in no case to yield any of our claims. I appreciate the bother of the matter and even the possibility of trouble, although I think if we put a sufficient number of troops up there the miners will be kept in check."[5]

The fact that the Canadians had increased their claim in the area from 1888 to 1898 annoyed him immensely: "In a spirit of bumptious truculence... the Canadians put in this wholly false claim. They now say that as they have got the false claim in, trouble may come if it is not acted on. I feel a good deal like telling them that if trouble comes it will be purely because of their own fault." And although trouble "would not be pleasant for us," the President wrote, "it would be death for them."

Months of polemic and a quick visit by Laurier to the White House finally produced a treaty in 1903 providing for six "impartial jurists of repute," three to represent the United States, and three, Britain and Canada. The rub was there: in the words "impartial jurists of repute." Roosevelt had no intention of honouring that phrase. One of his appointments was Senator George Turner, a man so impartial that he already had publicly condemned the Canadian position and had taken an annexationist stance toward Canada. But in comparison to the next appointment, Turner seemed a man without prejudice. Henry Cabot Lodge was a very close friend of Roosevelt's. He was an annexationist. He was rabid in his opposition to Canada and England. He had written on the Alaska question the following: "If we should agree to arbitrate there is nothing to prevent Spain from setting up similar claims in Florida, France in Louisiana or Great Britain on the borders of New York."

News of the selections rolled across the Canadian border like a hailstorm. Laurier labelled them "an outrage."

Jettisoning the established protocol of the day which still called for him to deal through the British ambassador in Washington, Laurier fired off a sharp rebuke to Secretary Hay: "... These gentlemen under existing circumstances cannot with any fairness be styled 'impartial jurists.'... They could not approach the question with an open mind, both having expressed their convictions that one side of the case is so strong as to render almost facetious the mere presentation of the other side." For Ottawa to grant legislative approval to the make-up of such a tribunal would be "humiliating."

Hay responded that Roosevelt had unsuccessfully tried to get Supreme Court justices for the tribunal. He didn't mention that the president knew they wouldn't accept before extending the invitations. He argued further that it was impossible to find people without an opinion on the controversial subject. By impartial jurists of repute, Hay said, "we take it to mean men learned in law of such character for probity and honor that they will give an impartial verdict." At the same time, however, the secretary of state was transmitting his real feelings in a letter to Henry White: "Of course the presence of Lodge on the tribunal is, from many points of view, regrettable and, as if the devil were inspiring him, he took occasion last week to make a speech in Boston, one half of it filled with abuse of Canadians." Mr. Hay added that "the infirmity of his mind and his character is such that he never sees but one subject at a time.... Of course you know his very intimate relations with the President.... He insisted upon his appointment on the tribunal."

The appointments put the United States in a dim light overseas as well as on the northern half of the continent. It seemed as though the president, in the words of historian Tyler Dennett, was, throughout the boundary affair, "delivered into the possession of his most evil genii." Laurier, pushed by the public outcry, scourged the appointments in the House of Commons, blasted London for tolerating them and, in a move which prompted action by the president, argued vociferously the Canadian case in the dispute, staking out the position he hoped the Canadian commissioners would make in the hearings.

President Roosevelt was then prompted to issue personal instructions to the American side. "I write you now because according to reports in the public press Sir Wilfrid Laurier, the Canadian Premier, has recently in open Parliament made a speech...which is, in effect, a mandate authoritatively and officially given by him to the two Canadian members of the Tribunal." Laurier, he said, was turning his tribunal members into advocates instead of judges. Because this behaviour is "as far removed as possible from the judicial I feel that I should briefly call your attention to my view of the question which you have to decide."

His instructions? "In the principle involved there will of course be no compromise." By "principle" Roosevelt meant boundary. "The question is not in my judgment one in which it is possible for a moment to consider a reconciling of conflicting claims by mutual concessions."

While the Canadian protests raged on, the British government went ahead and, in what the London *Saturday Review* called a "pitiful abandonment" of the Dominion, ratified the treaty establishing the tribunal. Laurier said that the move was "nothing short of a slap in the face." It had the effect of galvanizing Canadian opinion against Britain as it already was against the United States. Writing to Canadian journalist J. W. Dafoe, Clifford Sifton said the Downing Street decision represented "the most cold-blooded case of absolutely giving away our interests.... My view in watching the diplomacy of Great Britain as affecting Canada for six years is that it may just as well be decided in advance that practically, whatever the United States demands from England will be conceded in the long run."

A few months following the British ratification an impatient Roosevelt perceived Canadian-inspired delays in the progress of the arbitration. In a move which clearly disturbed his secretary of state he then threatened to "bring the matter to the attention of Congress and ask for an appropriation so that we may run the line [boundary] ourselves." At this even Hay, so bothered by Canadian diplomatic behaviour during his tenure, thought the president was taking things too far. In a strongly worded letter, he sought to cool Roosevelt down:

"Dear Theodore.... I do not think they are acting in bad faith. They are availing themselves of every possible pretext the treaty gives them of demanding more time to patch up their deplorably weak case.

"I do not think any threats are at this time advisable or needful. We shall be as hard on them as is decent — perhaps rather more so."

The Canadian tribunal consisted of Sir Louis Jetté and A. B. Aylesworth, both prominent lawyers, and one British member, Lord Alverstone, the chief justice of England. Henry Cabot Lodge, who viewed Canadians as "a collection of bumptious provincials" and told Roosevelt they were "perfectly stupid," surveyed the situation and warned the president that his only hope was Lord Alverstone. Roosevelt, ignoring warnings from Hay that the case was sub judice, gave directions to his tribunal members, and through the use of conduits such as famed jurist Oliver Wendell Holmes, pressured the British government, insisting that if a favourable decision was not reached, he would use force in Alaska.

"I wonder if the jacks realize," he wrote Hay, "that while it may be unpleasant to us, it will be far more unpleasant to them if they force the alternative upon us: If we simply announce that the country is ours and will remain so, and that so far as it has not been reduced to possession, it will be reduced to possession, and that no further negotiations in the matter will be entertained."

The tribunal sat for seven weeks, the crucial question being whether Lord Alverstone would side with the Americans. Otherwise there would be a stalemate. In the corridors, Alverstone met with U.S. representatives and let it be known that if they would yield on some small points, giving the Dominion a couple of islands, he would go their way. Roosevelt agreed, Alverstone voted with the Americans, and the final decision gave Washington almost everything it wanted.

The verdict, which was reached in October 1903, gave Canada only a non-strategic canal and two insignificant islands. It stunned Jetté and Aylesworth because they had been led to believe that Alverstone was with them on a number of important points. In 1871, Prime Minister Macdonald had voiced his opposition while signing a treaty with Washington. Now, Jetté and Aylesworth, with the support of Laurier, would go a step further. Having gathered in the cabinet room of the British Foreign Office, the tribunal members began signing the papers. Lord Alverstone handed the documents to Jetté and said, "Sign this, Sir Louis." Jetté demanded, "What is it?" Alverstone said it was the award. "You know I will not sign it," said Jetté. Aylesworth, his partner, broke in: "I thought we made it plain we would not sign."

"Oh, I thought you would," replied Alverstone. "And so did I," Senator Lodge added. With that the two Canadians withdrew from the room, the necessary majority of four remaining to seal the deal. A statement was then released by Jetté and Aylesworth: "We... have been compelled to witness the sacrifice of the interests of Canada. We were powerless to prevent it."

At a ceremony at Buckingham Palace, the Canadians were presented by Alverstone to King Edward. The King made a strong effort to get the two men to say they accepted the treaty but they would not budge. They shook hands, bowed, and moved away.

In Ottawa, Laurier spelled out the results to the House of Commons, placed a map open on his desk and, as members from all parties gathered around him, sadly illustrated the line the boundary would take.

Press reaction was scathing. "Led Like a Lamb to Slaughter," roared one Vancouver *Daily Province* headline. "The Line Which We

Have To Toe," said another. The Toronto *World* cited Laurier's desire to settle the question on a give-and-take basis. "It has turned out that way," the paper said. "The United States giving and Canada taking it in the neck."

The Buffalo *Evening News* said the award demonstrated the craziness of those thinking there could be a North American union. "Canada detests this country most cordially and is now nearly wild with grief and rage because our contentions have been upheld." In London, the *Express* headlined the story: "The Great Surrender—Canadian Interests Sacrificed."

Laurier lashed out at the British as well as the Americans, saying that the episode was a prime example of what made "British dipomacy odious to Canadian people." The defeat, even though he recognized the weakness of the Canadian case, would anger him for many years. Lord Grey, the governor-general, would meet with Laurier on Christmas Day, 1907. He would note "the general attitude of the United States has wounded Sir Wilfrid deeply. He referred again, only last night, with much bitterness to the inexcusable action of the United States in appointing the three political partisans as jurists of repute, to the Alaska Boundary tribunal."

In Washington, Roosevelt and Hay celebrated, the president calling it the greatest American diplomatic triumph in a generation and excoriating the behaviour of the two Canadian commissioners in failing to sign as "outrageous alike from the standpoint of ethics and professional decency."

Hay paid tribute to Lord Alverstone, calling him the "hero of the hour. No American statesman would have dared to give a decision on his honor and conscience directly against the claim of his own country."

The secretary of state wrote his wife: "I can hardly believe my eyes and ears when I see how perfectly all my ideas in this great transaction have been carried out....

"I do not wonder that they [the Canadians] are furious. But as Will Thomson used to say: 'Serves 'em right, if they can't take a joke.'"

From the same Christmas conversation with Laurier, Lord Grey was to note how deep ran the prime minister's disappointment with Washington. For Laurier it had become a one-way street. Ottawa was according the United States respect while the United States didn't seem to care. "He has more than once of late commented, and with great feeling," said Grey, "on the marked difference between American and Canadian actions in relation to each other. He is proud, and justly proud, that since he took office 11 years ago, there has been no act on the part of Canada which has not been prompted by the greatest consideration for the government of the United States...I wish it were possible to say half as much for the Government of the United States."

After Alaska, Roosevelt seemed prepared to reconcile his differences with Laurier and Ottawa. He came to respect the prime minister, he grew excited about the country's potential, and he began treating Ottawa with civility. He sent warm, laudatory letters to Laurier, one of which began: "As an admirer of you personally and of the great and wonderful country at the head of whose government you stand...." When Laurier was in New York at one point, he invited him to come over and spend a night at the White House. In the period following his presidency Roosevelt poured praise on the Canadian war effort in World War I, saying that the contribution of his own country wasn't nearly comparable. To enthusiastic crowds he gave many speeches in Canada, one as a favour to Prime Minister Robert Borden. He was impressed by the way the country was governed, remarking in 1914 that "if Mexico governed herself as well as Canada she would not have any more to fear from us than has Canada."

Laurier, however, kept his distance. He could never reciprocate the warmth. The single clash over Alaska was too much to overcome and a shadow hung over the relationship between the two men, just as later one would hang over Lester Pearson and Lyndon Johnson following their 1965 clash over Vietnam.

The poisoned atmosphere did not mean there was no progress. Elihu Root, the third American member of the Alaska tribunal, was the new secretary of state and, taking a keen interest in Canadian problems, he sat down one day and typed out seventeen full-length pages on what he considered the sixteen major difficulties. Negotiations were opened on many of them and the groundwork was laid for important settlements which were made after Roosevelt left office. Root visited Ottawa in January 1907 and dealt nimbly with the Alaska issue and his role in it, showing some of the diplomatic ability which would see him win a Nobel Peace Prize in 1912. Despite the differences, he remained a big admirer of the prime minister. To Root "Laurier was a very wise and fair-minded man and his character had a great deal to do with the fact that when the Great War came in 1914, there were no controversies left unsettled between the United States and Great Britain."

One main issue that arose before Roosevelt was finished was Japanese immigration. The Japanese government was allegedly overissuing passports, and immigrants were flooding the Canadian and American west, getting jobs that citizens of the countries were not getting. Roosevelt was stunned one day when a Canadian visitor told him that the western Canadian provinces and the Pacific states were prepared to separate and set up a new republic if Washington and Ottawa didn't act to stop the Japanese tide. The president was struck by the quality of the visitor: "...a very capable, resolute fellow...a gentleman...made a very favourable impression on me."

The fellow was young William Lyon Mackenzie King and he was beginning, in an obviously impressive fashion, his rise to the top. On assignment as Canadian commissioner of Labour and Immigration, he had headed directly for the White House, unaware that the required first stop was at the office of British Ambassador James Bryce. The president commented on the oversight: "Canadian diplomacy, like much of the diplomacy of my own native land," he wrote, "is much on the *sans gêne* order, which has its advantages in getting work done quickly, but which can be carried to an extreme. I was much amused (this of course you must not repeat) that King had no idea he was to call on Ambassador Bryce. I of course told him that he must do so at once."

In formulating a heavily restrictive policy toward Japanese immigration, Roosevelt followed the direction advised by Laurier in a letter to him. The prime minister said the contact of Asiatic labourers with Caucasians always led to serious troubles and therefore the contact had to be prevented. Roosevelt couldn't agree more, saying there was no way Japan would allow masses of Canadian and American workers into its labour force.

King was immediately taken by the impetuous president. "A man of strong impulses, but they are true impulses....I must say I like his impulses." He heard Roosevelt speak to the Gridiron Club about his "walk softly, carry a big stick" policy. Roosevelt told the audience that the idea was to "deal politely, be conciliatory but carry a big stick." He went on to add, King noted, "politeness was all right up to a certain point, but if advantage were taken of it, then it was time to send your fleet into the Pacific."

In Ottawa the government leaders were concerned that King, whom they were trying to groom for great things, would get a swollen head through such eminent contacts. "I hope they won't make him conceited," Lord Grey told Laurier. "I know him well enough to give him a word of caution on this point."

Perhaps King needed a word of caution. His ambition was sent soaring by his meetings with Roosevelt. He observed every inflection and gesture of the president's, recording each one: "His delivery was clear, concise and direct. He speaks slowly, carefully, enunciating each word and with a sort of musical utterance at times. He has a habit of showing all his teeth both when he laughs and speaks. At the dinner he entered into the fun like a boy. He keeps himself erect and firmly set. His whole manner and appearance bespeak force and determination. There is an undoubted impulsiveness and strong tendency to combativeness.... I have the greatest possible admiration for him."

Roosevelt had startled King with words on the impending danger of war. The wide-eyed visitor concluded that indeed the world was on the verge of a major conflict and he elicited from his talk with Roosevelt a message for himself, a grandiose message.

"I feel it has been a golden day lined with cloud all over it," he wrote in his diary. "But the meaning of it has found its way to my heart. It looks as though I was to help preserve peace between nations."[6]

CHAPTER FIVE

The Missing Tact of President Taft

MOST LIKELY NO United States president loved Canadian soil so much as William Howard Taft. Most likely no president would be hurt so much by a decision of the Canadian people.

In 1892, Taft, then an Ohio judge, rented a summer cottage on the banks of the St. Lawrence in Murray Bay, Quebec. The place and its people immediately captivated the huge, affable man with the walrus moustache. Through the next four decades he would return almost every summer to eat hearty meat breakfasts, sharpen his imprecise golf game and delight the French Canadian townfolk with tall stories.

His cottage porch overlooked the river and each afternoon Taft would slowly pilot his 310 pounds into a yawning chair. He would sit there for hours breathing the pure air, following the flight of the gulls, watching the whitefish dance on the running blue waters.

When he became president in 1908, custom commanded him to refrain from foreign travel. Three months into office he was thinking about how he was going to miss his Canadian summers. "There is no place like Murray Bay," he wrote his brother, Charles. "If I only have one term, as seems likely in view of the complications that will be presented during that term, one of the great consolations will be that I can go to Murray Bay in the summers thereafter.

"Tell Annie [Charles' wife] that every once in a while when she breathes her lungs full of that delicious air, she shall think of me and know that I envy her opportunity."

The habitants of the little village loved Taft. They would fondly refer to him as *le petit juge* and when he entered town they would raise their caps. Taft's birthday on September 15 was the closing event of every summer season. The Quebeckers would fill his cottage and celebrate through the night. When he was gone in the winters, they would stage skits with the largest, most jovial villager honoured to play *le petit juge*. But no disrespect was shown. Taft was their hero. Later when Teddy Roosevelt split the Republican ranks, thereby ruining Taft's re-election bid, they spat in disgust at how their friend had been betrayed. When Taft died in 1930, sadness swept Murray Bay. The townspeople lit candles in his honour.[1]

The feelings in this little corner of Quebec did not mirror however the feelings of the rest of Canada. Nor did the wonderful village diplomacy of Taft extend to the rest of the sprawling Dominion. Just like Franklin Roosevelt, another president with a Canadian cottage, Taft wanted to forge a special, new relationship with the neighbouring country. His idea was a comprehensive free-trade agreement which, in economic terms, would forever weld the two countries together. For Taft, it was to be "the most important measure of my administration." It was to be "an epoch in our country's history."

Had he been able to work more closely with Laurier, and had the president and the prime minister communicated better, such an "epoch" may have come about. What did come about was not an epoch in Taft's country but an epoch, a declaration of independence, in the other country.

The free-trade issue had been somewhat dormant since the miscarriage of 1898. In the following years Canada was prosperous, riding a wheat boom. There was little pressure for change. In Washington, Roosevelt had been personally interested in an agreement but didn't like his chances in the still largely protectionist Congress. But by 1910, there was a change of drift. Duties were going up, a tariff war threatened, and American complaints about the high cost of living were increasing. Taft needed something to buck the slumbering image of his administration. The thought of open Dominion markets was appealing.

One day, while vacationing in Washington, Reverend James A.

Macdonald, the Toronto *Globe* editor, was introduced to the president. Not an average introduction, this one soon found Macdonald in Ottawa at the office of the prime minister. "Taft was almost in a panic," Macdonald revealed, "over what he could do to secure exemption for Canada from the effects of the bill the high tariff gang are forcing on the country. He wanted to know if I thought Sir Wilfrid would meet him to consider a reciprocity measure."

Taft wanted a meeting with Laurier in Albany, New York in March. Laurier, either ill or feigning illness, said he couldn't make it. Earl Grey, the governor-general, and Finance Minister W. S. Fielding went in his place. (The Dominion had an External Affairs department by this time. In 1909, Laurier had created one atop a barber shop on Bank Street. It consisted of a deputy minister, two clerks, a secretary, and an annual operating budget of $14,950. But there was no External Affairs minister to represent Canada in foreign countries. In Washington the British ambassador was still handling the duties.)

Taft's message was that there must be a special arrangement with Canada. "I am profoundly convinced," he told his visitors, "that these two countries, touching each other for more than three thousand miles, have common interests in trade and require special arrangements in legislation and administration which are not involved in the relations of the United States with nations beyond the seas. We may not have always recognized that in the past but that must be our viewpoint in the future. Say that for me to the people of Canada, with all the earnestness and sincerity of my heart."

Lord Grey echoed Taft's sentiments. "Although living under different forms of free and enlightened government we are, so far as the real big things of the world are concerned, practically one people."

Taft and Grey got along famously. While behind closed doors the general points of a vast trading arrangement were being debated, up front and for the newspapers the president was challenging Grey to a golf match for the executive championship of North America. Taft, who took Grey as a special guest in his train compartment to New York, boasted that he had recently shot less than 100. But, the New York *Times* reported on page one: "the Earl was nothing daunted at this and accepted the challenge forthwith."

The Taft trade proposal was a call for the removal of tariffs on all natural products as well as some manufactured items. Lower rates would be applied to secondary food products, agricultural implements, and some commodities. Touring the west in the summer, Prime Minister Laurier, now sixty-nine, found support for such a measure, particularly from disgruntled farmers who resented the extent to which high tariffs favoured eastern manufacturers. Like Taft, Laurier felt his complacent government needed a dramatic initiative. The defeat of the Liberals in the 1891 election when they proposed free trade was having little carry-over effect. It was a long time ago. Support in Laurier's party caucus for the measure was strong, support in the United States this time was strong and, as far as Laurier could ascertain, support in Canada was strong. On January 21, 1911 following a long series of bilateral negotiations, a comprehensive agreement between the governments was signed, leaving final approval to the respective legislatures.

In Washington, where a sardonic reporter described the agreement as "Taft's first policy," the president began selling it to Congress. In 1910, of $376 million in total Canadian imports, $223 million had come from the United States. "The reduction in the duties imposed by Canada," said Taft, "will largely increase this amount and give us even a larger share of her market than we now enjoy, great as that is."

The Dominion, he asserted, "has greatly prospered. It has an active, aggressive, intelligent people. They are coming to the parting of the ways. They must soon decide whether they are to regard themselves as isolated permanently from our markets by a perpetual wall or whether we are to be commercial friends."[2]

His reference to "the parting of the ways" was largely overlooked by the press. But unfortunately for Taft, he liked the phrase, would use it often, and reporters would pick it up. Initially the president reaped favourable press treatment on reciprocity. One reason was that the agreement would mean cheaper imports of newsprint from Canada for U.S. newspaper publishers. Beneath the surface, however, Taft worried. "I send you a copy of my message on Canadian reciprocity," he wrote Horace, his brother. It will "suit you, I think, though it may not suit any other of the 90 millions of people."

His real concern was laid out in a striking letter to Teddy Roosevelt dated January 10, 1911, eleven days before the pact was even signed. Taft knew then what the problem was going to be. He also knew that it was a legitimate problem. The letter read:

"The amount of Canadian products we would take," he wrote, "would produce a current of business between western Canada and the United States that would make Canada only an adjunct of the United States."

He continued: "It would transfer all their important business to Chicago and New York, with their bank credits and everything else, and it would greatly increase the demand of Canada for our manufactures. I see this as an argument made against reciprocity in Canada and I think it is a good one."

His forecast was accurate but despite his awareness of the impending problem Taft was unable to work to alleviate it. Instead, his words and the wayward words of a congressional leader would only do the opposite. While in the cabinet of Teddy Roosevelt, Taft had always impressed the president with his diplomatic touch. "With Taft sitting on the lid," Roosevelt used to say in mock reference to Taft's ample girth, "everything will be okay." But this was not an accurate characterization of Taft, particularly in respect to reciprocity. The Cincinnati-born, Yale-educated man with the sparkling blue eyes that dashed from side to side with unusual speed, was as apolitical as any president. Taft abhorred the chicanery of politics. He had never craved the Oval Office. He always wanted to be a Supreme Court judge. There, his considerable intellectual powers and unchallenged integrity could be used in greater quantity. There he would not have to play so many political games.

In the Congress Taft had a man who sometimes didn't know how to play the political games any better than he did. James Beauchamp Clark was the Democratic party leader in the House of Representatives. Because his party had won a majority in the 1910 midterm elections he was about to be officially named the second most powerful man in Washington—speaker of the House. The Missouri-born Clark, who was nicknamed "Champ" in the United States and was to be nicknamed "Chump" in Canada, joined in a raucous February 14 debate on the reciprocity bill. He spoke the most damaging words of support that any Canada-U.S. legislation has ever received. "I am for it," cried Clark, "because I hope to see the day when the American flag will float over every square foot of the British North America possessions clear to the north pole!

"They are people of our blood. They speak our language. Their institutions are much like ours...I do not have any doubt whatever that the day is not far distant when Great Britain will see all of her North American possessions become a part of this Republic. That is the way things are tending now."

A congressman named Norris wanted to make sure of what he was hearing. "As I understand it," Norris said, "the gentleman favors this bill for at least one reason; that it will have a tendency in the end to bring Canada into the union."

"Yes sir," said Clark. "Have no doubt about that."

The speech had no immediate negative impact in the United States. The House voted shortly after it to approve reciprocity. In Ottawa, news of the vote, not news of the speech, arrived while the Commons was sitting. Government members interrupted the business of the day to applaud for several minutes. Prime Minister Laurier joined in. The opposition Conservatives were visibly nonplussed. They thought the reciprocity package would be a winner for the Liberals. "There was the deepest dejection in our party," Tory leader Robert Borden later recalled. "Many of our members were confident that the Government's proposals would appeal to the country and would give it another term of office."

Amazement and indignation accosted the news of the Clark remarks. Laurier decried the speech, British government officials ravaged it, and Taft issued a statement to clarify the situation saying: "No thought of future political annexation or union was in the minds of the negotiators on either side. Canada is now and will remain a political unit."

Sensing that this was not enough, Taft then arranged for Secretary of State Philander Knox to wipe away remaining doubts. "The United States recognizes with satisfaction," said Knox in a landmark speech on Canada-U.S. relations in Chicago, "that the Dominion of Canada is a permanent North American political unit and that her autonomy is secure." After forty-four years, Washington was issuing an official, unqualified, categorical statement of Canadian autonomy. Knox continued: "It is probably more true today than ever before that the weight of sentiment and opinion both in Canada and the United States, while desiring closer relations in all other respects, is crystallized in a belief that the present political separation is desirable and will lead to the best development of each nation and to better and more satisfactory relations between them."

In 1938 Franklin Roosevelt would be credited with the first formal declaration pledging American military support of Canada in any time of peril. But Knox, a Pennsylvanian and an attorney-general under McKinley, did virtually the same thing in his Chicago speech. "In the higher atmosphere and broader aspects of the situation, it is certain that if there should be any great world movement involving the continent, Canada and United States would, as a matter of course, act in the most perfect concert in defense of the common rights of a common blood of civilization."

Despite the assurances, Taft was clearly apprehensive: "That speech of Clark's," he told his personal physician, "has unquestionably sounded the death knell of the reciprocity pact and it was the plan nearest to my heart."

"Bosh!" he cried out in a speech to newspaper editors in New York's Waldorf-Astoria on April 27. "The talk of annexation is bosh. Everyone who knows anything about it realizes that it is bosh. Canada is a great strong youth anxious to test his muscles, rejoicing in the race he is ready to run.

"The United States has all it can attend to with the territory it is now governing, and to make the possibility of the annexation of Canada to United States a basis for objection to any steps toward their great economic and commercial union should be treated as one of the jokes of the platform."

At the same time he was trying to beat down the annexation bogey, the president continued to make insensitive remarks that nullified his gains. "The bond uniting the Dominion with the mother country is light and almost imperceptible," he said in the same New York speech. And, on another occasion: "Now is the accepted time. Now Canada is in the mood. She is at the parting of the ways."

Such were the comments that were highlighted in the Canadian press. In the United States, they were not damaging. There, after a Taft speaking tour to promote the package, after he called a special session of Congress to deal with reciprocity alone, and after strained political infighting, reciprocity was approved. In a strange departure from the norm, Taft's Republican members in both the Senate and the House of Representatives voted predominantly against the bill. But most of the Democrats supported the president on it. The Democrats traditionally represented lower tariffs, but in this case many were inclined to support Taft because they thought reciprocity would ultimately do him more harm than good.

The focus turned to Canada. Laurier had been so confident in the early spring: "The country is decidedly with us." Time would bring with it a better understanding of the policy, he thought. Some more beating up on the annexation stuff would take its toll; the Liberals, in power for fifteen years, would continue their run.

"I don't understand," Laurier told his people, "that kind of logic which says that a man will lose his manhood by trading with a good neighbour. We stand on our manhood.... This talk of annexation is simply beneath the contempt and beneath the attention of a serious people.... Rather than part with our national existence, we would part with our lives."

The eloquence was splendid, but as time passed, the Conservatives were finding increasing hostility in the population toward the reciprocity plan. Railroad, manufacturing, and banking interests of the East were lining up and organizing against it on economic grounds. And the "little man," as much as Laurier told him no, was receptive to the annexation argument. So the Tories brought on filibusters and assorted delaying tactics to stem the rush of the prime minister's legislation and, still confident, Laurier decided to challenge them at the polls on it.

"Bet on the old cock," he told voters in Trois-Rivières, Quebec on August 17. "Soon I shall be 70 years old and rest, which I have not known for so many years, would be most grateful to me. But I should be ashamed of myself if I did not devote what talents I may have, and all my strength, to the service of the country."

"I do not know what the future holds. It is said that the most uncertain things in the world are horseraces, elections and cockfights. But if I were a betting man I would bet on the old cock which has been winning for the last 15 years."

He had tried to get through to Taft in order to have the president do more to diminish Canadian fears, but he didn't do this by writing. Curiously, the two men exchanged a few letters on trivial concerns but not on the reciprocity issue. Instead, Laurier used an intermediary named John Hays Hammond. Caution Taft, Laurier told Hammond, "against creating the impression that there is political significance in this treaty."

After its initial rejection of "Champ" Clark's remarks, the White House found it difficult to understand how the fear of absorption could be such a grand concern in Canada. Indeed, Americans generally found the fear difficult to understand. Writing at the time, Teddy Roosevelt, in typically graphic form, explained the situation: "No human being seriously thought that this was a step toward annexation. Unfortunately three or four prize idiots of importance, including the Speaker of the House, indulged in some perfectly conventional chatter which, although universally understood here as being a rehearsal of 'letting the eagle scream' on the fourth of July, was apparently accepted seriously in Canada. And poor Taft seemingly cannot learn anything about foreign affairs and made some remarks that were as thoroughly ill-judged as was possible."

The election date was September 21, 1911. It was no secret what the thrust of the Conservatives' campaign would be. "I beg Canadians," said Borden in a speech typical of many, "to cast a soberly considered and serious vote for the preservation of our heritage, for the maintenance of our commercial and political freedom, for the permanence of Canada as an autonomous nation of the British Empire."

The question for Laurier and for Taft, who also had a large stake in this election, was how to allay the annexation fears. In modern times when the leaders could pick up telephones and discuss such things or pay a routine visit, strategy formation was not so difficult. In 1911, when telephones weren't around, and presidents didn't visit foreign countries, the chances of misunderstanding and miscalculation were great. Laurier wanted Taft to speak out and yet he didn't want him to speak out. Taft wanted to speak out and yet he didn't want to speak out. It could backfire if he did, and be construed as interference in a foreign country. The Conservatives might profit.

But conversely, would not a grandly staged, intensely publicized, blanket refutation of the insinuations kill the spread of the fire? The president hadn't issued a major denial since April and he had done much to spoil that denial by more talk in the intervening period about "the parting of the ways." Was not another statement mandatory?

The pressure on Taft began in the summer. S. R. Richard, a former Liberal member of Parliament from western Canada, cabled Charles Hilles, the executive assistant to the president, recommending an unequivocal statement from Taft on the meaning of "the parting of the ways." Otherwise, the Liberals might lose, he said.

"The President is willing to make his position very emphatic," the response from the State Department said, "but will not interfere without their [Laurier officials'] full knowledge and an intimation as to what they would have him do. Would it help the cause to have him explode annexation talk on a western trip in Michigan, Minnesota or elsewhere?"

A state department official, Charles Pepper, contacted Ottawa cabinet members. President Taft talked to British ambassador James Bryce. James Bryce talked to Laurier. Laurier was cool. Bryce told the president as much. Taft held back.

By September 7, the election two weeks away, the Tories gaining ground, Laurier, less confident of winning, had changed his mind. That day, campaigning in Sudbury, Ontario, he met Henry Appleton, a friend. A statement from the President, he told Appleton, could move thousands of votes to the Liberal column. Could you contact the White House?

Appleton contacted Pepper and Charles Osborn, who was the governor of Michigan and a good friend of Taft's. The president was planning a speaking tour before September 21 that would take him to Sault Ste. Marie on the American side. Laurier "personally desired me," Appleton wrote the Michigan governor, "to ask you and President Taft if it would be possible for you to give the public in your addresses at the Soo the correct version of reciprocity." He told them of the damage the "parting of the ways" commotion was causing: "I need only tell you that your addresses will be quoted largely on the 20th as it is the day before the election in Canada and, as Mr. Laurier has well said, if the right word was said at that time it would mean thousands of votes.... Trusting that you will not consider me presumptuous to present the matter as it was presented to me, I am...."

The governor telegrammed Taft: "Your parting of the ways speech... is being used emphatically in Canada against reciprocity. Is it possible you would come to refer to the subject publicly in Detroit in a manner calculated to convey most clearly what you meant so as to disarm those who are misinterpreting it and thus taking unfair advantage?"

Pepper then wrote Taft's executive assistant on the timing of a possible speech. "Do it for the Saturday afternoon papers because they have no Sunday papers of importance in Canada," he advised.[3]

The president at this time was worried about a challenge from Robert La Follette to his renomination to lead the Republicans. He wanted the reciprocity win badly because it was an approach he wished to try with other countries and because the boost would help distance him from the challenger. "If we can only carry reciprocity in Canada," he wrote his brother Horace a week before the election, "we can put our whole case on an actual test." William Hoster, an acquaintance of Taft staying at the Windsor Hotel in Montreal, received a letter from the president about the same time. Taft wrote, "I am really very anxious to have Sir Wilfrid win and am very hopeful that he will because I do not think the people of Canada have felt the necessity for the uplift [from reciprocity]."

The plans for a blockbuster Taft speech appeared ready. But only a few days before the election, executive assistant Hilles was given some impressive news by a friend named John Stewart. "I have recently been in Canada," said Stewart, "and lunched with the Liberal manager who gave me the result of his canvass of the Dominion on the reciprocity question. It may interest you and is as follows...Liberal Majority—49."

Now the question arose—Was there any need for a speech by the president? Would it not be a reckless gamble? The Liberals were going to win anyway.

In Secretary of State Knox's office, a cable then arrived from John G. Foster, the U.S. consul general in Ottawa: "Confidential. The newspapers report President contemplates discussing reciprocity at Sault Ste. Marie and other frontier posts before the Canadian elections. Conservatives are trying to make out a case of American interference and will undoubtedly misconstrue if possible any utterance on this subject."

Knox forwarded the message to Hilles. Hilles informed the president. A decision was made. The president would not make a speech on reciprocity.

On September 19 he arrived at Sault Ste. Marie where he was greeted by large crowds including many Canadians who had come across the border, as some of them said, "to meet the man who was going to annex Canada."

Taft was friendly. "A gentleman from Canada. Glad to meet you Sir." He was pressed on the reciprocity issue. It is "sub judice" he declared. "I have sufficient sense of propriety to say nothing on the subject but merely to say that I am in a state of prayer and hope." Being on the boundary, he did what virtually every president and prime minister of the twentieth century would do: he paid tribute to the undefended border. "That 4,900 miles of boundary has no forts. We have no battleships. There is nothing here to mark the difference between the two countries save custom houses and some natural boundaries. Now that presents an example that might well commend itself to all countries and all nations."[4]

In Canada, as one of the most emotional elections moved toward verdict time, the big names were wheeled out. "The Americans are a great people," said Stephen Leacock, an economist and great man of letters, "but fifty years ago we settled the question as to what our lot was to be with respect to them. We have decided once and for all that the British flag was good enough for us."

Rudyard Kipling issued a statement in the Montreal *Star:* "It is her own soul that Canada risks....Once that soul is pawned for any consideration Canada must inevitably conform to the commercial, financial, social and ethical standards which will be imposed upon her by the sheer admitted weight of the United States." Americans had already dissipated their resources, he said. Now "they are driven to seek virgin fields for cheaper food and clothing."

On election day, President Taft was in Battle Creek, Michigan. "They say we want to annex Canada. Huh," he said mockingly: "Gentlemen, my experience in this government has taught me that we have enough territory without enlarging borders."

He lashed out at some of the treatment he had been receiving: "I know that some irresponsible newspapers have called me a trickster and a swindler and say that I in some way deceived or played unfairly with the ministers of Canada to secure the treaty." But, "there wasn't any trick about it. The cards were laid on the table."

He told his aides that afternoon that he thought reciprocity would win. In the evening he moved on to Kalamazoo, Michigan, where he attended a banquet. White slips of paper were frequently passed to him at the head table and, with each, his countenance grew more grim. "Canadian election very close," a telegram at 8:40 P.M. warned him. "Conservatives now have 14 majority overall. Five cabinet ministers have been defeated including Fielding and Patterson, the framers of the pact. Result will be in doubt until the west is heard from."

At 9:08 P.M. there was no doubt. "Laurier Government and reciprocity beaten."

President Taft moved his large body sadly to the podium. "I have just been informed that reciprocity has failed in Canada," he announced. The audience members were against reciprocity. They applauded his words and then there were cries of "hush, hush." Taft chuckled a little bit. "I know there are a lot of people in this vicinity who want to see reciprocity defeated," but, he said, "for me, it is a great disappointment. I had hoped that it would be put through to prove the correctness of my judgment that it would be a good thing for both countries. It takes two to make a bargain however and if Canada declines I suppose that we can still go along still doing business at the old stand." The people applauded him then and Taft waved his hand in appreciation of their consideration.[5]

A few days later he wrote indelicately to Horace: "The Canadian contest which was raging when you wrote has been settled. ... We were hit squarely between the eyes and must now sit tight. Of course I am very disappointed because I should like to have had this scalp dangling at my official belt even if I am only going to wear the belt for four years."

In Ottawa, Laurier was graceful in defeat, while new Prime Minister Borden saw little that was anti-American feeling in the Canadian vote. "In rejecting reciprocity, Canada has simply affirmed her adherence to a policy of national development which she has pursued for many years. The verdict was in no way dictated by any spirit of unfriendliness to the great neighbouring republic. No such spirit exists."

The Laurier cabinet met for the last time on September 26 and it concluded that the prejudice against the United States, inspired by Taft's "parting of the ways" speech and Champ Clark's mouthings, was the cause of the loss. "We have been beaten," Laurier said, "but I say again I have nothing to regret. We could not have refused that offer [reciprocity] and been true to ourselves. We have been beaten but we can keep our heads erect." Young Mackenzie King learned a lesson. "The moral," he noted in his diary, "is to make no appeal in good times for something better. It is only when people are hard up that they see the advantage of change."

Speaker "Champ" Clark was unrepentant. After his House speech had sparked the furor, he had tried to beg off, saying that his remarks were only half serious. Now a few weeks after the election in Fremont, Nebraska, he declared: "Nine tenths of the people in this country favor the annexation of Canada and I don't care who hears me say it. I am willing to make this proposition. You let me run for President on a platform calling for the annexation of Canada, insofar as this country can accomplish that end, and let President Taft run against me, opposing annexation, and I would carry every state in the nation."

President Taft ran for re-election the following autumn. He was ransacked, winning only two states. The only consolation for *le petit juge* was the granting of the wish he had expressed in the letter early in his presidency. He was now free to return to spend his summers in the place he loved—Murray Bay. In that corner of Quebec, Canadians were more friendly to him. He returned there every summer until 1930 when the habitants lit the candles.

CHAPTER SIX

Borden and the
Fight for Recognition

EARLY DECEMBER, 1911, ten weeks after victory, Prime Minister Borden journeyed to New York where he lunched with Teddy Roosevelt. "Mr. Prime Minister," said Roosevelt respectfully, "I do not expect you to make an admission but I am confident that in your heart you are profoundly grateful to my friend Mr. Taft for some of his utterances with regard to the effect of the reciprocity proposals."[1]

The prime minister concurred. Borden had won on the trade issue but he realized fortune had played a paramount role. Despite his own truculent opposition to reciprocity, Borden did not feel, deep down, that it was such a bad idea. Once, during the campaign, President Taft warned that if Canada didn't move commercially closer to the United States, it would be forever locked into a disadvantageous British imperial preference system. Hearing that, Borden told friends: "The most serious feature of Taft's utterances is their profound truth."

Now Canada's eighth prime minister, worried about negative American reaction to the vote, was anxious to reassure the country of Canada's friendship. "I recognize the duty of Canada," he told an audience on the New York trip, "to become more and more a bond of goodwill and friendship between this Great Republic and our Empire. It may well be said that for the cause of kinship and neighbourliness, Canada owes this to you. But I would rather put it on higher ground;

that for the cause of Christianity and civilization, she owes it to herself."

His campaign rhetoric had championed the British connection, but in office Borden would pursue a different course. He would try to reduce dependence on Britain, so that in future dealings with Washington, Canada could speak for Canada. The problem, as he put it in a letter to his wife, was that Canada was "a nation that is not a nation." The Dominion was independent in domestic policy but a vassal of Britain in foreign policy. This status was reflected on occasions such as the Paris Peace Conference which concluded World War I. French President Clemenceau, arranging for a session with Britain that would include Dominion representatives, told Lloyd George, the British leader; "Come—And bring your savages with you."

With Borden's stewardship, the pressures for change had grown strong. With survival on the continent, economic health, the trans-Canada railway, and with a significant contribution in World War I, the Canadian sense of nationhood and Canada's desire for an independent voice in the world, particularly in the United States, had been enhanced. The Canadian experience in Washington was a critical factor in giving rise to the demand for control of foreign policy, in expanding on that demand, and in bringing it to fruition. On many occasions, the most serious being the Washington Treaty (1871) and the Alaska dispute (1903), Canadian prime ministers or their associates had been compelled to negotiate with the White House as part of a British team and had been defeated and embarrassed as a result. The prime ministers had come to feel that if Canada was to lose to Washington, Canada was going to lose of its own accord.

The calls for independent negotiating status actually started soon after Canada was born. The pressure increased step by step, almost year by year, but it would be more than half a century from Dominion Day before the rights in Washington were won.

L. S. Huntington introduced a bill in Parliament in 1870 proposing that Canada be given the right to negotiate commercial treaties in the American capital. Prime Minister Macdonald, who had yet to undergo the Washington Treaty experience, blocked the bid. In 1877, Sir Alexander Galt, who was representing Canada at the Halifax negotiation on a price for the fisheries, warned the prime minister that it was time for seeking diplomatic status because "as colonials these arrogant insulars [British] turn up their noses at us all." Later, during the 1888 negotiation with the Cleveland administration, a frustrated Charles Tupper squeezed Macdonald on the issue again: "I confess that from my experience in Washington the crass ignorance of everything Canadian among the leading public men makes me attach the greatest importance to our having an able man in a position to dispel that ignorance."

The presidents themselves did not actively seek to perpetuate Canada's colonial bargaining status. Many would have preferred to negotiate with the Dominion alone. British shelter for Canada, some felt, made the task of achieving a good, quick settlement much more difficult.

Secretary of State Bayard, the man who said in 1877 that the building of the railway had brought the United States face to face with a nation, explained the Washington view of Canada's diplomatic status in a letter to Tupper the same year: "In the very short interview afforded by your visit, I referred to the embarrassment arising out of the gradual, practical emancipation of Canada from the control of the Mother country.... The awkwardness of this imperfectly developed sovereignty is felt most strongly in the United States which cannot have formal relations with Canada except directly as a colonial dependency of the British Crown....

"Nothing could better illustrate the embarrassment arising from this amorphous condition of things than the volumes of correspondence published severally this year relating to the fisheries by the United States, Great Britain and the Government of the Dominion. The time lost in this circumlocution, although often most regrettable, was the least part of the difficulty, and the indirectness of the appeal and reply was the most serious feature, ending, as it did, most unsatisfactorily."

President McKinley and Secretary Hay were frustrated in 1898 by having to find solutions to Canadian problems that satisfied both Canada and Britain. Teddy Roosevelt told Canadian lumber executives in 1906 that he was surprised Canada hadn't modernized its antiquated system of representation. William Taft wished he could have dealt more closely with Canadians on reciprocity.

Had Alexander Mackenzie, the first Liberal prime minister, stayed in power longer, the drive for change likely would have been much stronger. Macdonald, despite his annoyance with dealing through the

British, chose to resist such a move because he felt the support of London in Washington still gave Canada more leverage than she would otherwise have.

In 1892, however, the House of Commons passed a resolution requiring negotiations with England to begin on the subject. The British, feeling that the Empire would quickly be destroyed should Dominions like Canada be given independent treaty-making power, were reluctant but did make gradual concessions strengthening Ottawa's ability to make autonomous commercial agreements.[2]

The Alaska boundary decision, viewed widely in Canada as a farce, gave tremendous impetus to the push for more power. Laurier caused a stir in both London and Washington with a candid appraisal in the House: "I have often regretted Mr. Speaker, and never more than on the present occasion, that we are living beside a great neighbour who, I believe I can say without being unfriendly to them, are very grasping in their national acts and who are determined upon every occasion to get the best in any agreement they make. I have often regretted also that while they are a great and powerful nation, we are only a small colony, a growing colony, but still a colony. I have often regretted also that we have not in our hands the treaty making power which would enable us to dispose of our own affairs.... Our hands are tied to a large extent owing to the fact of our connection."

Laurier's creation of the Department of External Affairs was a partial response to the problem. In the same year, 1909, the International Joint Commission was formed for the purpose of arbitrating boundary disputes between Canada and the United States. Britain took part in negotiating the agreement but the IJC was a precedent breaker for Canada in that it was a foreign body in which Britain had no input on the Canadian side.

More strides might have been made under Laurier if not for the inspired performance of British ambassador James Bryce who eased tensions by looking after Canada's interests in Washington with far greater effectiveness than the likes of Thornton and Sackville-West. By 1912 Bryce was saying that "about 90 percent of all my official duties at Washington are purely Canadian business transactions." He felt that a Canadian minister should be appointed in his place, and so did the newly-elected Robert Borden.

The prime minister from Nova Scotia, earnest, even, and able, presided over a quiet first two years on the bilateral front. The annexation furor had died down, the long-standing fisheries dispute had been settled by a tribunal at The Hague in 1909, the Bering Sea controversy was put to rest to Canada's satisfaction in 1911, and the new IJC was quietly solving problems that previously had been the bailiwick of clamourous, high-profile joint commissions.

But no sooner had the plate been cleared than World War I broke out, engendering new antagonisms in Canada-U.S. relations and thrusting aside minor business, such as a representative for the Dominion in Washington. The United States was three years behind Canada in entering the carnage, its per capita contribution in manpower tiny compared to Canada's five hundred thousand, and when U.S. War Secretary Newton Baker had the temerity to suggest that his country was "now in the dominant moral position in the war," there was considerable resentment in the Dominion. Roosevelt, the old Canadian enemy, jumped to his neighbour's defence. "We have no right to consider ourselves at a standing level with Canada until we have placed five million men in the field."

Borden took the same stand, promoting the Canadian effort on trips south of the border, while pausing occasionally to keep his wife Laura up to date on the latest fashions in Manhattan. "The New York ladies are arrayed in the most stunning frocks I have ever seen," he wrote on a 1916 visit. "But some of them are mightily abbreviated." However, he didn't travel to Washington to meet Woodrow Wilson until February, 1918. Before the visit, he was warned by an associate named James Dunn that Wilson, the former Princeton University president, was "the most stubborn man in the world. No matter how wrong he may prove to be, he never changes his views." Others viewed the president, Dunn reported, as "a Bolshevik at heart." The prime minister's own first appraisal had not been flattering: "Great rhetorician but a weak and shifty politician." It was to get worse.

On Secretary of State Robert Lansing, Borden had been warned by ambassador Bryce that talking to the man was like speaking through the telephone with the connection cut off. The prime minister's own experience with Lansing, the New York lawyer who had stated the concluding arguments in the Alaska boundary arbitration, confirmed this view.

The visit, which featured discussions on how to win the War, bilateral cooperation in the War effort, and Borden boasts on the Canadian contribution, went smoothly—but was somewhat disfigured by an event north of the border. William Jennings Bryan, the perennial presidential candidate and Wilson's first secretary of state was shouted down and forced to stop his speech by an angry mob in Toronto's Massey Hall. Many spectators opposed Bryan's prohibitionist leanings while others felt he was too sympathetic to Germany in the War. More than one hundred people wore gas masks. Bryan, a brilliant orator, was stunned. He tried to calm the audience with appeals to continental brotherhood: "The same blood pulses through our veins." He then used a phrase which John F. Kennedy would later get credit for coining: "God has made us neighbors." But there was no hope, and Bryan left complaining bitterly to a reporter; "There isn't a city in the union where there is any danger of my being intercepted" like this. The incident received front-page coverage in many U.S. papers, compelling Borden to issue a statement: "I observe with deepest regret the occurrence at Toronto last night but was glad to note it was due to various small portions of the audience."

Borden would next meet Wilson at the Paris Peace Conference in early 1919. American claims that "we won the War" rankled the quiet prime minister as they did his population. His effort was to get Canada what he felt was due recognition — independent voting status in the peace settlement and eligibility to the council of the nascent League of Nations. Wilson was his main opponent on both counts and Borden got straight to the point, sending him a souvenir edition of the Montreal *Standard,* extolling Canada's War effort. The president was hardly enthusiastic. "It is very interesting to have such a record of the important part taken by Canada in this war," he responded.[3]

The initial peace conference plan called for five voting delegates from each of Britain, United States, France, Italy, and Japan, two from each of the smaller allied nations, and none from the Dominions. Borden, normally a stranger to the employment of wit, muttered to associates about the need for Canadians to "hold our own with Patagonia."

He found Wilson "very tiresome" and "obstinate as a mule," and Lansing was "arrogant and disagreeable." The secretary of state remarked condescendingly: "Why should Canada be concerned in the settlement of European affairs?" Lloyd George promptly reminded him that Canada "lost more men than the United States in the War."

A spirited lobbying effort, spearheaded by Borden, led the way to recognition. The Dominions won the right to be represented by two delegates each, and the right to sign the peace treaty in their own names.

In the League of Nations battle, Borden again directed the effort, demonstrating a passion for battle that few realized he possessed. A stinging memo from the prime minister declared that "the people of Canada will not tamely submit to a dictation which declares that Liberia or Cuba, Panama or Hejaz, Haiti or Ecuador, must have a higher place."[4]

When the name of President Wilson was raised during a Borden conversation with Lloyd George, the prime minister berated the president with such indignation that Lloyd George implored: "For heaven's sake, don't look at me like that."

Borden was more diplomatic in a note he sent Wilson about Canada's proposed changes to the League covenant: "...You will understand, I am sure, that it is my desire to be helpful and not critical. I fully realize the immense difficulties which have been overcome in presenting to the world this supremely important document upon which the future of humanity so greatly depends. I appreciate also the danger of undertaking amendments which may renew differences that the committee found it difficult to compose...."

With a big assist from Lloyd George, Borden succeeded in convincing Wilson that representation for the Dominions would not mean domination of the post-war world by the British Empire. The victory was tarnished, however, when the U.S. senate rejected American participation in the League, partly on the grounds that Britain would wield too much power. A disgusted Borden concluded: "In foreign affairs the politicians of the United States act like children and do not recognize their responsibilities to their country and to the world."[5]

The peace conference taught Borden the difficulties inherent in being "a nation that is not a nation." In reflecting on that anomalous position he wrote Laura: "It is about time to alter it." And in the context of U.S. relations that is the field to which his battle now shifted.

Near the close of the War, a Canadian mission had been established in Washington for the purpose of coordinating war-related activities. The end of the fighting removed its purpose, but instead of disbanding the mission, Borden wanted it replaced by a Canadian office with a minister enjoying full diplomatic status. Wilson did not object, saying that if it was okay with Britain it was okay with him. The president, despite being so exasperating for Borden at Paris, held no grudge against the Dominion. At a cabinet meeting in September 1920 he defended the Canadian pulp and paper industry, shooting down colleagues who were grumbling about high import prices. He said he sympathized with Canadian conservation efforts and, according to Navy Secretary Joe Daniels, argued that "newspapers had too much paper now." Daniels countered that "Canada was not trying to conserve but was robbing publishers." Wilson spurned him.[6]

Borden won 10 Downing's approval for a Canadian minister in Washington but there were catches. The Canadian would sometimes have to report to the British ambassador. When the latter was absent, the Canadian would have to move into the British embassy in his place. As a result, opposition Liberals decried the idea. Canada would be "establishing a kindergarten school of diplomacy," argued W. S. Fielding. "If Canada sends an ambassador to Washington he will degenerate into nothing better than a clerk under the British ambassador." Another member of the Opposition said it would take more than "pink teas and 10 o'clock dinner in Washington to make Canada a nation."

But Borden assented to the arrangement and on April 26, 1920, Robert Lansing, his American adversary, announced that the United States had agreed to Canada having direct diplomatic relations.

But strangely, after the long battle had been won Borden did not follow through with an immediate appointment. When he stepped aside due to ailing health, the promising Arthur Meighen succeeded him. Meighen, tied down by a sick economy, couldn't find a suitable candidate for the Washington appointment. Again it was delayed, though not due to any distaste for the idea on his part; later in 1921, he would rock the Imperial Conference with the declaration that "in all questions affecting Canada and the United States, the Dominion shall have full and final authority." But the Conservative prime minister wasn't in office long enough to put his assertion to the test.

Mackenzie King beat him in 1921 in yet another election in which U.S. tariffs played a big role. The Republican administration of Warren Harding was increasing the duties at a rapid clip and Meighen went to the country advocating a "brick for brick" customs wall to keep pace. King, aware of the lessons of the Laurier period, didn't push free trade but "freer trade," and won narrowly.

A man more continentally inclined than any prime minister before him, King would greatly change the face of the North American relationship in his amazing twenty-two years of power. Countries that were friends in name, and only sometimes, would become friends in deed. Canada and the United States would become, quite arguably, the world's greatest neighbours.

But before all this, in the initial years, when King was still feeling his way around and there was not a man in the Oval Office with whom he could closely connect, the bilateral initiatives were few. It would be six years before he moved ahead with the appointment of the minister to Washington — an extraordinary stall for a country that had so long complained about British representation and for a prime minister intent on tying the continent closer together. Among the explanations were: opposition in the Canadian Parliament; lingering antipathy in Britain; the lack of an appropriate man for the job; and the issue of total independence for him.

The major advance of the early King years was the signing of a bilateral agreement in 1923, signalling the coming to Ottawa of independent treaty-making power. To the displeasure of the British, Ernest Lapointe, Canadian Fisheries minister, and Charles Hughes, Secretary of State to Warren Harding, signed the Halibut Treaty, which regulated fishing in the North Pacific to preserve halibut stocks. It was generally recognized that such treaty-making power for Canada was overdue, and about to happen, but British ambassador Auckland Geddes wanted his name on the documents. Lapointe, with the strong backing of his prime minister and the support of President Harding, proceeded on his own.

The signing served to strengthen arguments for a Canadian resident minister in Washington, and King finally went ahead with the appointment of Vincent Massey in 1927 during the prosperous presidency of Calvin Coolidge. Coolidge was consistent in the bilateral context with his overall image — quiet, formal, boring. Massey found out how "extremely formal, even stiff," he was during the historic February 20 ceremony at the Executive Mansion marking his appointment.

"On arrival at the White House," he recalled in his diary, "we were met by a covey of footmen.... When the summons came that the President was waiting we all fell in, according to a prearranged plan and moved into the audience chamber like a squad of guardsmen at

Wellington Barracks. On arriving we bowed low at the door, advanced across the room, bowed again and stood still—how still!"

Massey was then introduced to the president as "His Britannic Majesty's Envoy Extraordinary and Minister Plenipotentiary to represent the interests of the Dominion of Canada." Massey read his address, Coolidge read his. "Then we shook hands and there followed what was alleged to be an 'informal' conversation," which, Massey noted, "resembled two public speeches delivered in alternate sentences to two audiences composed of one person each. The President asked where I came from, whether Toronto was near a lake and if this was the first Canadian diplomatic mission. I told him that my people came from Massachusetts originally and then came to Canada after a short time in Vermont. He said his people came from Massachusetts, moved to Vermont but stayed there. I suggested that there was only one lap left to be made. I gave him a personal message of friendship and goodwill from the King.... He replied in a stiff jointed sentence. After I could bear it no longer and the time seemed to have arrived to move, I begged leave to present my staff.... We then retired with Prussian rigidity."

Summing up, Massey said, "the ceremony struck me as having stiffness instead of dignity and where it was meant to be impressive it was simply pompous. In other words, the participants were oppressed by their ritual."

Prime Minister King visited Coolidge in November of the same year. Tom King, the Washington correspondent for the Toronto *Globe*, had warned the prime minister of the dour New Englander's frugality and lack of emotion. The joke was that Coolidge had been weaned on a pickle. On arrival in the capital city, the highest dignitary present to greet the prime minister was the State Department's second secretary. It was a step up from 1871 when the only person to meet John A. Macdonald was the British ambassador's valet. King, accompanied by Massey, was introduced to Coolidge who stood motionless in a black morning coat. The president asked King if there was snow in Ottawa. He asked how long the prime minister was staying. He said he was glad to see him. The conversation continued in the same vein, until the prime minister bowed as he prepared to leave. The president asked again if there was snow in Ottawa. Said King: "It was the most formal ceremony I have ever been through."

The next day, however, King was more impressed. Coolidge

"invited me after lunch to walk with him to the verandah of the White House looking towards the Potomac; told me it [the river] used to come near a present fountain, that Adams used to go in bathing there before breakfast and that once a woman reporter held him up for an interview while he was in the water. He said that if I had been Adams, I should have got out and put on my clothes and told her to make a story out of that."

The anecdote and subsequent conversation changed the prime minister's opinion. The president, who King described as dressed to "the pink of perfection," was a man of "much clearer vision and thought than I had believed, a man very well informed, very careful in all his utterances and exceedingly astute...I regard him as anything but a silent man only."[7]

The bilateral business of the day centered mainly on the issue of the construction of the St. Lawrence Seaway. A proposal being advanced eagerly by a cabinet secretary named Herbert Hoover was to deepen the existing waterways of the St. Lawrence and build canals circumventing falls and rapids so that ocean vessels could move up the river all the way to the Great Lakes and the heart of the continent. Since part of the St. Lawrence served as the Canada-U.S. border, joint negotiations were necessary. Coolidge pressed King on the matter but the prime minister was wary on both political and economic grounds. "I spoke of the situation being parallel to that of reciprocity and that every evidence of eagerness from the side of the U.S. was certain to make our path more difficult. This he recognized very clearly and said so."

From Ottawa, King wrote Coolidge, thanking him profusely and remarking how the opening of the Canadian legation marked "the beginning of a new era in Canada's international relations." Exaggerating, as he would often do with presidents, he continued: "It was our hope that it might be a beginning of closer friendships on the part of Canadians with their neighbours to the south. Such it has proven already to a degree that could scarcely have been anticipated."

Not one to sidestep self-promotion, the prime minister sent a little gift to the president: "Under separate cover I am venturing to send you a copy of a book just published which contains a few of my recent addresses. When your official duties are over, its pages will let you see—should there be a chance even to glance them over—how greatly we on this side of the international boundary value all its expressions of international amity and good-will."

CHAPTER SEVEN

The Last Voyage
of Warren Harding

THE 15,000-MILE JOURNEY of Warren Harding, a journey which would include the first visit of a United States president to Canada, began on a hot day in July, 1923.

Almost everything about this excursion into eternity for Harding was wrong from the outset. The world of the twenty-ninth president was collapsing from without and from within, and he knew it more than anyone. He wished only to play poker and bridge and to forget the sordid circumstances of his life.

From without, he was being helplessly whirled into a slimy kickback scandal brought on by friends he had appointed to high office; friends who took advantage of his soft heart, friends who were swindlers, confidence men, influence peddlers. "I can take care of my enemies all right," President Harding confided before his train left Washington station. "But my damn friends. My goddamn friends!"[1]

From within, the overweight, fifty-seven-year-old Republican suffered from an enlarged heart, high blood pressure, shortness of breath, extreme fatigue and a torn family life. He had fathered an illegitimate child. His relationship with Florence, his wife, was in turmoil. In recent months doctors had warned he was in perilous condition. His flesh had come to look like wax. Shortly before the trip, as if he knew the end was near, Harding sold his Ohio newspaper, reorganized his investments, sold his farm, and made out a new will. "He was a corpse," a journalist wrote, "essaying a pre-mortem tour."

To the public however, the world of Warren Harding was all well. The emerging scandal, the health problems, the family problems were masked. To Americans, and to Canadians, Harding was a popular, attractive president. He had all the exterior trappings. He looked, acted, and sounded the part, he was tall and strong, his face had a carved-of-stone imperious look, and his voice was deep. His words, embellished by his training as a newspaperman, were mellifluous and majestic. He was a president who inspired confidence but who had none.

The tradition-breaking trip would take him through the American west by rail, up the coastal waters aboard the U.S.S. *Henderson* to Alaska, and home by way of Canada—a one-day stopover in Vancouver, British Columbia. In the 134 years since George Washington's first presidency in 1789, not one chief executive had travelled to Canada. It wasn't until 1906 that an American president travelled anywhere outside his country. A 1790 statute required all central government business to be conducted in the nation's capital. Another required the president to act on all bills passed by Congress within ten days. In the pre-jet era this meant the Chief Executive couldn't allow himself to get too far away from home. The tradition developed, the tradition remained, and President Chester Arthur discovered how serious it was when he went fishing in the Thousand Islands near the Ontario border in 1882, accidentally ventured into Canadian territory and, in so doing, sparked a controversy in Washington.

Not surprisingly, it was the brash Roosevelt who formally broke the tradition in leaving the country to view progress on the Panama Canal or, in his own words, "to see how the ditch is getting along." Taft also slipped down to see the canal, making an official stop in Mexico on the way, and the only other foreign excursion before Harding's Canada visit was Wilson's post-war peace trip to Europe. So bothered were some congressmen that a president would go so far away, they introduced a bill to have Wilson declared out of office while in France.[2]

Harding, the president who became noted for advocating a return to "normalcy," had no compelling reason to visit Canada. He admired the land, what he knew of it, and was most impressed by the country's performance in the War. He remembered in this context a "brave lad" who worked for him while he was publisher of the Marion, Ohio *Star*. The United States had yet to enter the war but the boy was restless and he decided to go and do battle wearing Canadian colours. Harding gave him encouragement and best wishes. The lad went to the front and never returned.

Plans for the western trip did not include Canada initially. But after an invitation and further prodding by the government of British Columbia, Harding, in a decision which would prove unwise, chose to go.

From the beginning, accident, mystery and tragedy marked the tour, the Vancouver stop becoming one of the most controversial. In the first week, an automobile carrying two journalists of national reputation plunged off a Colorado embankment, killing both. Then Harding's railway engineer dropped off the president in Tacoma, just before running his train headlong into a landslide. He too was killed.

Aides tried to get the fatigued Harding to rest in the early days of the journey but he couldn't sleep. Instead, he stayed up nights playing cards. Poker was one of his favourite diversions. Every week in the White House he would have an all-night big-money game, and people such as Herbert Hoover, who felt the White House merited more dignity, would be disgusted.[3]

Despite the long games and the lack of sleep, Harding held up on the land segment of the trip. He was loved in rural America and the adulation of the crowds nourished his wavering frame. Rather than passing up opportunities to make speeches and meet the people, he made them all. Rather than let the advisors write all the drafts, the president did many himself.

But when he got away from the people and boarded the boat to Alaska, he became overpowered by gloom. Hoover, accompanying Harding, found him "exceedingly nervous and distraught." No government business was transacted. All that transpired was card-playing, around-the-clock cards. "As soon as we were aboard ship," Hoover recalled, "he insisted on playing bridge, beginning every day immediately after breakfast and continuing except for mealtime often until after midnight. There were only four other bridge players in the party, and we soon set up shifts so that one at a time had some relief. For some reason I developed a distaste for bridge on this journey and never played it again."

One day after lunch, the president asked Hoover to come to his cabin. "If you knew of a great scandal in our administration," Harding asked him, "would you for the good of the country and the party expose it publicly or would you bury it?" Hoover suggested that he should "publish it, and at least get credit for integrity on your side." Harding said it would be politically dangerous.[4] He described some of the corruption his aides had been involved in, the most notorious of which was to become the Teapot Dome scandal.

As the melancholy journey flagged on, Harding, receiving reports from home, became convinced the scandals could not be contained and his depression grew deeper. At Sitka, Alaska, the last stop before Vancouver, a military aide brought a box of giant crabs back to the *Henderson*. The president and other members of the party feasted on them. Shortly thereafter, one by one, they started to fall sick.

At 10:45 A.M., Thursday, July 26, 1923, a U.S. president officially set foot on Canadian soil for the first time. The welcome was stunning. More people, more enthusiasm than Harding had received from the American cities. Vancouver hadn't seen anything comparable in decades. The visit of the Prince of Wales three years earlier was a lesser spectacle. Estimates put the crowd totals for Harding for the day at 250,000. Little could explain his popularity but for the fact that he was a U.S. president who cared enough to come to Canada. "CITY FALLS TO HARDING" the headline across the top of the Vancouver *Sun* screamed.

The president was in a tailcoat and for the first time on the trip, his silk hat. Prime Minister Mackenzie King, who had met Harding a year earlier in Washington, was not present, deciding that the short stopover did not warrant a long trip for him across Canada. J. H. King, the prime minister's Public Works minister, greeted the president who, after stepping off the *Henderson*, made a brief statement: "I cannot let this moment pass without saying how gratified we are to come here and how gratified we are at being so cordially received. This is the first visit of a President of the United States to the Dominion of Canada and I hope it may serve to rivet the friendship between the two peoples which has always existed."

Harding was always good at cloaking his inner feelings in a cover of geniality and although some members of his party sensed he was falling apart, it was not apparent to the Canadian crowds. From the docks, the president moved through the joyous throngs to a gathering of fifty thousand in Stanley Park where he made his major speech of the day, the inaugural address of a president in Canada. With the sun brilliant, and the area festooned with American flags and colours,

Harding, though not as animated as when in peak form, delivered an eloquent, touching and, in parts, beautiful declaration of friendship.

"Let us go at our own gaits along parallel roads, you helping us and we helping you. So long as each country maintains its independence and both countries recognize their interdependence, those paths cannot fail to be highways of progress and prosperity....

"Our protection is our fraternity, our armor is our faith; the tie that binds more firmly year by year is ever increasing acquaintance and comradeship through interchange of citizens; and the compact is not of perishable parchment, but of fair and honorable dealing which, God grant, shall continue for all time."

In the years to come, many of the words of Harding would be repeated so often as to become clichés. But to the people in Stanley Park who loved the speech, they were not old words:

"What an object lesson of peace is shown today by our two countries to all the world. No grimfaced fortifications mark our frontiers, no huge battleships patrol our dividing waters, no stealthy spies lurk in our tranquil border hamlets. Only a scrap of paper, recording hardly more than a simple understanding, safeguards lives and properties on the Great Lakes and only humble mileposts mark the inviolable boundary line for thousands of miles through farm and forest....

"We are not palsied by the habits of a thousand years. We live in the power and glory of youth. Others derive justifiable satisfaction from contemplation of their resplendent pasts. We have relatively only our present to regard.... Therein lies our best estate. We profit both mentally and materially from the fact that we have no 'departed greatness' to recover, no 'lost provinces' to regain, no new territory to covet, no ancient struggles to gnaw eternally at the heart of our National consciousness."

The president moved from the park through the crowded streets to a luncheon where he wasn't scheduled to speak but was moved to do so by the glow of the reception. Canada was where he could go to "borrow eggs," he said, and "I don't know anything better than a good neighbor to whom you can go to borrow a couple of eggs."

It was a warm day and now the worn-out Harding was on his way to the Shaugnessy Heights Golf Club for a match with his Canadian hosts. Spectators were only allowed around the first tee and the last green. The president was scheduled to play a full round of eighteen or close to it. But after only six holes, he moved over to the eighteenth and finished out there. At the clubhouse, he jokingly told onlookers he had "been licked." They cheered him and he left quickly for his hotel, where his wife Florence waited. A year later Florence would reveal that on the golf course Harding had suffered the beginnings of a heart attack. She said those who knew he had grown ill kept it "a close secret" for the rest of the day. Later, reports also said that Harding gave up on his abstinence pledge on the Canadian links and drank heavily.

The press noted nothing untoward in the president's behaviour after the golf game, or during speeches in the evening. Articles said he played twelve holes and was in most jovial spirits at the conclusion.

The itinerary called only for his attendance at the state dinner that evening, but hearing that the local press was having a reception for the visiting press, Harding, already behind schedule, didn't want to pass it up. His surprise appearance was dramatic and the outpouring of affection from the press members extreme. "I hope that none of you will ever get it into his head that the newspaper game is a rotten one," said Harding, "because it is not. It is the best and the biggest game in the world.... I entered the Presidency as a newspaperman and if the high office that I now fill has changed me, I feel that I am not worthy of that office." The journalists cheered wildly.

"I feel I could just be one among you all," Harding continued. Then he looked at the coordinator of the group and said, "I don't think it would take up too much of your time, would it, if I shook hands with all the boys?" He went through every one there. The "boys," as he called them, responded by singing "Hail, Hail, the Gang's All Here." They gave him three cheers and a tiger and Harding, the biggest newspaperman among them, left happily for the dinner.[5]

To Hoover, the president appeared "very worn and tired" in the hot crowded dinner hall but to journalist Joe Chapple, who wrote a book on Harding, he was "the embodiment of manly strength and vigor, bronzed by the summer sun of Alaska, with his premature gray hair... one of the handsomest men I ever looked upon."

Shortly after the meal, Harding had what doctors thought was an acute gastrointestinal attack. The initial belief was that it was brought on by the bad crabs and soon the diagnosis was that he was suffering from ptomaine poisoning.

That night his boat slipped out of Vancouver at 10:00 P.M. and headed into a thick fog. A destroyer moved ahead as its guide but in the middle of the night, the *Henderson* rammed it. The president, who had gone to bed immediately on boarding, was startled, as were the other passengers. Major Arthur Brooks, Harding's valet, went directly to his room and found the president still in bed, face buried in his hands. When Brooks told him that the boat had crashed, Harding replied, "I hope it sinks." He got up and went to the deck. Order was restored and the *Henderson* deemed still fit enough to keep moving until morning.

In Seattle the next afternoon, Harding decided to go ahead with a major speech. He faltered badly in the oppressive heat, dropped the manuscript, grasped the podium and, with Hoover picking up the pages and prompting, struggled to the finish. Further engagements were cancelled, and the president was put into bed on a special train headed for San Francisco. A White House physician abided by the ptomaine diagnosis and said all would be well in a few days. But when specialists checked him on arrival in San Francisco, they discovered that in the last few days Harding had suffered a heart attack. By Thursday, six days out of Vancouver, his condition was reported to have substantially improved. By Friday, Warren Gamaliel Harding was dead.

His wife, who along with two nurses was the only person in his suite when he passed away, allowed no death mask to be made. No autopsy was performed. The belief was that the immediate cause of death was apoplexy.

Within a year, Mrs. Harding burned thousands of her husband's personal papers. Also within a year the president's physician died of strange causes while Mrs. Harding was alone with him in a room. Rumours that foul play was involved in Harding's death surfaced but none were proven. Gaston Means, a discredited ex-Justice Department investigator, published a book in 1930 strongly suggesting that Mrs. Harding poisoned her husband because of infidelity. He also hinted at strange occurrences during the Vancouver stop.

On the day President Harding died, thousands of shocked Vancouverites poured onto the streets looking for the latest newspapers, shaking their heads in bewilderment. In the Hotel Vancouver the people talked, the *Sun* reported, "in hushed tones of the big calm man whose purpose it had been to assuage the turmoil in a troubled world with his gospel of rationalism. They felt that his gospel was the true one and that had he lived to complete his work he would have done great good for his country and the world."

Ten thousand people in the city showed up for a memorial service in Stanley Park in the same place Harding had spoken nine days earlier. Vancouver journalists had an oil painting done of the president and presented it to President Calvin Coolidge, who hung it in the National Press Club in Washington. At the ceremony, Coolidge said he had just read Harding's speech in Stanley Park and was moved by it.

In Ottawa, prime minister King wrote to Hewitt Bostock, speaker of the Senate: "I am so glad that the reception of the late President at Vancouver was such a splendid one and that it has left so many pleasant memories. In view of Mr. Harding's death, the incident has assumed an international significance much greater than could have been anticipated...." Bostock had written the prime minister from Vancouver shortly after the visit to tell him about the glorious reception. "I hope we can manage that you get the proper credit," he added.

In 1928, after thousands of donations from Canadians had been gathered, a ceremony was held in Stanley Park. The people of Vancouver unveiled the Harding International Goodwill Memorial. It was a tribute to the first president Canadians ever saw. It was a signal, following many decades of suspicion, that there was a place in the Canadian heart for Americans.

CHAPTER EIGHT

Hoover Wagons, Bennett Buggies

A NATURAL TENDENCY among the prime ministers was to seek the favour of the popular presidents and to seek distance from unpopular ones. No prime minister was more eager in the coat-tail game than R. B. Bennett, who faced Presidents Herbert Hoover and Franklin Roosevelt. But Bennett's misfortune was his striking similarity to the disdained Hoover and his equally striking dissimilarity to the admired Roosevelt. In party, in pedigree, in philosophy and in some respects in appearance, the Conservative prime minister was a Hoover, a Depression-ridden Hoover. In the same respects he was the opposite of FDR. The predicament called for a face lift and Bennett chose to undergo one. But unfortunately the Canadian people were not fooled. They could see behind the disguise.

Much more successful at the game was Prime Minister King. Beginning with Theodore Roosevelt he had personal contact with seven presidents. The experience, combined with his political savvy, made him adept, particularly during the FDR years. But, before Bennett's hard times with Hoover, King's mettle in dealing with the presidents was also toughly tested by the depression president.

A millionaire, an engineer, a humanitarian, Hoover initially had a favourable reputation in the Canadian capital. The Iowa Republican was considered knowledgeable, decisive and positively disposed to the Dominion. But, as a Canadian journalist in Washington warned

King, Hoover was a "rampant protectionist." He won the 1928 election running on higher tariffs for agricultural products, a policy which would be disastrous for Canadian farmers, and a policy which Prime Minister King himself noted would create "a deplorable attitude and feeling between the peoples of the two countries."

To save his own re-election chances in 1930, King had to find a way of convincing Hoover to exempt Canada from such a tariff. His plan was to make a trade-off, to employ a seldom used tactic in bilateral relations—linkage.

A necessary ingredient for the execution of such a strategy is the availability of something for the president, something to trade off. King had just the item—the St. Lawrence Seaway. By happy coincidence the man in the United States most interested in the securing of an agreement for the joint development of the St. Lawrence Seaway was Hoover. This had been his goal since his days as commerce secretary in the Harding administration. He pushed for it then and, under Coolidge, he was chairman of the St. Lawrence Commission. To Canadian objections, he released a report enthusiastically endorsing the scheme. The deepening of the St. Lawrence, he felt, would enable 90 percent of the world's ocean shipping to reach into the Great Lakes. "Its completion," he wrote later, "will have a profoundly favorable effect upon the development of agriculture and industry throughout the Midwest. The large by-product of power will benefit the Northeast. These benefits are mutual with the Great Dominion to the north."

Throughout the twenties, the Canadian government had been cool. The costs would be tremendously high. Ottawa had already invested large sums in a railway transportation system. Montreal would lose its status as the inland seaport. But with the crippling U.S. tariff threatening, King was prepared to reconsider. At least he was willing to suggest to Washington that he might move ahead on the St. Lawrence if he received an exemption on the agricultural tariff.

In a diary notation shortly before Hoover's swearing-in, the prime minister sounded like he was in soliloquy. "Hoover makes his inaugural speech on Tuesday, a week hence. If I can win his confidence— which I do not think I have at present—I may be able to save the tariff being put up against Canada and a tariff war developing. In any event my clear duty is to do all possible to prevent this and go just as far as I can in indicating our intentions to proceed with the St.

Lawrence development...Hoover is wedded to that project more than all else."

In order to ingratiate himself with the Hoover White House the prime minister warned how tough relations would be with the opposition Conservatives under Bennett. The Tory leader had been making pointedly anti-American speeches. In case the Hooverites hadn't heard about them, King, quite capable of disreputable behind-the-scenes work, wrote William Phillips, the U.S. minister to Ottawa. "I think we may assume they [speeches] foreshadow a campaign of prejudice and antagonism on the part of the Opposition toward the United States, having in mind the feeling that may be engendered should the tariff later be raised against Canada. Every effort will be made by the Conservative Party to foster retaliation and to make as impossible as can be joint negotiations over the waterways."

King sent Trade minister James Malcolm to Hoover to work out a Seaway-tariff deal. Hoover showed interest but while King wanted a discreet, unpublicized arrangement, the president wanted blatant linkage. He was willing to have a provision in his tariff bill which would stipulate that a Canadian exemption be put into effect as soon as Ottawa gave the Seaway the official go-ahead.

King wasn't in a position to provide such a cold, hard assurance on the Seaway. The Hoover proposal, he told Vincent Massey, would be viewed as a Washington attempt to force Canada to accept something it didn't want. But before he could quietly decline the first offer and go for something better, a story, hinting at the arrangement and embarrassing King, was leaked to the press. Now the prime minister had to make a public stand. Had he been seeking a trade-off? Was he willing to let the Americans have their way on the Seaway to prevent the possibility of a higher tariff being introduced by Hoover and gaining assent in Congress? There was no such deal in the works, no such possibility, declared the prime minister. In words which may well have astonished Herbert Hoover, he told the House of Commons that he could "conceive of no greater misfortune than that the question of the St. Lawrence waterway should be mixed up in any way with the tariff." Each issue, he asserted, "must be dealt with separately on its merits."

Hoover subsequently introduced his tariff. It was rejected the first time but made it through prior to King's 1930 re-election bid. King, suffering because of it, was swept aside by Bennett who promised to "blast a way" for Canada into world markets. But it was a most propitious period for another intermission in King's record stretch as prime minister. The early thirties were the wrong years for anyone to be Canada's leader.

Bennett had the misfortune of settling in at the same time the Great Depression settled in. The Americans soon had automobiles drawn by mules because there was no gas. They were called Hoover Wagons. Soon Canada had the same things and they became known as Bennett Buggies. In the United States empty towns multiplied and they came to be known as Hoovervilles. In Canada ghost farms multiplied and they came to be Bennett Barnyards. The links were natural not only because of the similar conditions in both countries, but also because of the resemblance of the two leaders. They both offered the same prescriptions. They were believers in the free market. There was no need for government intervention. With time, they thought, Adam Smith's invisible hand would go to work. All would be well.

"Gentlemen," Hoover told a group of relief-seeking visitors in the early days of the depression, "you have come too late. The depression is over." To another group, he said "nobody is actually starving. The hobos, for example, are better fed than they ever have been. One hobo in New York got ten meals in one day." To others: "What this country needs is a great big laugh. There seems to be a condition of hysteria. If someone could get off a joke every ten days, I think our troubles would be over."

Bennett was less vivid but spoke essentially the same line. "I cannot make up my mind," he told Albertans, "why this country between the lakes and the mountains should experience the depression, why people who have lived here for years should now find themselves without an accumulation of goods."

"Governments cannot do everything," he told others. "They can tax you and you can pay taxes, grudgingly or otherwise. But you must look beyond that."

Hoover and Bennett had as much in common as any other president and prime minister. But the theory that resemblance breeds rapport did not apply here. The Conservatives under Bennett were like the Conservatives under most previous prime ministers. They looked east, not south. They were, as assistant secretary of state William Castle warned Hoover in Bennett's first year, "less friendly disposed to the United States than the Liberal Party." Because of this political imperative, Castle told the president, "Mr. Bennett frequently finds it advisable to criticize us despite the fact that he is personally friendly to the country."[1]

Hoover was still determined to get the St. Lawrence Seaway built. He wanted to overcome any unfriendliness. He worked directly with Hanford MacNider, the U.S. minister in Ottawa, so much so that MacNider made a point of apologizing to state department officials for going over their heads. At one point MacNider had wanted to make a strong series of statements in support of the Seaway. But Bennett was in Britain and, out of respect for his absence, Hoover rejected the idea. MacNider was annoyed. "Now I suppose I must go around mumbling platitudes which is not my idea of a good time."[2] The minister was soon given another assignment. Worried that Canadians had the wrong impression of the U.S. attitude, Hoover wrote MacNider on October 17, 1930: "It seems to me that we should think up some particular method or occasion by which we can mark our real feelings toward Canada and try to impress them with it."

The first two years in office had not been easy ones for Hoover but he was by no means derailed. Hume Wrong, Canadian chargé d'affaires in Washington, on his way to becoming one of the country's exemplary diplomats, analysed Hoover for the prime minister in the fall of 1930:

"My own belief is that the problems of the 1932 election are occupying Mr. Hoover's mind to an inordinate degree. The great administrator, in elective office for the first time, is harassed and oppressed by the difficulties, the nature of which he is unfitted by his training and character to comprehend. He has as yet done nothing which will permanently prejudice his future; but he has also done little to confirm the reputation which he brought to the White House. If he is to accomplish great things (and of this I am growing more and more doubtful) they are likely to be postponed until his second term."

Whatever the prime minister's own opinion of Hoover's future, one thing was certain—he wanted to have as little to do with the president as possible. So shrouded was Bennett's one visit to Washington that the press called it the "mystery tour." Secretary of State Henry Stimson found the Bennett act incredible. So anxious was the prime minister to be "incognito," Stimson told reporters, that he wore a derby hat instead of the more formal silk hat the occasion would normally have warranted.

The ultimate snub occurred on the White House lawn. Twenty-five photographers prepared to take the standard picture of the president and the visiting dignitary. It was customary to do so. But Prime Minister Bennett stopped them. It would be "an honour" to be photographed with Mr. Hoover, he said. But since the visit is "unofficial," pictures should await another occasion. The problem, as most top officials there realized, was that Bennett did not want to be seen on the front page of Canadian newspapers with Herbert Hoover.

The meeting with the president did not go well. The president pressed Bennett on the St. Lawrence Seaway. The prime minister responded evasively, went to a press conference and told more than fifty anxious scribes virtually nothing. "What about the St. Lawrence?" asked one. "I believe it is still there," Bennett replied. He did make one formal statement but added that it was not for publication.

The Washington *Star*'s front-page story reflected the obscurity: "The confusion and uncertainty which has surrounded the visit to Washington of Prime Minister Bennett deepened last night as he prepared to leave for Ottawa. Even a trip by the Premier to Arlington cemetery to place a wreath on the Canadian cross there was surrounded by secrecy. Legation officials declined even to confirm that the Premier would lay such a wreath. A photographer who followed the Premier was requested to refrain from taking pictures."

Most press reports took the same tack and they stung Bennett. He had been annoyed on arrival when reporters asked pointedly whether he or members of his party had taken advantage of diplomatic immunity to bring liquor into the United States, a country then in the throes of prohibition. His advisors responded testily that the prime minister had given explicit instructions against taking booze.

When the Associated Press, reputed for its objectivity, ran an article on his furtive behaviour, Bennett instructed Hume Wrong to fight back. Wrong wrote A.P. President Frank Noyes, complaining that Bennett's footsteps were "dogged wherever he went," that one reporter jumped into his car and tried to interview him and that reports were "filled with rumours of mysterious and quite non-existent negotiations."

"...I can assure you," said Wrong, "that these reports gave an entirely distorted version of what took place and were a wide departure from the usual standards of accurate reporting maintained at the Associated Press."

Reporters would not believe there was truth in the announced purpose of the visit—an inspection by the prime minister of the Canadian legation. Hanford MacNider, besieged by the doubters in his Ottawa office, spent two hours fending them off. Undaunted by Bennett's clandestine debut in the capital, the Washington press corps tried to get him to appear at its annual Gridiron dinner. MacNider said there was little hope. "He naturally doesn't want to be running back and forth from here to Washington because he has been accusing Mr. Mackenzie King of the same thing through all the past years."

President Hoover was irritated. From the disappointing meeting he felt he had at least elicited a small promise from Bennett to appoint a preliminary commission on the Seaway. "I was under the distinct impression," he wrote Stimson, "that the matter would be taken up at once upon his return and that we would have some results. Nothing has happened..." He instructed the secretary of state to get the Canadians moving. MacNider told the president that the problem was that Bennett was trying to run a one-man government and had not taken the time to acquaint himself fully with the St. Lawrence situation. There was dissatisfaction among party members over his domineering ways, he reported, but "he shows no sign of changing his procedure."

MacNider devised a plan. William Herridge, the extremely influential brother-in-law of Bennett, was taking up his new posting as minister to Washington. MacNider suggested that Hoover take Herridge away with him for a couple of days out of the capital and do the hard sell on the St. Lawrence. But the State Department, arguing hotly that every other ambassador in town would expect to go on trips with the president, rejected the idea. "It seems to me," the under-secretary of state told Hoover, "that there would be plenty of opportunity to discuss the St. Lawrence Waterway with Mr. Herridge right here in Washington."

After months of pressure, the Bennett government finally agreed to open negotiations on the project. Conditions were changing, the Opposition forces were softer, and the prime minister saw some political advantage in moving ahead with the job-creating scheme if the terms were right. In July 1932, four months before the presidential election, a treaty for the development of the waterway was signed. Hoover was ecstatic, calling it "the greatest internal improvement yet undertaken on the North American continent."

But like so many other agreements notched between the leaders of the two countries, this one had a decidedly short life span. In the election, Hoover was crushed by Franklin Roosevelt. The Senate, which had not moved on ratification of the treaty before the vote, now rejected it.

Bennett, to his joy, had a new man in the White House. For that, the loss of the St. Lawrence agreement was not too high a price to pay. Just seven weeks into the Roosevelt term, he was in Washington to see FDR and the contrast was glaring. Now Bennett catered to the press, and sought out picture opportunities with Roosevelt. Now there was no scoffing at the prime minister's derby hat but rather, references to his sartorial splendour—particularly to his stylish, pearl-buttoned gray vest.

From the outset Bennett appeared to realize that he was dealing this time with a man on the verge of greatness. Bill Herridge, whose role would be critical in the next two years, had sized up Roosevelt for him in the following way: "There is no doubt that Mr. Roosevelt is confronted with a great opportunity and that he is eager to seize it. The country is begging for leadership.... Talk is growing of the need for a dictatorship; Mr. Roosevelt, if he has the skill, could assume the position of a constitutional dictatorship much as Mr. Wilson did during the war.... The country is anxious to take sides with the President against Congress in the perennial conflict which is inevitable under the constitution; and Mr. Roosevelt has both the authority within his party and a gift of popular appeal which are denied to Mr. Hoover."

Before the Bennett visit, the State Department had provided the president with an analysis of Bennett and Canadian-American issues. Among the points: Bennett's conservative high-tariff views had mellowed somewhat during the past two-and-a-half years and he is convinced that economic nationalism all over the world has gone too far; Bennett alone is powerful enough to obtain approval in Parliament for any program he wishes; Herridge has more influence with him than anyone; the financial community in Canada is teetering, the situation with the banking executives being that of a "small group of drunk men with their arms around one another, no one of whom could stand alone." A smelter company in Trail, British Columbia, was spewing poisonous sulphur across the border causing heavy damages; Canada must get moving on compensation.

Roosevelt wanted a trade requirement reducing the high Canadian barriers. It was to be part of an American free-trade push the world over. But the State Department warned against feeding the Bennett ego by negotiating the first agreement with Canada: "Mr. Bennett would in such circumstances be in a position to say to the people of Canada that he had brought the United States to its knees by tariff retaliation and forced us to sign a trade agreement."[3]

As it turned out the two men came to an agreement in principle to work toward a trade treaty. Bennett, the New Brunswick lawyer who had campaigned strenuously against reciprocity in winning a seat in Parliament in 1911, was now steering his government toward such a path. He found Roosevelt to be "kindness itself." The president ordered tea for two and as the delicate fragrance of Washington's pink cherry blossoms drifted by the sun-spanked White House columns toward them, the two leaders discussed, as Grattan O'Leary put it, "the hundred and one things the two countries have in common." Several world leaders were in town that April week taking part in a World Economic Conference. But Roosevelt made sure Bennett received priority treatment. As the prime minister was headed for an embassy reception one day, Roosevelt turned to him and said: "Bennett, where are you lunching?...I wish you would stay here and have a bite with me."

Bennett did, and by the end of the trip he was motivated to tell a national radio audience in the United States that Roosevelt was a man of "wide vision, unselfish purpose, steady courage and sincerity, rare patience and determination."

But no one expected that Bennett would become so taken by the man and his policies that he would undergo a political reincarnation.

Herridge was the catalyst. Beginning with Vincent Massey, the prime ministers would have a series of illustrious men representing them in Washington, but none would be so close to the prime ministers or quite so influential as Herridge. In the words of Dean Acheson, a future secretary of state who was then undersecretary of the treasury, Herridge was one of the ablest and most popular diplomats the United States ever received: "The first central and all important fact about Herridge was his vitality. It poured out of him.... Whatever he did was done with verve and often with a good deal of noise. To be with him was to be alive, to be moving, to be breathless."

The New Deal, Roosevelt's massive use of federal planning and government programs to relieve unemployment and the plight of the farmer and businessman, began in the spring of 1933. By the fall, Herridge, the master salesman, was trying to pawn a facsimile off on Bennett. The Roosevelt program, Herridge felt, was more bull than butter, but the important fact was that the public was buying it.

"This New Deal," he wrote the prime minister early in his hard sell campaign, "is a sort of Pandora's box from which, at suitable intervals, the President has pulled the N.R.A. (National Recovery Act) and the A.A.A. (Agricultural Adjustment Administration) and a lot of other mysterious things. Most of the people never understood the N.R.A. or the A.A.A. any more than they understood the signs of the Zodiac, but that did not matter much; they were all part of the New Deal and the New Deal meant recovery because the President had so promised....

"We need a Pandora's box," he continued. "We need some means by which the people can be persuaded that they have a New Deal, and that the New Deal will do everything for them in fact which the New Deal here has done in fancy....

"It has been said that on March 4, 1933, President Roosevelt was given a national instrument of extreme sensitivity upon which to play. It has been argued that we cannot reasonably conceive of a parallel situation in Canada, and that, at any rate, none such exists. I do not know how much truth there is in this, but I believe there is in Canada today a situation which can be almost amazingly influenced by the right treatment. I believe that the national heart at this time is highly responsive and will incline with profound fervour to the right sort of lead...

"That alone you can give."

A young civil servant named Lester Pearson was also "intensely interested" in Roosevelt's New Deal. He watched as Herridge, in several trips to Ottawa, put the pitch to Bennett: "I was on the outskirts of those discussions, some of the most vigorous of which used to take place at lunch in the cafeteria of the Chateau Laurier, which became kind of a poor man's Rideau Club, for threshing out radical ideas for a Conservative Government in a deepening depression." He wrote a speech for Bennett that contained thoughts "more likely to be popular with a socialist than a tory. I assumed that the Prime Minister would drop or alter them but when I got on the train with him...I found that he had not had time to go over my draft." To the astonishment of party regulars and Pearson, Bennett gave the speech almost as written.

The election of Liberal Mitch Hepburn in Ontario was further evidence to Herridge that "old fashioned Toryism is dead." In his correspondence with Bennett he then became extraordinary: "We are now the Progressive Party. And by God, we must keep on the move until we find the answer to the question, 'what's wrong with Canada!' This is your job and no one can take your place. It is indeed, a trust! If we should let go now, Canada would sag back into a 'slough' which would rot her. Ease the strain and we fall to pieces. Hand over to inept, colourless and medieval leadership these fine people and they will break and turn upon one another. The Destiny of Canada is up for decision. And you are the judge.

"Deep down in your heart, you know that is the truth. And deep down in my heart I know what your course will be...I believe this—that you alone can save the day for Canada."

Whether Bennett was going to ape his New Deal or not was of no great matter to Roosevelt. What concerned him in respect to Canada was the Trail Smelter case and the St. Lawrence issue. He had William Phillips, undersecretary of state, meet for ninety minutes with Bennett in Ottawa over the pollution matter. Phillips won a promise that the prime minister would try and jawbone the offending company into behaving. But Bennett wanted the president to know that the problem was not Ottawa's fault. "I fully appreciate your difficulties," he wrote Roosevelt, "It might be well however if the residents and officials of the State of Washington would bear in mind that any injury which they consider they have suffered is not due to any act of the Canadian Government, but to the operations of a corporation in the province of British Columbia over which the Dominion as such has no jurisdiction."

Don't worry about the statement, Phillips told Roosevelt, it is "only for the purposes of the record and should not, therefore, be taken too seriously. He [Bennett] took the position that willy-nilly the Canadian Government was saddled with the problem." On the St. Lawrence, the president had modifications made to the treaty, submitted it to the Senate again, and the Senate rejected it again.

Finally, after hint upon hint throughout 1934, R. B. Bennett succumbed to the influence of Herridge and made the desperate lunge to the left. To open the new year he announced the Bennett recovery program. It called for a series of acts, some constitutionally assailable, which would control prices, working hours and wages, provide unemployment insurance, and provide greater oversight on banking and marketing and mortgage foreclosures. It was a mini New Deal.

"If you believe that things should be left as they are," Bennett announced, "you and I hold contrary and irreconciliable views. I am for reform. And, in my mind, reform means government intervention. It means the end of laissez-faire. Reform heralds recovery. There can be no permanent recovery without reform. Reform or no reform! I raise the issue squarely. I nail the flag of progress to the masthead."

The announcement engendered incredulity. Socialists such as J. S. Woodsworth called the program a "deathbed conversion." The Montreal *Gazette* asked: "Is Mr. Bennett endeavouring to humbug himself or the people of Canada?" Liberal leader Mackenzie King, truly disgusted, bolted to the attack, calling the program one part unconstitutional, one part fascist and one part stolen from Grits of old.

In his diary he wrote: "It was really pathetic the absolute rot and gush he talked—platitudes, unction and what-not, a mountebank and a hypocrite.... If the people will fall for that kind of thing there is no saving them: they will deserve all they will get."

King did not have to worry. The people were not as gullible as he feared they might be. The belated attempt of R. B. Bennett to turn himself into a Franklin Delano Roosevelt was a dismal failure. The election result? Liberals—171 seats. Conservatives—39.

CHAPTER NINE

The Best Bilateral Years: Franklin Roosevelt and Mackenzie King

PRIME MINISTER KING was in his bed in Ottawa when the vision came to him. "It seemed to me the late spring or early summer. I was sitting on the grass in the sunshine. President Roosevelt was seated almost immediately opposite to me. A lady was standing nearby talking to both of us. The President had in his hand a new straw hat. It had a narrow cord hanging from it and he played with it in his hands. There was no band on it. The style was closely woven straw."

The president threw his hat to the prime minister. "I placed it on my head and, to my amazement, found that it fit me exactly. I said to the lady nearby that I had thought the President's head was much larger than mine. I was surprised to see his hat was a perfect fit."

As King awoke the vision was clearly etched in his mind. The need for more sleep beckoned but so did the message of the dream. The prime minister pulled himself out of bed. He took out a pencil. He quickly wrote down what he had seen.[1]

What he had seen in Franklin Roosevelt was the good neighbour, maybe the best neighbour. He saw a president whose head was never too big for Canada or its crafty, sometimes neurotic, leader: a president who took the continent's two rival parts and did more than anyone to make them partners.

Like William Howard Taft, Franklin Roosevelt came to know the Dominion of Canada by spending time there. The year following his birth in 1882, his affluent parents purchased a summer residence. It was on the small New Brunswick island of Campobello, which was nine miles long and populated by less than one thousand people. The breezes were cool in the summers and the blue Bay of Fundy waters cold. The rambling cottage had comfortable balconies, porches, hammocks, and big armchairs, around which the servants sorted the books and magazines.

The Roosevelts spent all their summers on the island and Norman Lank, a sailing instructor, took early notice of an eager youth named Franklin. "When he was just a boy," Lank said, "he could sail like a man of fifty. I knew then there was something more than common in him."

Charting his boat, the *New Moon*, bird watching, and golf occupied most of young Roosevelt's holiday time. Like his cousin, Teddy, he thrived on physical exertion. As well as being secretary and treasurer of the local golf club at the early age of eighteen, he acted as its greenskeeper, rebuilding tees and putting surfaces. Politics was the subject for the folks who gathered beside the sagging wooden benches outside the general store. Franklin frequently joined in and was there to hear some blistering debates over the Laurier-Taft reciprocity deal.

As his political career took shape, as he moved from New York state senator to under secretary of the Navy, he cherished the Campobello breaks, and in the summer of 1921 he was particularly anxious to get away from the Washington cauldron. A Senate committee investigating homosexuality in the Navy had put him through a messy, gruelling few days, charging that he had knowingly allowed service investigators, or "fairy chasers" as they were called, to act as agent provocateurs in catching homosexuals.

Unnerved and exhausted, Roosevelt reached Campobello after captaining a yacht for too many hours through fog-bound Fundy waters. The next day he was fishing in the hot sunshine when the accident took place. "I baited hooks, alternating between the fore and the aft cockpits of the motor-tender, crossing beside the hot engine on a three inch varnished plank. I slipped—overboard. I'd never felt anything so cold as that water. I hardly went under, hardly wet my head, because I still had hold of the side of the tender, but the water was so cold it seemed paralyzing. This must have been the icy shock in comparison to the heat of the August sun and the tender's engine."

He did not feel right the rest of the day or the next morning. But rather than rest, he ran, he swam, and fought a forest fire on a nearby island. The fight took many hours. Roosevelt chopped down evergreen branches for himself and his children and they thrashed away at the flames. "Our eyes were bleary with smoke; we were begrimed, smarting with spark-burns, exhausted," he said. Back at the cottage, the "glow" he normally felt after a hard day's work was missing. He took his mail and a few newspapers, and "sat reading for a while, too tired even to dress." It "never felt quite that way before." He went to bed, thinking he had a slight case of lumbago. But as he tried to get up in the morning, his left leg lagged. "It refused to work," then the other leg felt laggard and it, too, refused to work. His temperature shot to 102°F. His wife, Eleanor, sent for Doctor E. H. Bennett, an old friend. No more than a bad cold, said Bennett. Next day, Roosevelt couldn't move either leg. His hands were so weak he could barely write. He felt paralyzed from the chest down. A specialist came to the island, diagnosed a blood clot in the lower spinal column, prescribed heavy massaging, predicted recovery, went home, and sent in a bill for six hundred dollars.

Recovery didn't come. Roosevelt remained in bed, got his massages and felt worse. His spirits blackened. He felt God had abandoned him. Finally, two weeks after the fall from the boat, a Boston doctor specializing in a relatively unknown disease called poliomyelitis arrived. He informed the thirty-nine-year-old Roosevelt that he had it. He said it was not an overly serious case and complete recovery was a possibility. [2]

Roosevelt lay on the Canadian island, immobilized, for another two weeks. The pain was agonizing. It was in his back, in his arms and in his bladder which was paralyzed and had to be regularly catheterized.

The public was sheltered from the news. Reporters inquiring on Campobello were told he would be all right. In early September, about a month after the illness occurred, the Roosevelts stealthily had him removed from the island to New York city where the press was told he had temporarily lost the use of his legs below the knees but that there would be no permanent injury. At this point Roosevelt had already determined that he was not about to let the disease destroy his political career. When the New York *Times* carried a front-page story saying he would recover, Roosevelt wittily wrote Adolph Ochs, the publisher: "While the doctors were unanimous in telling me that the attack was very mild and that I was not going to suffer any permanent attacks from it, I had, of course, the usual dark suspicion that they were just saying nice things to make me feel good. But now that I have seen the statement officially made in the New York *Times* I feel immensely relieved because I know, of course, it must be so."[3]

That September, when he left Campobello on a stretcher, was the last time Roosevelt would see his beloved Canadian summer home for twelve years. He simply did not wish to return. When he finally did, on June 30, 1933, he was president. "Memories of Campobello," said his son Elliott, "had been too painful, I believe, until this day. He decided that this was the time to exorcise the memory."

The emotional return of FDR to Campobello, marking only the second visit of a sitting president, was not without a specal drama. As he did in 1921, Roosevelt had to pass through foggy waters to get to the island and, as before, he took control of the yacht himself. Visibility was so impaired this time that it was feared his boat would not be able to pass through Rogue's Bluff, off the Maine Coast, and that the homecoming would have to be cancelled or, worse, that the yacht would crash.

Eleanor Roosevelt waited on the island with concern. There had been no word from the presidential party. Residents and visitors, clustered at the dockside, worried a little, but were mostly optimistic. "Franklin will be here," someone would say, "he won't let us down." Slowly the fog began to lift and the doubts lifted with it. When word came that the presidential party was only fifteen miles away, tiny Campobello grew excited. The fisherfolk were in their Sunday best; the children waved flags and pennants; the anxious old friends of the president told stories while waiting to clasp his hand; the well-to-do summer residents, very much "Park Avenue" on this day, readied their cameras.

Since it was not an official visit, no Canadian government representatives were present. But practically everyone on the island was there and, from the site where polio had seized him, the welcome was rousing and genuine. "We well remember," said John Calder, a local official, in greeting Roosevelt, "the young man who roamed our shores, fished our streams and battled with Old Fundy's tides in his little sail boat."

The president looked back: "I was brought here first because I was teething, 49 years ago. From that time on I came every summer until

12 years ago.... When we came out of the fog at West Quoddy today the boys said there was land all ahead. I started full speed ahead because I knew it was Luebec Narrows. That is one of the things Captain Lank taught me here when I was a youth."

The welcome was "the finest example that could be given of permanent friendship between nations. I am glad that Norman Davis, our official delegate to the disarmament conference, is with me," said Roosevelt. "Now he can go back to Geneva and tell them what a border without fortifications means between two great nations."

Roosevelt spent much of the weekend with old Canadian friends. He boasted to Captain Lank about the crack American fishing schooner, the *Gertrude Thébaud*, adding that he had a large, framed picture of it. "We got better ships than that in Canada," said Lank. The captain presented him with a picture of the *Bluenose* and Roosevelt said he would put it in his study alongside the *Thébaud*. Chesley Allingham, the proprietor of the general store, was called in and he and Roosevelt reminisced about the store-front debates.

"I'll be back next summer," said the president on leaving. He took away many fond memories but also a dreadful cold which lingered for a week. He left behind a most gratified island population, a group of Canadians who sensed, although he was just four months into office, that this man was not an average president. "There is every promise," the Saint John *Telegraph-Journal* rhapsodized during his stay, "that he will occupy a place in his country's gallery of the greatest, alongside Washington and Lincoln. The phenomena of the last few months are as yet barely apprehended."

The popularity of the president was not a fact that would escape Mackenzie King at this time or at any time during the thirteen-year stewardship of FDR. After he won re-election in October, 1935, it took only one day before King was at the door of Norman Armour, the American minister to Ottawa, asking for an audience with the president. Specifically, he wanted to open negotiations for a new liberalized trade agreement which would help alleviate the depression. He was prepared to go to Washington right away, he told Armour. He explained how he thought Canada, in future, could be of great use as an intermediary between the United States and Great Britain. He wanted to have far closer relations with the United States than had past Canadian governments. "I am not in favor of annexation," he told the minister, as if it was still considered a viable option. "I don't think that would be good for either country. Certainly you have enough troubles of your own without wanting to add us to them." But closer economic and political cooperation was vital, he said, and the trade agreement was the place to start. The prospect of Canada and the United States proclaiming a trade agreement within a few weeks, while Britain looked helplessly on, "seemed to give him almost malicious pleasure," Armour recalled.

Two weeks later, King was in Washington and it was here, during the first of eighteen visits, that the friendship began. The two leaders had one big thing in common. They were Harvard men. King attended the illustrious institution at the close of the nineteenth century, Roosevelt at the beginning of the twentieth. Although their frequent future references would make it sound like they were classmates, they never met as students. They met at Harvard only once, during the war, when King was there to receive an honourary degree and Roosevelt was a member of the board of overseers. That was the only in-person contact prior to 1935. In 1929 King, as prime minister, had communicated by letter with Roosevelt, then governor of New York but it was a rebuff. Roosevelt had written, saying he would like to stop by and discuss the St. Lawrence Seaway proposal. King said no: "The leader of the Opposition and the conservative press...assert that I am prepared if need be to sacrifice Canadian interests.... Any act on my part which in any way is capable as being construed as one having a bearing upon the existing controversy is bound to be misinterpreted and magnified out of all proportion."

Before the visit advisors had told Roosevelt about King's nature. "Inclined far more to play the game with us," was one description. "Inclined to indulge in poetic licence," was another. King's "pet idea," as they put it, was to nourish Canada's role as the go-between on U.S.-British relations.[4] There were no references to the bizarre underside of the prime minister—to his trust in his dog Pat, his contact with the spirits, his omnipresent superstitions, and to his excessive lust for being among the world's greats. These aspects of his makeup were well sheltered. The only reference to anything odd about the man was a statement in a memo that on reaching Washington he requires a day's rest period before feeling capable of doing business properly.

It was during his rest period before the first session with FDR that another vision came to King. This one featured him and the president driving golf balls around a White House room. Two others were present, and Roosevelt was more interested in watching them than in playing himself. As for the prime minister: "I was feeling a little reticent about not having played the game before, but prepared to join in."

The significance of this vision for King was that in the game of public life, he and Roosevelt should see primarily to their figurehead roles while letting the experts in the game take care of the details. It was a lesson that neither would heed.

On meeting, the president and the prime minister went on at length about their Harvard days and forever after, Roosevelt, in alluding to King, would almost always draw the link, sometimes going so far as to suggest they were teenage buddies. ("As you know," he wrote Australian Prime Minister John Curtin, "I have been close to Mackenzie King almost since we were boys." Had he been so close he would have known that no one called the prime minister by the first name "Mackenzie.") After the chat, the president wanted to exercise his afflicted limbs with a swim in the White House pool. He invited the prime minister to come along. But as King would do virtually every other time he was asked swimming, he declined. This time it was because he was tired, in need of yet more rest. Eleanor, who spoke admiringly of Quebec's Gaspé peninsula, showed King to his room, pointing out that it was the one in which Lincoln signed the proclamation for the emancipation of the slaves. King was shaving when Roosevelt's son, home from Harvard for a couple of days, came in for a bath. Talking to him, King found it all quite extraordinary. "It recalled to my mind the circumstances of the descendants of Wolfe and Montcalm becoming acquainted in a bathroom at the Chateau Frontenac about three hundred years after."

After dinner, Roosevelt gave a toast. "Having an old friend here and one who comes from a neighboring friendly country, I should like to propose the health of the sovereign, King George,"[5] he said. "We all rose and drank to the King's health," Prime Minister King noted. "When one recalls that the United States was lost to England, and to one of the Georges, with Washington the leader of the struggle for American independence, it was a rather striking circumstance that another King George's health should be proposed, the occasion being what it was."

Following a White House movie, Roosevelt asked King and Secretary of State Cordell Hull to join him in a room off the hall. The president, as King recorded, "was assisted to his seat on the sofa by an attendant and when sitting down, knocked over the ashtray. Both his lower limbs are between steel supports. He manages pretty well with a cane but it is with the greatest difficulty that he gets up and down."

On the couch, Roosevelt beckoned, "come and sit here, Prime Minister." He meant next to him on his right side. Always when they spoke, the president would want King in that same place. But King, feeling uncomfortable, would frequently get up and move to a chair directly across from him. He never realized until the end that Roosevelt only had one good ear—the right one.

The conversation opened with Secretary Hull holding forth on what a great smoker he had been until his tonsils were removed, compelling him to give it up. Having talked about so many other subjects, King was anxious to get on to trade. When FDR was interrupted by the telephone, King asked Hull if it would be wise to start in on it. Hull advised patience, but when Roosevelt finished, he opened the trade subject himself. The three then entered into a long detailed discussion about cream, lumber, potatoes, and cattle. Roosevelt knew the particulars of trade in respect to them all and King realized then that here was a man who could golf his own way around a room.

An agreement for reciprocal trade had eluded all presidents and prime ministers since Confederation. The last pact was the treaty of 1854 which was abrogated in 1866. The years of trying had brought years of turmoil. King himself had found his 1930 re-election chances badly weakened by the record-breaking Smoot-Hawley tariff of the same year. Bennett had tried unsuccessfully for a tariff agreement with Roosevelt to bolster his 1935 election bid but couldn't pull one off. Smoot-Hawley, in combination with the depression, had sent bilateral trade spiralling downward to the point where by 1934 it was only one third of the 1928 level. Both sides realized that increased trade would mean increased prosperity. Roosevelt wanted an agreement, Hull was an ardent free-trade advocate, and in Ottawa, the United States had a much respected representative who was convinced that the time was critical. Go now, Norman Armour advised the White House in a significant memorandum, or Canada would be forever drawn into the British orbit: "Is it not vitally important for our political future that we have next to us a Canada interested in developing her trade with the United States, interested in supporting our policies in regard to Latin America, possibly as a member of a Pan American Union, the Far East and elsewhere, and feeling that in a thousand and one ways they are bound to us in practical things even though sentimentally and politically they are part of the British Empire?"

High tariffs, he argued, were leading to the Canadian development of competitive products and industries: "It does seem to me inevitable that this development should continue to such an extent that Canada, equipped with low-priced French-Canadian and other labor, may become before long our most intensive competitor abroad in many spheres of agriculture and industry.

"There is still time, while the Canadian economy is in a formative stage, to shift the impetus away from highly competitive production to complementary production."

This memo was to William Phillips, the undersecretary of state. Arguing that it would be a "real tragedy" if the opportunity was not grasped now, Armour asked forgiveness for being so personal and pleading in his remarks.[6]

Concluding the long discussion with King on the trade commodities, the president then said to him: "Mr. King, all these three, cattle, cream and potatoes are political. If the campaign were over, I would feel we would have no difficulty with regard to them." He was referring to his own 1936 re-election campaign. King, who knew American politics, was prepared for such a line of argument. His strategy was to seal the deal that very weekend so that the question would not ride unsettled into the election campaign. He felt an added lure was the fact that it was Armistice Day weekend. If the agreement was reached on the Monday holiday, he told the president, it could be a lesson for the world. He described his argument in his diary: "If we could give to the world an object lesson of the new world developing the arts of peace, while the old world was bent on destruction, it might be the means of changing the whole world situation....It would certainly point the way to the breaking down of the false doctrines of economic nationalism, which were the main cause of war."

Roosevelt loved the Armistice Day symbolism. "That would be a great stroke," he said. Plans were made to have the respective staffs sort out the fine points over the following two days, Saturday and Sunday. King, delighted, did not want to keep the president up any longer. It was almost midnight but Roosevelt stretched the conversation for another forty-five minutes. In the morning, the prime minister felt sufficiently unabashed to produce a copy of his book, *Industry and Humanity*, but Roosevelt surprised him saying he already owned a copy and knew it well. He had a secretary bring it in so that King could sign it. King could hardly have been more impressed.

That day, Roosevelt met with his cabinet and told them he was negotiating a treaty with King that was distinctly to the advantage of the United States. He later ordered all cabinet secretaries to attend the signing. Most did so willingly except for the woman member, Labor Secretary Frances Perkins, who wouldn't stop talking throughout the ceremony, greatly annoying colleagues like Harold Ickes with her criticisms. "I hope," said Roosevelt, in making the Armistice Day announcement, "that this good example will reach around the world some day, for the power of good example is the strongest force in the world. It surpasses preachments; it excels good resolutions; it is far better than agreements unfulfilled."

King was in wonderland. In his diary he said the treaty was "the greatest political achievement of my life and one of the greatest of this continent in a century or more." He sent the first of many absolutely fawning letters to Roosevelt: "May I say that no visit anywhere, at any time, has left memories which will be longer cherished.... May I add how delighted I was to renew with yourself an acquaintance having so memorable an association with Harvard University, and to have it grow into what I hope you will permit me to believe is a very real friendship."

Roosevelt didn't respond to the adulatory missive for almost five months. "When you get to know me better you will come to understand that though my letters are few and far between, my heart is in the right place," he finally replied. The Republicans, as FDR suspected, tried using the treaty against him in the campaign of 1936. Hoover mocked the pact, saying that the more abundant life Roosevelt promised Americans was apparently to be provided by Canadians. But Roosevelt was confident at the time of the King letter that the worst was over. "In a sense," he wrote him, "we both took our political lives in our own hands in a good cause and I am very happy to think the result has proven so successful."

With just one meeting King had been able to secure a major trade agreement that had eluded all predecessors, and establish a form of rapport with a president that had never happened before. Roosevelt's personal connection with Canada was an advantage, as was the Harvard connection. The shared ideals of the two men were a factor. And the climate of war, and eventually the war itself, was something that almost compelled cooperation.

To the men who were around King through the Roosevelt years there were many reasons for the forging of such a splendid partnership. To Jack Pickersgill, who worked for King, "Roosevelt had so few people around he could talk to who didn't have an axe to grind," and King was one. "He liked to have King around to bounce his problems off him."[7] It seemed to Liberal Paul Martin that Roosevelt took King under his wing because the prime minister was an exceptional veteran statesman and political leader whose advice was very valuable.[8] To James Reston of the New York *Times*, it seemed a case of Roosevelt marvelling at the vast potential of the grand land to the north and wanting to be as close to it and its leader as possible.[9]

And, as Mackenzie King was to find out during his next meeting with the president, Roosevelt admired him because of his early background, his writing, and his education. While Roosevelt was off speaking to the governor-general, an associate who had talked to the president told King that Roosevelt was impressed because King was "about the only one left of the university men who had held on to politics as a career and kept his place with the people—a man of education who continued to command their confidence."

The meeting, in Quebec City in July 1936, marked the first time a president and prime minister met one another in Canada. Roosevelt wanted to see his good friend, Governor-General Lord Tweedsmuir, he wanted to further his relationship with King, he was in an election campaign and a Canada visit wouldn't hurt. As King put it, there was also the hope that a further display of friendship might have a "quieting effect upon the situation in Europe where international friendliness and goodwill seem to have lost their footing altogether."

As the president's train pulled in at 9:30 A.M. King observed a "fairly tired man and one who had been through a bit of brutal battering. Soon his face broke with a smile, and the dark or sombre expression was lost in the radiant one—he is very brown. It is quite amazing how he manages with his infirmity. His son, James, at his side, was a fine picture of filial devotion."

The reason for Roosevelt's success? "I think the President is reaching the people more through his infirmity, his determination of will, and with family scenes—than in any other way."

A weather-perfect visit, crowded with homilies about the unde-fended border and so on, it excited the prime minister because he was beginning to feel a harmony with Roosevelt. "How completely his views are in accord with my own," he would soon record. "Anyone can see by reading my *Industry and Humanity,* the whole Roosevelt program is there." He was smart enough to attempt to learn from the chief executive. When Roosevelt was preoccupied, he badgered his advisers about their man's *modus operandi:* "It is clear to me his methods and point of view are not unlike my own re preparation of speeches and correspondence but he has an infinitely better organiza-tion and has an infinitely better capacity to delegate work and to take off time from work completely."

In conversation Roosevelt recalled that several senators had recently asked him what he would do if Japan attacked British Columbia. The U.S. forces would move in to prevent Japan from getting a foothold, he replied. Someone then asked, well what would he do if Japan attacked Australia? "Australia is a hell of a long way off," Roosevelt said.

In his public remarks, Roosevelt inaugurated the practice of the presidents saying some words in French, a practice that brought grief to many. Roosevelt carried it off splendidly, however, his staff supply-ing him with a long memo when he got home on the excellent press and public reaction to it.

Somehow, Prime Minister King was led to believe that these nice meetings with Roosevelt would have a healing effect on the acrimo-nious spirit of war-bound Europe. "It was all just as wonderfully beautiful as it possibly could be," he noted in the diary. "One kept continually contrasting in one's mind the condition of Europe—the fear and hate there and the confidence and goodwill here. I think the proceedings will do great good, are bound to have an effect in Europe...I believe my speech will help in all this. It is a means of attacking the problem of international strife and unrest from the Christian side with Christian methods because of reason and understanding."

Somehow too, King was led to believe that the president would likely be assassinated: "It is a truly horrible and contemptible cam-paign and he is a courageous man to face it all, doubly so with his physical condition....It will be a miracle if he escapes assassination. If he should be assassinated, it would mean instant civil war in the U.S. —Spain over again."

The relationship between the two men became close and personal when they met in March 1937 at the White House. It was on this occasion that King read to Roosevelt in bed, shared with him private thoughts, and advised him on a number of issues. With Europe on the verge of conflict, Roosevelt was trying to organize a world peace conference in the United States, but was having his doubts about such a venture. King laid out a plan whereby the conference could be held in Geneva in conjunction with a League of Nations gathering. Roosevelt asked for more details and King came to his bedside the next morning with a written plan. Very excited about this development, King attributed it all to guidance from above: "This I am sure is divine planning of things working together for good by unseen spiritual forces." His mission, he believed, was "a holy one, that God's spirit was guiding—that Christ's purpose was being fulfilled, that I was acting as an agent to help fulfill his Holy will." Roosevelt was under one of the most stinging attacks of his career because of his ill-advised attempt to change the rules governing Supreme Court appointments so that he could get a court more amenable to his New Deal legislation. He was lying down, reading the bad reviews in the morning papers. The prime minister told him that his policies were Christian, and "the world would find Christianity was a virile thing." He complimented Roosevelt on his moves toward world peace. The president told King he had helped take his mind off other things and the prime minister "left with the President urging me to be careful about my health, I doing the same to him, each with a wave of the hand to the other—like brothers."

One of the subjects discussed during the visit was the readiness of Canada to defend itself. It was a short discussion. King suggested that many of his countrymen seemed to think that the Monroe Doctrine was sufficient protection for Canada and that Ottawa therefore didn't have to worry about defence preparations. He added that no self-respecting government could countenance such a view. The president quickly got down to the basics of the situation. His demands were not great. "What we would like would be for Canada to have a few patrol boats on the Pacific Coast."[10] Don't worry about the Atlantic, he said, leading King to assume that Washington and Britain could protect him there.

Earlier in the evening when other guests were present "the President said in a joking way that he and I were going to toss a coin to see whether I should give him the maritime provinces, or whether he should give Canada Maine and Vermont; he was quite evidently joking at the part of America which had gone against him."

The president, sensing that in King he did not have a drinking mate, explained to him that the reason he drank was because of his polio. His feet often became cold and in order to keep the blood circulating down there, doctors had recommended pre-dinner cocktails. Then he told King his view of the King Edward-Wallis Simpson affair. He hoped Mrs. Simpson would make a good wife, but knew her type. "In a few years, she would become pretty plain looking and be a different person." The conversation was another during which King was not aware of Roosevelt's hearing disability. The president, as usual, had him sit on the same sofa by his right side. But King soon moved, thinking he was being considerate. Some of the ideas exchanged were ones which would have made the press shudder. With respect to the advent of radio, the prime minister said that governments could not afford to turn over to private organizations the control of what was being said over the air. Roosevelt agreed entirely.

Already, the personal nature of the diplomacy between the two was beginning to aggravate other politicians and the press. King was so close-mouthed after his summits that White House reporters, in their frustration, concocted a rhyme: "William Lyon Mackenzie King—Never tells us a goddam thing." They sang it often, and FDR passed the news of it along to the prime minister. The two of them wanted to get together again in 1937, but King wrote to Roosevelt suggesting that perhaps too many suspicions were being generated: "I expect to be told, as soon as the debates of the session begin, that all kinds of deals with respect to trade between Great Britain and the United States, the St. Lawrence Waterways and the export of power and much else have been made between the two of us, and that already in some mysterious way we have tied the hands of the members of Congress in the United States and the members of Parliament in Canada." But "no one except yourself," King added, "knows better than I do how much in the interests of both countries it is that you and I should have frequent opportunities to talk together."

Roosevelt was of the same mind. "It was father's hope," wrote son Elliott, "that the day would come when he and Mackenzie could 'drop in and visit' with each other as casually as members of the same family."

Ulysses S. Grant. (Public Archives of Canada.)

The British High Commissioners, 1871. Standing, left to right: Lord Tenterden, Sir John A. Macdonald, Montague Bernard. Seated, left to right: Sir Stafford Northcote, Earl de Grey & Ripon, Sir Edward Thornton. (Public Archives of Canada.)

President Chester A. Arthur during his visit to the Thousand Islands, 1882. (Public Archives of Canada.)

Sir Wilfrid Laurier at Red Deer, Alberta, 1910. (Capital Press Service.)

Teddy Roosevelt, c. 1905.

William Taft, 1908. (*The Globe and Mail.*)

Warren Harding on his way to Vancouver, B.C., 1923. (United Press International.)

Harding on the golf links in Vancouver where he fell ill. This was the first official visit of a president to Canada. (United Press International.)

Richard Bennett (left) meeting Franklin D. Roosevelt (centre)
at the White House, 1934. (Public Archives of Canada.)

Franklin Roosevelt at Queen's University, August 1938. (*The Globe and Mail.*)

FDR and Mackenzie King at Ogdensburg, New York, 1940. (*The Globe and Mail.*)

Harry Truman and Mackenzie King during the president's visit to Ottawa, June 1947.
(*The Globe and Mail.*)

Truman with King and Mounties at a press conference in the Laurentians, 1947.
(*The Globe and Mail.*)

Truman shares a joke with (left to right) Ray Atherton, U.S. ambassador to Canada, Mackenzie King, and (right) Staff Sargeant C. W. Graham, during a visit to the Seigniory Club at Montebello, Quebec, June 1947. (Public Archives of Canada.)

Truman greeting Louis St. Laurent in Washington, 1949. (Wide World Photos.)

St. Laurent and Dwight D. Eisenhower at the Augusta
National Golf Club in Georgia, 1956.
(Wide World Photos.)

John Diefenbaker with Eisenhower and Secretary of State John Foster Dulles in
Ottawa, 1958. (Wide World Photos.)

John F. Kennedy arriving in Ottawa, 1961. (Wide World Photos.)

Kennedy addressing a joint session of Parliament in Ottawa, May 17, 1961.
(Wide World Photos.)

Kennedy during the tree planting where he wrenched his back, 1961. (Canadian Press.)

Reception at the U.S. embassy at the close of Kennedy's 1961 visit. From left: Kennedy, Governor-General George Vanier, Jacqueline Kennedy, Mrs. Vanier, John Diefenbaker, and Olive Diefenbaker. (Wide World Photos.)

Lester Pearson and John Kennedy at Hyannis Port, 1963.
(Wide World Photos.)

Pearson with Lyndon Johnson at the president's ranch in Texas, 1965. With them are Lady Bird Johnson and Maryon Pearson. (Wide World Photos.)

Pearson and Johnson at the Camp David meeting where Johnson rebuked the prime minister for his speech on Vietnam, 1965. (Wide World Photos.)

Pearson and Johnson at a press conference in Ottawa following Johnson's visit to Expo '67. (Canadian Press.)

Nixon and Trudeau in a discussion prior to the signing of the Great Lakes Water Agreement in Ottawa, 1972. (John McNeill, *The Globe and Mail.*)

Nixon addressing Parliament in Ottawa, April 1972. (*The Globe and Mail.*)

Pierre Trudeau's first visit with Jimmy Carter, at the White House, February 1977. (Wide World Photos.)

Pierre Trudeau and Ronald Reagan in Ottawa, 1981. (Erik Christensen, *The Globe and Mail.*)

Reagan addressing Parliament in Ottawa, March 12, 1981.
(United Press Canada.)

A casual drop-in was made by Roosevelt at Queen's University in August of 1938 and a casual remark was made. At least he considered it a casual remark. "I give to you the assurance," he told a large crowd in the football stadium, "that the people of the United States will not stand idly by if domination of Canadian soil is threatened by any other empire."

The statement, to his great surprise, became a landmark one in Canada-U.S. relations as it was considered the first defence commitment of the United States to its neighbour. "What I said at Queen's was so obvious," FDR wrote Tweedsmuir, "that I cannot quite understand why some American President did not say it half a century ago." A similar commitment, though not heralded by the press as such, had been given by Secretary of State Knox twenty-seven years earlier. A few days later, King reciprocated Roosevelt the best he could by pledging that hostile powers would not be allowed to base operations against the United States from Canada. In his diary he made reference to the Roosevelt commitment but gave equal prominence to the fact that Roosevelt alluded to "our both being from Harvard, using, in this connection, the expression 'Mackenzie King and myself.'"

The next time they met, King, always sensitive to the political value of the association, announced that it was no exaggeration to say that "the relations between the United States and Canada have never been happier than in the three years that have elapsed since November, 1935." The occasion was the reaffirmation and the extension of the 1935 trade agreement. The health of the president, of great concern to King since he met him, jolted the prime minister. Roosevelt had lost many, many pounds, his eyes were terribly weary, and King was frank with him in saying how poorly he looked and how he wished he would get some rest. After a long series of meetings, Roosevelt told King he had arranged for them to dine alone. This was something the presidents and prime ministers rarely did. According to King, Roosevelt told him that "he liked this so much better, and could relax with me."

A rumour spread at this time that the bachelor prime minister had a greater interest in the White House than his relations with the president. He was quite taken, reports said, with FDR's social secretary, Marguerite LeHand, or Missy as she was called. A tall, dignified, reasonably attractive woman, Missy was a personal favourite of the president's and believed to be romantically involved with him. In his diary account from the visit of November 1938, King refers to Missy throwing him a kiss. "She is a very fine woman," he wrote, "I can see what a great help she must be to the whole family."

At the White House, though Eleanor could never understand what her husband saw in him, the prime minister was gaining the status of a close relative. At the State Department, where Cordell Hull was a deep admirer of King's, the same was true. "If I had belonged to the department myself, I could not have met with more in the way of recognition along the way," said King. "Darkey messengers and porters, as well as members of the staff, all seemed to know me."

Hull, a Tennessean, an architect of Roosevelt's Good Neighbor policy, was so kind and benevolent that when listening to him King got the feeling that "he was just thinking out loud. Two or three times however, to my surprise, he used the expression 'Christ Almighty.'"

FDR had confided to the prime minister that he did not intend on seeking re-election in 1940, and that although he was hesitant because of Hull's age (then sixty-nine), he wanted him to be the next president. But Roosevelt did not personally broach the subject to Hull. He chose as his intermediary in important internal American politics none other than the prime minister of Canada.

On April 29, 1940, King told Hull that it was not really his business but that "for the sake of the world," he should run and become the next president. He said that Mr. Roosevelt was looking to him to succeed. Telling the secretary of his Canadian electoral successes, King even offered advice on how he should run his campaign. Use radio instead of travelling, he offered, and don't hesitate to use a picture of yourself with a dog. King felt posters of him and his mutt, Pat, had been a substantial political plus. He said that he thought "the people at this time would appreciate a campaign carried on in that way in the U.S." Hull doubted his capabilities in domestic affairs and was reluctant considering his age but, as FDR chose to run again, he never got a chance anyway.

He was delighted to hear from King that he was the president's choice. Then, and in the years to come, he invited the prime minister to his apartment for informal lunches and dinners. His analysis of King? "I found him a very serious-minded person, thoroughly agreeable in his relations with others, philosophical, unpretentious and sanely liberal. He possessed great vision and constructive ability. Not an impassioned orator, he was nevertheless a fluent, forceful and captivating speaker. I never knew a more unselfish patriot or a man who loved humanity more."

The advantage of close ties with Washington for the Canadian head of state was evidenced in the summer of 1939 when King George VI was planning a historic visit with Roosevelt in the United States. The prime minister, who would be seeing the king in Canada anyway, really had no business being on the U.S. leg of his tour but there was an opening for a minister-in-attendance. A Canadian election was only months away, and coupled with his great yearning to be part of historic occasions, King could use the wonderful shower of publicity for political purposes. He knew that the British weren't really considering him for the role, but realized that President Roosevelt might have some input. "I understand," he wrote in a slyly worded letter to FDR, "that before a final decision is reached by his Majesty as to who, if anyone at all, is to accompany him as Minister or Ministers in attendance, it is proposed to ascertain your own wishes and to be guided by them.

"In these circumstances, it would, of course, not do for me to express any opinion as to what may or may not be best from the point of view of the United States." But, "I have thought I should let you know at once that I shall be acting as Minister in attendance upon the King throughout the period of his visit to Canada, and that nothing would give me more pleasure than to accompany his Majesty in the same capacity in the course of his visit to the United States."

Roosevelt, against the stated wishes of London, lobbied strongly for King and won him the position. King George went so far as to mention during the visit that initially he had someone else in mind. "Mackenzie and I," Roosevelt told him, "know each other so well that I was most anxious he should come." For this trip, the president even helped the prime minister with his appearance. King was a dour dresser and with discretion, Roosevelt wrote: "If it is terrifically hot can't you discard that very good looking gray morning suit and light gray hat and design for yourself a white naval uniform, with gold maple leaves to denote Prime Minister rank?" Throughout the visit Roosevelt, sensitive to the prime minister's needs, sensitive to the fact he would continue to need his support, made a point of seeing to it that the Canadian leader was right next to himself and King George for all the well-photographed ceremonies.

Despite King George's initial coolness to his participation, Mackenzie King soon ingratiated himself, and it wasn't long before the two of them and Roosevelt were sharing gossip about such figures as Winston Churchill. Roosevelt felt Churchill was one of the only leaders who realized the magnitude of the problems ahead, but unfortunately "Churchill was tight most of the time." He said that when Sumner Welles, his undersecretary of state, visited him, Churchill drank whiskey throughout, then made a speech of an hour's length, at the end of which "he had become sober." King George said he wouldn't wish to appoint Churchill to any high office unless it was absolutely necessary in time of war. "I confess I am glad to hear him say that," the prime minister recorded, "because I think Churchill is one of the most dangerous men I have ever known." He described his behaviour with Welles as shameful: "It is that arrogance and the assumed superiority that some Englishmen have that have made so many nations their enemies today."

Although the king's visit marked yet another successful outing for the prime minister with the president, King still wasn't confident enough to address Roosevelt by his first name. He opened a letter following the occasion with his usual formality: "My Dear Mr. President." In his first sentence he said: "I almost wrote My Dear Franklin, for so indeed I feel, but my Scotch reserve gets the better of me." With typical excess, the prime minister went on to say, in describing the visit, that "nothing fraught with so great significance or good has happened since the great schism of the Anglo-Saxon race." The only regrets were the consistency with which the "darkey waiters" kept dropping trays of expensive china and, as he pointed out in the letter, his failure to join the president and the king for a swim. When FDR called for him to join in, King declined because he felt there would be a big party of swimmers. He went off for a ride with Miss LeHand and another gentleman. When later he heard that the swim was an exclusive affair, he was upset for weeks. "I am afraid I missed one of the great events of my life."

His relationship with Roosevelt was not distinguished by harmony alone. There were moments when the quality of the bond would be put to tough testing, the worst clashes coming in the early stages of the war. Roosevelt was clearly bothered by Canada's inadequate defence, saying it presented a danger to the United States. King said he was doing his best but admitted the best wasn't much. The slow nature of British war preparations bothered Roosevelt more however. "Now I will ask you something," he said to King. "You have Canada. You get

Australia and New Zealand and all of you put a burr on the tail of the British. They are so slow about everything." King agreed. "Well, Mackenzie," said Roosevelt, "if there is more trouble you will not mind if I ring you up." In an unnecessary gesture of politeness he turned to Loring Christie, the Canadian ambassador in Washington: "You will not mind if I go over your head and talk straight across the phone to Mr. King."[11] But the next request of the president to the prime minister did not come directly. In May, the Germans were toppling France. England could be next and Roosevelt and Hull were doubtful she could defend herself. The president told H. L. Keenleyside, a Canadian External Affairs emissary, that he believed Hitler might make an offer of settlement based on Britain relinquishing her colonial empire and sea fleet in exchange for her salvation. Such would make Germany superior in military power to the United States. He gave Keenleyside instructions to relay to the prime minister: Line up the Dominions to bring concerted pressure on England to reject any soft peace and, before making any settlement, disperse her fleet to the United States and the colonies so it would remain out of German hands. Not only was King to orchestrate Dominion pressure on London but also to personally notify Churchill of Roosevelt's wishes.

King was shocked. He had always promoted and enjoyed playing the role of intermediary between the two big powers, but this was too burdensome. Although he had often been accused of being anti-British, and although he had even been referred to as "the American" in the quiet corridors of diplomacy, he was thinking now that "the U.S. was seeking to save itself at the expense of Great Britain," and he didn't like it. "I instinctly revolted against such a thought," he wrote in his diary. "My reaction was that I would rather die than to do aught to save ourselves or any part of this continent at the expense of Britain."

He sent Keenleyside back to Washington to make sure the instructions were perfectly clear, to make sure the president meant what he had said. Yes, Keenleyside reported back, the message was to be delivered to Churchill. In anguish, the prime minister decided to go ahead with the assignment. He set about wording a letter that would "appear to be from myself rather than from him [Roosevelt], while at the same time taking care to see that it was wholly his point of view that I was putting over and not my own."

The key paragraph of his message read: "The United States cannot, it is considered, give immediate belligerent aid. If however Britain and France could hold out for some months, aid could probably then be given. If further resistance by the fleet in British waters became impossible before such aid could be given, the President believes that, having ultimate victory for the allies and the final defeat of the enemy in view, it would be disastrous to surrender the fleet on any terms, that it should be sent to South Africa, Australia, the Caribbean and Canada...."

Churchill was affronted by the message. He shot back a telegram: "We must be careful not to let Americans view too complacently prospect of a British collapse, out of which they would get the British fleet and the guardianship of the British empire minus Great Britain.... Although President is our best friend, no practical help has [reached us] from the United States as yet." Then he asked King to do some lobbying the other way: "Any pressure you can apply in this direction would be invaluable."

The prime minister, who instructed Keenleyside to provide the news of the rebuke to Roosevelt, was becoming exasperated. His finance minister, J. L. Ralston, found him working in his office at 2:00 A.M. one morning on another telegram. He told Ralston that he was played out, finished, couldn't carry the load and was on the point of quitting. "Chief, you've got to go through," Ralston told him. "The despatch you are working on may mean victory."

King satisfied himself that he was too indispensable to the world at the time to consider stepping aside. The president and Mr. Hull were his "intimate, personal friends," he told his Liberal party caucus. "If they learned tomorrow that this government had gone and I had ceased to be its leader, I do not know just what effect that would have on all relations of confidence not only between Canada and the United States but between the States and Britain."

The danger to Britain meant danger to Canada and King was compelled to brood upon the vulnerability of his country's negligible defences. There was Roosevelt's informal Kingston pledge and other casual assurances from the president that Washington would offer protection, but there was no North American alliance as such, and King wanted one, or something close to one. The way it came about was classic King-Roosevelt.

In June of 1940, the prime minister had requested some low-level talks. Roosevelt, concerned about preparations in the North Atlantic, told Canadian ambassador Christie on August 15 that he was thinking of sending three officials to Ottawa for discussions. But there was no urgency in his conversation and little indication that any breakthrough was imminent.

At the time of the Christie conversation, the State Department received a memo from its distinguished minister in Ottawa, J. Pierrepont Moffat. Canadian public opinion, he wrote, had gathered solidly behind the need for a joint defence understanding with the United States. "As a matter of practical politics the Prime Minister may ultimately be forced to recognize the existence of this popular demand.... The old fear that cooperation with the United States would tend to weaken Canada's ties with Britain has almost entirely disappeared."

The day after receiving the memo, and the day after the talk with Christie, Roosevelt phoned King. He said he was on his way to Ogdensburg, New York to inspect American forces and would like King to meet him there: "We can talk over defense matters between Canada and the U.S. together. I would like you to stay the night with me in the car [railway] and on Sunday I am going to a Field Day service at 11. We could attend it together."[12]

King met with his Defence Department officials, had a hair cut at the Chateau Laurier, and arrived in Ogdensburg at the appointed hour. Initially the president was preoccupied studying the first major campaign speech of Republican opponent Wendell Wilkie. But he then entered into a long discussion with King and War Secretary Stimson on continental defence. The talks continued the next morning whereupon the president took a sheet of paper and a pencil from a basket. He began drafting the first defence pact between Canada and the United States, an agreement which marked the first accord between the United States and a belligerent in the war, an agreement signalling a changed destiny for Canada—from the cloak of the Empire to the cloak of the continent. As custom with this president and this prime minister would have it, the creation of the Permanent Joint Board on Defense was an entirely personal venture. Neither the Canadian cabinet, the U.S. cabinet, the Congress, nor Winston Churchill were consulted about it.

When Roosevelt finished drafting the statement in the railway car he read it aloud to King. Roosevelt used the word "commission." King said "board" would be better. He questioned the president on the use of the word "permanent." Roosevelt explained that it was highly significant because the board was not just to be a response to wartime emergency, but a lasting institution.

Feeling that a press conference was unnecessary, the president called in an aide to get his script typed, had it mimeographed, and in ten minutes copies were handed to reporters. Stimson said it was a good day's work. King thanked both men with typical extravagance and remarked inaccurately on how Churchill would be so impressed.

The British leader soon wired: "I am deeply interested in the arrangements you are making for Canada and America's mutual defence. Here again there may be two opinions on some of the points mentioned. Supposing Mr. Hitler cannot invade us and his Air Force begins to blench under the strain, all these transactions will be judged in a mood different to that prevailing while the issue still hangs in the balance."

But in Canada where it mattered most for King, the agreement was widely praised. He commented in his diary at the time on what made him and Roosevelt tick: "A certain boyish interest in simple things...a thorough dislike of undue formality," and a shared view that "the really important things of life are very simple and that all that is needed is good will and sincere intent to effect any great end."

As King's rapport with the president developed, it did not bring him greater security. The sychophantic nature of his approach to Roosevelt only increased. After almost every meeting there would be a King letter to the effect that it was one of the great experiences of his life. After the signing of the Ogdensburg Agreement he may have been a little out of form. In his letter to the president, he could do no better than call it "one of the most far reaching agreements ever reached on this or any other continent." There were no references to the great Anglo-Saxon schism.

But if the approach aggravated Roosevelt, he didn't show it. The enjoyment he derived from being with King and talking to him was evidenced by his desire to have the prime minister join him on his holidays. Early in 1941, Archibald MacLeish, the librarian of Congress, was leaving the American minister's residence in Ottawa when King turned, came toward him, and "with a sudden and very real warmth," asked MacLeish to greet the president for him. "Give him my love," said King. MacLeish then wrote the president. "I have never heard words spoken with more sincerity."

As soon as he got the MacLeish letter, Roosevelt wrote the prime minister: "One of our mutual friends who saw you recently told me that he thought you looked a wee bit tired and that it would do you good to run down to the United States for a little while to 'get your gas tank refilled.'

"...I still hope to go to Warm Springs for a week or ten days starting the end of March. It would be grand if you could come down there again."

King wanted to see Roosevelt, not only for rest, but to ask for another favour. Canada was facing a balance-of-payments crisis. Usually Ottawa had a trade deficit with the United States, but a balancing surplus with Britain. With Britain at war however, London was unable to meet its dollar payments for Canadian imports, leaving the Ottawa treasury dangerously depleted. Ottawa mandarins had failed for months to negotiate more favourable terms with the Americans to make up the deficit and now Mackenzie King was about to do it himself. As soon as he left for the president's home at Hyde Park, New York, he knew God was on his side because when he awakened he noticed the two hands of the clock were on top of one another. King got very excited whenever this happened. This time, he felt it was a sign there was "a guiding hand in my mission."

FDR at this time was extremely well disposed toward the Dominion. In his 1940 election victory the French-Canadians on the eastern seaboard, for the first time, went solidly for him. He was planning a trip to Ottawa and agreed with the prime minister that he would probably receive a rousing welcome. On meeting, the two men congratulated each other on the wonderful jobs they'd done in respect to relations on the continent. King was delighted because the president didn't have his economic experts with him, meaning that it would be easier for the prime minister to sell the deal. Roosevelt, who invited King into his "cubby hole" study for a shirt-sleeved talk, didn't know much about international economics. King explained the problem and posed the solution—a Canada-U.S. defence production sharing arrangement whereby the United States would purchase more war supplies and munitions from Canada. Washington in turn would simply supply them to the British under the lend-lease formula. This way, Canada's exchange problem could be solved.

Roosevelt thought it was "a swell idea." He telephoned his treasury secretary and gave him a synopsis. He took a copy of a draft of a possible agreement that King had been cocky enough to prepare in advance and told his press secretary he could strike out the word "draft" and use it for the real thing. King asked if they should not have an official signing. "No, you don't need to trouble about that," said the president. "But let me write on one." In pencil, he scribbled on the original: "Done by Mackenzie and F.D.R. on a grand Sunday in April."

The president insisted that the prime minister be the one to give out the copies of the agreement to the press. King did so happily, climbed into his train car and went to bed at once. But he got up a few minutes later to see what he thought was the president sitting in his train car as it rolled by. In his pyjamas and dressing gown, King dropped to his knees to thank God for the marvellous day. But the excitement wasn't over yet. When he looked up at the clock, "the hands were absolutely across each other at about six minutes to 11. It was almost as though some one were speaking to me."

In Washington, some technical officials were dubious about what Roosevelt had signed. When King telephoned him one day he heard the president shouting instructions: "This is what I want done! Don't tell me why it can't be done. Just do it!"

The Hyde Park Agreement, as it was called, was one of King's greatest successes. It removed the currency crisis, aided Canada's economy, helped in the country's war effort, created a closer bilateral economic climate, and it gave King more political bonus points because the deal was clearly seen to be in Canada's favour.

But it was not long after the master stroke that the always insecure prime minister suffered his most tormenting episode in connection with FDR. It had been his habit to have the occasional drink with the president, but in 1941, he felt he owed it to his dog, Pat, to swear off the stuff. During a follow-up visit to Hyde Park he had to turn down the offer of a drink from the great president and for Mackenzie King it was "one of the greatest struggles of my life...I do not recall a time when I experienced more in the way of self-torture."

He described what happened: "I had had in mind for months past that when I came to pay this visit to the President that he would be expecting me to have a drink with him...I had wrestled with myself when little Pat passed away and made the vow I did then to give up taking anything to drink. I kept it firmly in England with Churchill.

"...Just before I left to dress for dinner the president said to Princess Juliana and myself, we will have a cocktail in my room before dinner—then to Princess Juliana—'you know Mackenzie King only takes a drink when he comes to see me.'"

King said at once, "You will have to let me off. I then explained that before going to England I had sworn off, knowing how much sherry and wine etc. was consumed there and that Churchill would want me to drink with him as he did."

Before dinner, cocktails were made and everyone stood around drinking them except King. Later, he wrote of the occasion: "I would have given anything for just one glass of wine or sherry as a cocktail but I held out. I said to the President that I felt I was spoiling the party and that I should not perhaps have made the resolution I did and should make an exception. But the President said quite firmly, putting up his hand—'You must not.' It was as if some force or voice was compelling him to speak."

At dinner everyone continued drinking and King only had water, although he would have preferred ginger ale. He then found it very hard to talk and remember names, and felt that instead of easing the president's burden he was adding to it. After dinner he retired to his bedroom and wrestled away the night:

"I was very restless, tearing my soul out wondering if I had made a great mistake in binding myself the way I had, wondering if I had not made relations between the President and myself more difficult for the future, in other words, really injured relations instead of helping them between our countries.... At one time I had a queer sensation as if the house had been bombed. I felt the house was being attacked and I felt real fear, but decided to stay; curiously enough the bomb seemed to me as if something had exploded in my own stomach. This was the way the night lasted till dawn.

"...I thought then I should look at the clock for evidence to see if someone was watching over me and if I was right.... To my delight and comfort the hands of the clock were together."

The anguish didn't seem to register with President Roosevelt. In a letter he told King the visit had been a joy and spoke again of how the continent was blessed with fortune.

Meanwhile, the prime minister was having more visions. In one dream, set near Queen's Park in Toronto, he was walking with the crippled Roosevelt who was using King as a support. The president was getting tired, the city was getting crowded, and King couldn't get a taxi. He stuck the poor president on top of a newsbox, or something like one, and left him there, sitting on it. King proceeded into the hotel to find a taxi but could only find a bunch of selfish, rich people. They were indifferent. They laughed at him and at what he told them.

The moral? Roosevelt was now "hard pressed, in a tight corner.... He had lost the sense of freedom which he had when we were together prior to the entry of the U.S. into the war."

U.S. officials complained in the early 1940s that, as Pierrepont Moffat put it, "Things move very slowly in Mr. King's mind."[13] Moffat was lamenting Ottawa's indecision in respect to playing a more active role helping the democratic forces in Latin America. His message about King's lassitude was forwarded to Roosevelt who, in an interestingly worded missive, tried to get the prime minister moving.

"As you know," he wrote King, "I have 'hunches'—not always good but sometimes accurate.

"This is for your information only. My present 'hunch' is that it would help if Canada could take a great part in the struggle between the forces of totalitarianism and the forces of democracy being waged in Latin America. They use somewhat different weapons down there—but it is a real fight.

"Canada can help."

Among Roosevelt's other hunches was one asserting that the territory known as Newfoundland was not fit for occupation. In a meeting with King and Churchill, the British prime minister suggested that with a military base there, the Americans might be considering taking the island over. Roosevelt said there were some things he might like to acquire but Newfoundland was not one of them. It was "suitable for raising sheep," he said.[14]

The president continued with favours for King. When Canadian troops landed with the Americans and the British on Sicily to begin a new campaign, the British War Office prepared to announce that only British units had arrived with General Eisenhower's Americans. His political fortunes depressed at the time, King was furious. His solution was to telephone Roosevelt and tell him the Canadian people were not going to tolerate being overlooked again. Roosevelt brought out his bat once more and sent an order overseas stipulating that the Canadians be included in the announcement.

In December 1942, King wanted a congratulatory letter from the president on the third anniversary of the British Commonwealth Air

Training Plan, a project in which Canada had played a large role. On this occasion a peculiar short cut was taken. Neither Roosevelt nor members of his staff knew much about the program or what to say in such a message. Finally, a White House assistant, without informing the State Department, approached the Canadian embassy for help. His idea?—Why don't you people write your own letter of congratulations and we'll have the president sign it? The embassy official approached was Lester Pearson. He was somewhat shocked by the absence of diplomatic propriety but agreed to it. On December 16, a beautiful, laudatory letter, signed by the president but written by a future Canadian prime minister was sent to the current prime minister.

Pearson was at his descriptive heights: "May this great Air Training Plan, which...has made Canada the aerodrome of democracy go from strength to strength. May it continue to send into the skies thousands of eager and courageous young fliers until the enemy is swept from the air and lies crushed on earth beneath the ruins of his own temple of tyranny." The unknowing King was deeply thrilled.

Although Roosevelt's interest in Canadian fliers was not engrossing, he and staff members had considerable concern for the Quebec problem and Canadian unity. Moffat was struck by the attitude of English Canadians toward the French. "They do not so much hate the French Canadians as despise them," he wrote the president in August 1942. The English are "increasingly talking of them as though they weren't even Canadians, merely a minority living in Canada."

The president took time off from his war deliberations to compose a lengthy letter to King on the French problem. His advice was to get moving on the assimilation process: "When I was a boy in the nineties I used to see a good many French Canadians who had rather recently come into the New Bedford area near the old Delano place at Fair Haven. They seemed very much out of place in what was still an old New England community. They aggregated themselves in the mill towns and had little to do with their neighbors. I can remember that the old generation shook their heads and used to say, 'this is a new element which will never be assimilated. We are assimilating the Irish but these Quebec people won't even speak English. Their bodies are here but their hearts and minds are in Quebec.'"

Today, he said, they have been absorbed. "They no longer vote as their churches and societies tell them to. They are inter-marrying with the original Anglo-Saxon stock: they are good peaceful citizens and most of them are speaking English in their homes....

"All of this leads me to wonder whether by some sort of planning, Canada and the United States, working towards the same ends, cannot do some planning—perhaps unwritten planning which need not even be a public policy—by which we can hasten the objective of assimilating the New England French Canadians and Canada's French-Canadians into the whole of our respective bodies politic. There are of course many methods of doing this which depend on local circumstances." Concluding, he said that "there would seem to be no good reason for great differentials between the French Canadian population elements and the rest of the racial stocks."

In the early 1940s when the defence of the continent was of primary importance to Americans, Canada received more attention than normal from Washington. This would change after the war when American responsibilities became global as well as continental, but for the time being the care and consideration were badly needed balm for King's fragile confidence. He was still fretful of calling Roosevelt by his first name. He confessed once to Roosevelt that he was afraid the president found him dumb. He would look up at the clock during conversations hoping that the hands would be forming the straight line.

In May of 1943, King got the first in a series of ego-boosters when he took part in a meeting at the White House with Roosevelt and Churchill. Initially he hadn't been invited, but with some foxy footwork was successful. Before the meeting King knew that Churchill wouldn't have time for a stopover in Canada but his strategy was to invite the British leader anyway, have the request turned down, and thereby gain leverage for having to join the meeting in Washington. Pearson, who wrote the telegram to Churchill, recalled: "It was evident that I was also delicately to convey to Mr. Churchill the impression that, if time made it impossible for him to come to Ottawa, Mr. King was prepared to accept an invitation to Washington. I got the point at once since I knew how Mr. King liked to convert these Big Two meetings into Big Three or even Big Two and a Half ones. Who could blame him?"

Roosevelt and Churchill praised King in their sessions, talking of him as the ideal man to moderate a post-war conference on reconstruction of the world. "Is it not a fact," asked Churchill, "that we three men who are at this table, now, have had more experience in government than any other men in the world today?" The status of the Canadian legation in Washington was being changed to that of a full-fledged embassy with an ambassador instead of a minister. FDR referred to the need for the prime minister to get consent from the king. Churchill rejected such an obligation, saying "Canada has complete control of her own affairs."

Roosevelt confided in the prime minister many of his deliberations with Churchill, among them the story of how the United Nations got its name. After a fruitless session with Churchill in search of a phrase to describe the countries fighting for freedom, Roosevelt went to bed one night and couldn't sleep. He wanted the word "united" in the phrase but couldn't come up with an appropriate companion word. Suddenly "nations" came to him and he knew immediately it was right. Excited, he couldn't wait until breakfast to tell Churchill and had his aide wheel him to the British leader's door at daybreak. He knocked and heard Churchill shout: "I'm in the tub." Roosevelt entered and the cherubic Churchill popped from the bath, "not a stripe on him." The president pointed a finger and declared, "Winston, I have it — The United Nations." Churchill agreed immediately that it was right. King told Roosevelt that the name had been "properly baptized."

In the planning for the first Quebec conference — the Roosevelt-Churchill parley which laid plans for the invasion of Nazi-occupied Europe — the question naturally arose as to the status of host Mackenzie King. Since Canada' war contribution was substantial and since the meeting was in Canada, it was argued, particularly by the British, that King should have full status at plenary sessions. Here, Roosevelt went against him, successfully reasoning that if Ottawa was let in many other countries would have to be let in. But King wasn't bothered. As long as the big two were coming and he was host, it would be "quite sufficient to make clear that all three are in conference together and will not only satisfy but will please the Canadian feeling and really be very helpful to me personally."

The conference went smoothly. King got in all the important pictures, the role of the Canadian forces was lauded by Roosevelt after Churchill had forgotten, the president was crazy about Quebec trout, and the "Big Two" finished the work they wanted on war plans. One of the only blights on the week, in King's view, was a showing of a film of the Group of Seven artists, featuring mainly the work of A. Y. Jackson. "I really felt ashamed of the exhibition being announced as

Canadian art," King wrote. The paintings, he said, destroyed and distorted many natural and beautiful Canadian scenes. The prime minister was also needled about his tea-drinking ways. As Roosevelt and Churchill enjoyed their scotches, Churchill told King he should forget about his silly resolution. But the problems were small stuff compared to the glories of a conference which, the prime minister said in a final statement, "helped to put our country on the map of the world."

Just as important for him were the next few days. Roosevelt proceeded from Quebec to Ottawa to become the first president to visit Canada's capital. It was seventy-six years since Canadian Confederation, and 154 years since George Washington's first presidency. Spectacular sunshine and a loving crowd of thirty thousand greeted the president on Parliament Hill. The House was out of session but the members had been called back to Ottawa so that Roosevelt could speak to them. He knew many of them because the U.S. embassy was in the habit of providing him with capsule summaries. In the cabinet, "Chubby" Power was "unfortunately a periodic drinker," Ralston was "too immersed in detail," and despite his sound common sense, Crerar was "definitely a 'has been.'" Among the Conservatives, R. B. Hanson was "none too friendly to the United States" and "completely uninspired."

For the size of the occasion, Roosevelt's speech was not a proper fit. His prose managed to sidestep Canadian and for the most part Canada-U.S. affairs, and focussed almost totally on the war and the evil Nazis: "Sometimes I wish that that great master of intuition, the Nazi leader, could have been present in spirit at the Quebec Conference—I am thoroughly glad he was not there in person. If he and his generals had known our plans they would have realized that discretion is still the better part of valor and that surrender would pay them better now than later.... We spend our energies and our resources and the very lives of our sons and daughters because a band of gangsters in the community of nations declines to recognize the fundamentals of decent, human conduct."

The way Nazis deal with their neighbour is "first to delude him with lies, then to attack him treacherously, then beat him down and step on him, and then either kill him or enslave him."

It was a speech that could just as well have been given in Kansas as Canada, but for King there was a reference which pleased him greatly. Roosevelt alluded to him as "my old friend" and added: "Your course and mine have run so closely and affectionately during these many long years that this meeting adds another link to the chain." The visit was not without its disappointments for the prime minister however. Beside the fact that the president's car broke down during a motorcade, King found, while showing Roosevelt through his Laurier House residence, that his favourite table had a cloth on it: "I took a look at the dining-room table while the president was having a wash. My heart fell into my boots when I saw the table had been set with a white cloth instead of being left uncovered with doilies and flowers." He made an effort to get it changed before Roosevelt emerged from the washroom but aborted the bid when he discovered there were no doilies.

The Ottawa visit was the last time that King was to see his friend, the president, in reasonably healthy condition. At the second Quebec Conference in September 1944, which was the next time they were together, King was shocked. While Churchill was "fresh as a baby," Roosevelt had lost thirty pounds and was worn out physically and mentally. King, however, worried most about his own mental deficiencies. Listening to Churchill and Roosevelt he would grow sad that he hadn't mastered history as he should have, that he hadn't kept more contacts with important men, that he had been far too much of a recluse: "It is a great opportunity of life largely missed....I continuously deplore not having been able to keep up with the events in different countries and not being more familiar with the history of Canada. I am woefully ignorant of questions on which I should be best informed, when associating with the President and Mr. Churchill."

But he was always confident of his political judgment and passed on advice that Roosevelt heeded. Before the presidential election of 1944, the president wanted a conference on the division of post-war Europe with the Soviet leader, Joseph Stalin. Pointedly, King warned that it would be a mistake. Rather than risk a failed conference, he said, make a campaign promise to have one afterward. Much less of a gamble, King told him.

Roosevelt won yet again and a few months later King had an election to think about, needed political help, and set out for Washington to get it. The State Department alerted Roosevelt to the real reason for the meeting. "Prime Minister King comes to Washington tried by the animosities aroused by the conscription issue in

Canada and on the eve of an election campaign which will be very tough indeed. He is seeking to rebuild his prestige and thus may want to meet the press here and capitalize discreetly on his friendship with you. As you know, Canadians would have voted for you to a man last November."

Roosevelt was only happy to oblige. "I would like to see him get more publicity," he told dinner guests days before the visit. The president had been through ten years with King as his neighbouring head of state and his relationship with him had been smoother and happier than with any foreign leader. With the warm rapport had come accomplishment. Canadians not inclined toward stronger continental ties would not see the many agreements as accomplishments, but men such as Cordell Hull regarded the relationship with Canada through those troubled years as being nothing short of the highlight.

"Throughout my twelve years at the State Department," said the secretary, "no sector of our foreign policy gave me more satisfaction or brought more fruitful results than our relations with Canada. In 1933 cooperation between the two countries had sagged to a low point; the depression, the Smoot-Hawley Tariff Act, and the Ottawa agreements had slashed their trade, and there was no adequate expression of the natural identity of the two countries, especially in the strategic and economic spheres. As I left office we had built a solid economic relationship through two trade agreements and a truly wonderful industrial cooperation during the war; we had assured the strategic interdependence of the two countries through the establishment of the Permanent Joint Board of Defense; and our relations in general had increased in extent and importance. They offered to the world the highest example of nations, bordering on each other and cherishing the same free institutions, working together for their mutual advantage."

King arrived at the White House a month before Franklin Roosevelt would die of a cerebral hemorrhage. The prime minister kissed him on the cheek and the usual confusion followed about the sofa, the right ear, and a chair directly across. At first King felt good about the president's appearance, but as the discussion wore on, he noticed that Roosevelt was repeating the same stories, that his eyes were not square, that he was thinking only on the surface, and that he was taking credit for things he didn't do. Pearson had visited Roosevelt earlier and been appalled by his condition. King felt that he had "pretty well lost his spring," but Roosevelt himself was thinking of the future. "Three years from now when I am through here I am thinking of setting up a newspaper which will be about the size of four pages of foolscap." It would have no editorials, he said, but just report the news truthfully and be distributed in every city in the country for the price of one cent.

King left the White House on Saturday, March 10 for a couple of days rest in Williamsburg, Virginia, but stopped by again on his way back to Canada. Roosevelt was having a press conference on March 13 and he wanted the prime minister there. King didn't want to go through the pressure of answering questions but wished to attend in order to pick up any available publicity points. Roosevelt, doing his last favour for the prime minister, told him to just come and sit there. He did and Roosevelt spoke at length to the press of the friendship, of the accords that had been reached and of the personal relationship that had translated into concrete achievements. "He spoke," wrote King, "as if I had been at the White House right along." The press reports in Canada were glowing.

The last conversation with the president was about politics. Roosevelt said if there was any way he could help in the election he would do it. King said that he did not think he would win, that he might even lose his own constituency. The president told him not to worry, that he felt he would be victorious.

In the late Ottawa afternoon of April 12 while he was being massaged, Mackenzie King was informed that Roosevelt had died. His reaction, curiously, was unemotional: "I seemed too exhausted and fatigued to feel any strong emotion. It all seemed like part of the day's heavy work. Just one more in fact. I was almost too tired to think of what, in the circumstances, I would be called upon to do."

Lester Pearson, ambassador to Washington, wrote the tribute on behalf of his country. "My country is Canada. We Canadians knew the President well and he knew us. He was, in fact, closer to us in a sense than any other President ever was. He spent his summers on our shores. He fished our northern streams. His fireside talks were heard in our homes. His ringing declarations lighted our hearts. He understood our problems and our possibilities."

On Sunday, April 15, Prime Minister King arrived in Hyde Park for the burial ceremony. "The fields were green," he noticed, "the little leaves were coming out on the trees, birds were singing. Many shrubs were already in bloom. Some blossoms on the trees. The sun shining brightly, the air fresh and balmy. It really filled one's soul with a feeling of delight.

"There came to my mind as we drove along the lines from the darkey song: 'When the birds were singing in the morning and the myrtle and ivory were in bloom and the sun on the hill was adorning, oh, it was then that we laid him in the tomb.'"

At the grave site, the prime minister, worried that he was wearing the wrong style hat, stood near Harry Truman, whose head was lowered. King had a wreath and, as the mourners gathered around the burial plot, he unwrapped it, left his coat and hat with Edward Stettinius, the secretary of state, and walked alone toward the grave. He stood motionless for a moment, dropped the flowers beside the bier, and walked slowly back. A man in charge of a motion picture crew came forward and asked King to do it again because it would make an excellent shot. King, encouraged by Stettinius, walked slowly to the bier again. He picked up the flowers and placed them down again. He returned slowly to his place among the mourners.

CHAPTER TEN

Life with Harry

WHEN HARRY TRUMAN, the haberdasher from Missouri, assumed the presidency in 1945, the United States held Canada in esteem. "Canada has developed during the war years into a nation of importance," the State Department asserted in a memo to the new president. "Her eleven and a half million people have demonstrated remarkable productive capacities and she has put a million men in uniform.... The strength of Canada's overseas armies was particularly remarkable." The Dominion had "played an effective and important role" in conferences establishing the United Nations and the International Monetary Fund and in providing international relief. The Canadian delegation at the United Nations Conference was a "conspicuously able group."[1]

The memorandum declared that Canada had now reached the status of "a leading Middle Power." In respect to U.S. interests, the country was playing a "useful, constructive role." The Canadian government, it said, "is quick to respond to considerate treatment by the United States, is sensitive to public opinion in this country, is anxious to stand on its own feet, paying its own way, but is naturally inclined to resent any situations in which Canada is taken for granted or overlooked entirely."

Truman was given a frank assessment of Prime Minister King: "As a speaker and a writer he is lacking the essential gifts of clarity, force and ease. On the floor of the House he is a past master at evasion in answering questions but in rough and tumble debate he scores many more points than he loses. He is primarily a student. He is a bachelor and devotes a large part of his leisure to reading and abstract thinking.

"... He dislikes publicity; avoids giving interviews and, in his occasional press conferences, is not only uninformative but over-polite to the point of seeming disingenuous. He is intensely loyal to his friends though quite willing to laugh at their foibles." Summing up, the State officials said the prime minister enjoyed little personal popularity but will "go down in history as a statesman."

Had the same officials who wrote flatteringly of Canada and interestingly of its leader seen what the powers in Ottawa were saying about Harry Truman, their reviews might have had a different tone. Lord Athlone, governor-general of the Dominion, spared no mercy in telling King what he thought of the beloved Roosevelt's replacement. Truman was, in his words, "a crook."[2] King acknowledged in his journal that "some persons have been seeking to convey that impression." His own view was not that he was a criminal but an inexperienced low brow, probably not up to the job.

Ambassador Lester Pearson shared the concerns. As vice-president, Truman had made him feel he had about as much status as an ambassador from "Upper Ruritania." He kept Pearson waiting for an hour for an appointment, seated with a peanut-chewing Missouri friend of the president's who was later charged with influence peddling. In the meeting Pearson was interrupted by the unannounced entrance of a senator who condescendingly assured him that, as usual, everything was fine with Canada. At the next encounter, a reception for Truman, the vice-president cracked a series of stag-party one-liners that Pearson found "more vulgar than funny." Truman then took to the piano with a sexy young actress who dangled more public leg than Pearson was used to seeing in 1945. "I was not amused or impressed. I thought, 'can this man rise to the awesome responsibilities likely to fall on him so soon?'"[3]

With Roosevelt gone, King realized he could not maintain the influence he had in Washington. Truman, who called the War of 1812 "the silliest damn war we ever had," knew little about Canada, had no previous contact, and seemingly cared little. Initially suspicious of him, King told his cabinet that he believed "the long range policy of the Americans was to absorb Canada. They would seek to get this hemisphere as completely one as possible."

The times were momentous. The United States suddenly stood unchallenged as the world's number one military and economic power. The rest of the world was so crippled from the War that Canada now stood fourth. The atomic bomb, the ultimate horror weapon, had been discovered, with Canada playing a significant role. A new world economic order and organization was in place. A multilateral free-trade movement was nascent. The globe was being severely split into communist and capitalist camps. The United Nations was in place, and soon there would be NATO and the Marshall Plan.

These vast changes meant that the mandate of the United States was no longer just the defence and the economic health of the continent, but the defence and the economic health of the noncommunist world. Relations with Canada had to be squeezed into this new perspective, and into the perspective of a stronger, self-assertive Canada. In 1931 the Statute of Westminster had put the Dominion on the same level as Britain in essential status, but not in function. But with its imposing performance in war and diplomacy, Canada was now functioning at the same level as well. Britain was no longer its military and economic protector, the United States having assumed the role. The FDR years saw the forging of a greater economic alliance with Canada through the liberalized trade and Hyde Park agreements and the dawning of a defence alliance with the Ogdensburg pact. The Truman administration leaned toward a further strengthening of both, a greater integration of the continent. Mackenzie King, now more infirmed by age, unable to maintain concentration over an extended period, was leaning toward a more isolationist Canada of the type he led before the war. He was less trustful of America without Roosevelt, wary of its new super-power status, tremulous over the advent of the atomic age. His cabinet and the shining breed of civil servants Canada was producing at this time were inclined in opposite directions—toward internationalism, collective security, and a closer relationship with Washington.

King spent his remaining three years as prime minister with Truman in Washington (St. Laurent dealt with the president for the following four). The first private meeting of King and Truman came seven weeks after one of the first of so many momentous decisions Truman would make—detonating the atomic bomb on Hiroshima and Nagasaki, marking the first and only occasion on which nuclear bombs have been used. The Hiroshima blast, August 5, 1945, killed roughly 100,000 people. The Nagasaki detonation, four days later, left 50,000 dead and historians perplexed over the rationale. Was not the first A-bomb and the threat of more enough to drive the Japanese to surrender? King feared that Truman did not fully grasp the horrific revolutionary nature of the new bomb. The prime minister, along with British leader Attlee, were the only two heads of state in the world to know in advance of the United States' plan to go nuclear. President Roosevelt told King during the Canadian's last visit in March of the decision and that August would be the likely date. The early consultation was in recognition of Canada's contribution to the building of the bomb and as a supplier of the vital ingredient — uranium. In the Quebec conferences, King, Churchill, and Roosevelt had reached an agreement on the development and use of atomic energy which, when later scrutinized by Truman, distressed him greatly. Among other things it required the United States to gain British permission before using the bomb. "Byrnes [secretary of state] and I discussed the Roosevelt agreement with Churchill and Mackenzie King on the Atomic Energy Program," Truman noted in his diary. "It is a mess. No one seems to have thought the thing would work out as it has. So I am the heir to a hell of a mess." He was somewhat consoled by the fact that the vast amounts of money spent on the development of the weapon produced something. "But I'm not blaming anyone. Suppose that 2 billion, 600 million dollars had been spent in vain. What a terrible mess that would have been! So let's be thankful for what we have."

On the day before the Hiroshima explosion, King wrote of the pending event: "It makes one very sad at heart to think of the loss of life that it will occasion among innocent people as well as those that are guilty. It can only be justified through the knowledge that for one life destroyed, it may save hundreds of thousands and bring this terrible war quickly to a close."

On the day after Hiroshima: "Naturally it created mixed feelings in my mind and heart. We were now within sight of the end of the war with Japan.... We now see what might have come to the British people had German scientists won the race. It is fortunate that the use of the bomb should have been upon the Japanese rather than upon the white races of Europe."

Before the prime minister could confer with Truman on atomic energy, he learned of another stunning development, this one even closer to home. In early September, Igor Gouzenko, an employee of Ottawa's Soviet embassy, appeared at the offices of King's top officials and revealed the existence of a Soviet espionage ring. The Soviets, fair-weather allies with the West in the war, had been moving away but few had suspected this and King was alarmed, fearing that secrets to the production of the bomb may have been stolen.

The revelation, along with the bomb, absolutely compelled a meeting with Truman but owing to the skittishness which accompanied King's dotage it almost never came off. The two leaders had talked briefly at the United Nations founding conference in San Francisco in the spring and Truman had invited King to the White House in June. But King was in an election campaign and the public relations value of a visit with the unproven president was deemed insufficient for the trip. Now, Truman wanted King to fly in Friday, September 28, spend the night in the White House and, since the president had a long-standing engagement in Missouri on Sunday, fly home on Saturday. King, however, had an important debate to attend in Parliament on Friday. Moreover, he didn't want to fly to Washington because he was going to be flying to London to see Prime Minister Attlee. He didn't like to do too much flying at once. He was over seventy.

Truman was so informed, stewed for a while, and decided he would be gracious enough to cancel his Missouri trip so that King wouldn't have to miss Friday's debates. King then determined he would not fly to Washington under any circumstances. He would take a train which would leave Friday night and arrive late Saturday. But then it was discovered that the trip would require the transfer of his railway car in New York at an additional cost of three hundred dollars. Outraged, King cancelled his train ticket. The biggest spy story in decades was demanding urgent action but the prime minister of Canada, a man of Scottish blood, was not about to spend an extra three hundred dollars to see to it.

King telephoned American ambassador Ray Atherton to give him the news. Too much money, he said. The expenditure might touch off a scandal. Can't go. Atherton, fuming, said that surely the excursion could be arranged in such a way that no one would know about the extra three hundred dollars. But King was intransigent. "I told him these things should not and could not likely be concealed. At any rate, I would take no chances." Norman Robertson, the highly regarded deputy minister of External Affairs, intervened to plead with the prime minister that it would be absolutely crazy to let the small amount of money get in the way of such an important matter. But King again held ground. "I told him I did not wish my reputation to be damaged by any false step."

Truman, becoming perplexed about this man, now un-cancelled his Missouri venture, deciding that if King couldn't make it by early Saturday, there would be no meeting. The prime minister would not change his mind on the train problem, but finally under considerable pressure resolved that, if the weather was excellent, he would fly down Saturday morning. It was and the Washington departure crisis finally concluded.

The hope expressed immediately as the two leaders sat down in the rather empty executive mansion, was that what had begun with King and Roosevelt could continue with King and Truman. Truman had been pleased with King's re-election, writing him about what a "source of deep gratification" it was for Americans. "We rejoice." The prime minister replied that his relationship with FDR was an important factor in the victory.

They referred to the spy matter as the Corby case, because the files on it were kept in a Corby's whiskey box. After a lengthy briefing from the prime minister, Truman emphasized repeatedly that he hoped King would take no unilateral action on Corby, that the two of them must get together with Attlee to work out a strategy, and that nothing should be done without consensus among the three. Ten Downing Street was suspected of wanting faster action—public disclosure and arrests—but Truman's recommendation was soft music for King. With advanced age had come advanced insecurity. His confidence was now so frail that he didn't feel up to the job. "I am too weary to meet situations as they arise," he wrote in his diary that fall. "The things that I was wholly familiar with this afternoon I could not find strength to express. This is a condition which no responsible leader should be in in times like the present." On Corby he didn't want to have to act alone.

Under questioning from Truman, he disclosed that the espionage net likely extended into the top level of the State Department. Truman did not react with great surprise. He wanted to get all the information possible, but the deferential prime minister, fearing he was taking up too much of the president's precious time, kept getting up as if it was time to leave. Truman, after the third or fourth flagrant King gesture, assented, suggesting that a further meeting to include Attlee was necessary.

The new parley was scheduled for the second week of November. Along with the espionage matter, the future of atomic energy joined the agenda. This was a subject the dire importance of which was fully understood by Mackenzie King. From England he wrote that he would return to the continent "ready to enter on a larger sphere of work than ever—a sphere of work which will identify me with this new age of atomic energy and world peace. It is the thing that I am sure is a part of the purpose of my life. All that I get from my own inner feeling through psychic sources etc. stresses this very clearly."

To Lester Pearson the meaning of the meeting was clear as well. A force that could destroy the world had been unleashed on it. A way had to be found to control that force. One of the days of the summit was Armistice Day, and for Pearson it "could never have been more relevant. I had not missed an Armistice Day silence since 1919 but never had the two minutes seemed so long, so pregnant with meaning, so evocative of memories or so challenging to a renewed and more resolute search for a better world."[4]

In damp, cool weather the leaders and their assistants boarded the yacht *Sequoia*, normally the venue for Truman's around-the-clock poker games, and sat around the green felt card table. After his annihilation of Japanese cities, Truman had written King thanking him for Canada's part in "this most terrific of wars." Now he asked the seven people around the table to speak in turn on what could be done to ensure that atomic energy would never again be used for destructive purposes.

King, whose diary account of these Washington days has never been found, stated his position, but Pearson felt compelled to elaborate. "I could...not resist the opportunity to plead for a deep and broad international effort through the United Nations to control this new and final threat to human survival, an effort which must be made before other atomic powers appeared. I emphasized as strongly as I could what seemed to be so obvious, that we could prevent global catastrophe only by global agreement of an unprecedented character, and that this would undoubtedly require some delegation of sovereign rights to a supranational agency."

The discussion was discursive, but there was agreement on the need for international rather than trinational action. Each side then wrote a draft of a suggested agreement and, with Prime Minister King playing a leading role in the final alterations, the three were combined into one. The major principles of the joint Declaration on Atomic Energy were that Canada, the United States, and Britain would share scientific information on the atom with other nations; that specialized information, which could lead to the development of the bomb, would be withheld; and that an international control commission would be established at the United Nations.

King was enthusiastic. He told Truman a great service had been rendered mankind. The president was encouraged as well. "The more I think about it, the better I like it." The principles embodied in the declaration were put forward at the United Nations but an agreement could not be secured with the Soviets, who wanted all stocks of atomic weapons destroyed within three months, and an international convention prohibiting production of all such weapons instituted. The United States, the possessor of a distinct military advantage because of the atomic capability, was not prepared to go that far. And of the poker-table agreement of 1945, Pearson was later left to muse: "These were fine words and noble sentiments. There was a solemn warning in them but there was to be little effective action to follow. Have they become merely the expression of another 'might-have-been' of history? Today the answer seems to be 'yes' and it could mean humanity's greatest and final failure."[5]

The spread of bomb technology was not controlled, nor was the effectiveness of Soviet espionage. Highly secret yacht talks led to an agreement on coordinated police action, although diplomatic relations with the Soviets were maintained. In Canada a royal commission was appointed and arrests made. Public reaction to the disclosures was vehement, the spy case becoming a catalyst in the genesis of the Cold War. Lewis Clark, an American official in the Ottawa embassy, reported to Washington: "At the moment the Canadians are like the brave little boy who has talked back to the bully [Russians] and is wondering what is going to happen to him."

The bully managed fine without having to retaliate. By 1950 when more Russian spying was uncovered, the Soviets had stolen enough secrets to develop their own atom bomb and, by 1954, the more powerful hydrogen bomb.

From the continental standpoint, the meetings in the autumn of

1945 at least produced some harmony out of a King-Truman relationship that had begun without promise. Following the *Sequoia* Conference, the prime minister was impressed enough to send the president a rare token of appreciation—one of his treasured dog pictures. "I should feel deeply honoured Mr. President if you would accept as a slight remembrance of this visit, and the events of the past week, the somewhat intimate photograph of myself and my old dog, Pat." It was, he pointed out, one of FDR's favourites.

"Your picture will occupy a place of honor in my study," Truman responded and, unless his wife Bess was diplomatically devious, he meant it. Two years later, Bess took King aside during a state visit to Ottawa. She told him that whenever the maids mixed up the photos on her mantle, the president would always make a point of rescuing the picture of King and Pat to the foreground. King was most gratified. He raved about it in his diary.

For Truman the most important aspect of relations with Canada was the planning and application of joint defence measures. A White House memorandum put the case simply to Truman in 1946. "Two world wars have demonstrated that an aggressor must destroy the power of North America or be defeated. Due to post 1945 technological advances, North America is no longer adequately protected by geography. Canadian and United States military advisers agree that in five years North America must be prepared to meet major enemy capabilities." The Americans wanted to integrate as much as possible Canadian military methods and planning but Dean Acheson, the deputy secretary of state, whose parents were from Toronto, realized there would be problems. "In view of Canada's traditional close association with the United Kingdom," he told the president, "the shift to an even closer association with the United States armed forces is a matter of great moment in Canada and one which involves considerable political risk for the present government. Some Canadians fear we would encroach on their own sovereignty and some fear that Canada might ultimately have to withdraw from the British Commonwealth."

But the Pentagon, as Acheson added, was "insistent on closing the gap between Alaska and Greenland and on pushing the defense of our industrial centers north of our own border. For this we are dependent on the cooperation of the Canadian Government." On the Pentagon's list of requirements were an air defence system to include bases in

Canada and meteorological and early warning communications facilities.

Ottawa officials were somewhat sympathetic, but not convinced of the immediacy of the Soviet threat. King, feeling that Canada was to be "a mere pawn in the world conflict," wanted to maintain strong defence links with Britain to avoid total reliance on Washington.

The prime minister had worried all along that, having established a military presence in Canada during the war, the Americans would be reluctant to dismantle it after the war. He had talked once to Vincent Massey about the process of disentanglement and Massey recalled that "The PM showed he had grave doubts as to whether international agreements on this which Canada had secured from the United States provided any practical guarantee against the United States' claims and pretensions. When I suggested that the Americans did not take us seriously enough as a nation, King said that Canadians were looked upon by Americans as a lot of Eskimos...."

In October 1945 King wrote that "If the Americans felt security required it" they "would take peaceful possession of part of Canada with a welcome of the people of BC, Alta., and Saskatchewan...." He was apprehensive about the loyalty of his western provinces. "I felt perfectly sure that once the Western provinces became alarmed in the matter of their security, they would look to the United States for protection, not to Canada or the Commonwealth."

In a wire to the State Department, ambassador Atherton labelled King's suspicions about American motives "traditional caution," adding that unfortunately the prime minister's control was such that he dragged the views of his cabinet and chiefs of staff with him. His recommendation was to have Truman meet King and "...assure Canada that joint defense with the United States will not lead to withdrawal from the Commonwealth."

In a White House session with King in October of 1946, Truman pushed his case for an American Air Force bomber base at Goose Bay, Labrador. King first pointed out that Labrador belonged to Newfoundland which was not, at the time, a Canadian province. He said he understood that the United States was thinking of stationing 10,000 men in Goose Bay and this would cause many Canadians to fear an infringement of their sovereignty. Truman argued that all he was trying to do was make aggression impossible anywhere but he was unable to move the prime minister, it being a meeting in which the most concrete development was that there should be another meeting. Truman, a man who could be blunt in his appraisals, a president who would later refer to Richard Nixon as "Squirrel Head," was not dismayed, however. "Mr. King was here last week," he wrote his mother a few days later. "He is an honest man. I can always get along with an honest man." The prime minister was also impressed, finding the Truman style most effective: "His whole appearance is that of a business executive who has himself well in hand, completely in training. He has a very disarming smile, very deep dimple in his right cheek when he smiles. Eyes kindly and sympathetic yet strong."[6]

A few months after the meeting, post-war principles of defence cooperation were enunciated, the outcome being a compromise falling short of the degree of integration Washington sought. Canada took the position that the granting of permanent or long-term rights to the United States for defence installations on Canadian soil was undesirable.

Nonetheless King wanted a favour from Truman. He would soon be celebrating his twentieth anniversary as prime minister and, for this "crowning event" as he called it, he wanted the president to come to Ottawa in June 1947. To lobby, he stopped by the White House following a vacation in Williamsburg, Virginia. Having left his advisers behind he hoped Truman would reciprocate so that he could have a one-on-one session. But an aide joined the president, leading King to grumble in his journal that Americans always like to have a third man present. "I do not think that as between the President and the Prime Minister that sort of thing is necessary."

The pitch to the president was that "the plain people" of Canada wanted to see him and cheer for him because he was courageous and fearless. To this, Truman responded: "I only try to do what is right; not to trouble about anything else." King's philosophy was somewhat different. He once told Pearson on a train trip to Washington that the secret of politics was not to do what is right but to avoid doing what is wrong. Pearson told the story to James Reston, and Reston never forgot it.[7]

King's second line to Truman was standard poetic excess. He said that the president's presence for his twentieth anniversary celebration would constitute such a sensation that he would then be prepared to part the world in peace. These blandishments were successful, and on June 10, 1947 Truman became the second president to come to

Ottawa. To mark the anniversary, the prime minister scheduled a portrait of himself to be unveiled in the Parliament buildings as the president looked on. A portrait of former Prime Minister Robert Borden was also to be unveiled. The governor-general, Viscount Alexander, would do the honours.

With an air of solemn dignity, the gushing preliminary statements were read. With the bespectacled Truman watching carefully, the call went out first for the unveiling of the Borden portrait. The governor-general, his grandeur appropriate for the occasion, walked gingerly to the covered picture as the sense of anticipation grew. He drew the cord and the wrong portrait appeared.

The governor-general, despite a rehearsal earlier in the day, had been led to the wrong spot and accidentally exposed the picture of King instead of Borden. The master of ceremonies turned deadly white. Viscount Alexander was led to the other portrait and this time Borden was unveiled. The master of ceremonies apologized for what had happened. There were apologies all round. Prime Minister King's great moment, the moment which was supposed to prepare him to leave the earth peacefully, was terribly tarnished. The unveiling of his portrait was re-enacted. There was a nice round of applause.

Otherwise, the Truman visit was a splendid success. The president was greeted by large, genuinely enthusiastic crowds. As he strode up the main walk to the Parliament on a sparkling morning, the band played the Missouri Waltz, his favourite tune. In a marvellous expression of friendship, the president and the prime minister joined arms and, to the delight of the sun-drenched thousands, began to skip along to the beat. It was a grand departure from King's normally strict behaviour, and inside he had another surprise. When Truman finished his speech, King brought him back to face the audience, and called for three cheers for the president: "Hip-hip-hoorah!" the House thundered. Hip-hip-hoorah! "Never in my life have I received such a cordial welcome as I had from your Parliament this morning," Truman told a luncheon. "You were kind to me. I have heard of people receiving three cheers and a tiger but it never happened to me before."

There were no immediate controversial issues. The visit was an exhibition of friendship. Truman praised the wisdom of King in his speech to Parliament. He said the unveiling ceremony was "wonderful." He lauded the Canadian war effort as "magnificent," and he said there was a lot more than luck to the Canada-U.S. friendship: "The example of accord provided by our two countries did not come about merely through the happy circumstance of geography. It is compounded of one part proximity and nine parts good will and common sense."

Canadians, he said, were broad in mind and broad in spirit. Americans "find that the composition of your population and the evolution of your political institutions hold a lesson for the other nations of the earth. Canada has achieved internal unity and material strength, and has grown in stature in the world community by solving problems that might have hopelessly divided and weakened a less gifted people."

The two leaders had a press conference at Montebello, Quebec. Truman sat down under a tree and said, "Let's have a drink." He asked for bourbon and branch water, his favourite. Someone told him there was no branch water, but Truman said not to worry about it, that he had brought his own. While the prime minister stayed dry and in the background, the president drank and fielded the questions. "I sincerely hope that Canadians will pay us a visit," said Truman. There isn't a chance in the world of our being able to give them the sort of reception that they have given me, but we do the best we can....The United States has but one objective in view and that is peace in the world and friendship with every nation in the world. And underline that every."

His daughter, Margaret Truman, accompanied the president on the three-day stop and was effusive in a later description. "The Prime Minister, Mackenzie King," she said in words which would have shocked many, "was one of the most charming statesman I have ever met, with a delicious sense of humor. We loved the old world charm of Ottawa. It was like a trip to London with only one-tenth the trouble."

In the same year, the prime minister, facing a dollar crisis similar to the one in 1941 which had prompted Hyde Park, began quietly, very quietly, to work toward the establishment of a free-trade area with the United States. It was one of the most top-secret negotiations in bilateral history. King appointed a small group of Finance Department officials to try and negotiate an agreement. They were to report directly to him. The Department of External Affairs was kept in the dark. A similarly shrouded group was set up in the Truman administration and by early 1948 a comprehensive agreement was produced.

It was, the Canadian team felt, a close approximation of what the prime minister wanted. It would now have to be approved by the U.S. Congress, and an agreement as sweeping as the one in 1911 would be on the books; Canada and the United States would take the lead in the free-trade fever Washington was trying to spread and Canada would be given a five-year head start on some central aspects. Goods flowing unencumbered across the forty-ninth would likely mean less need for American multinationals to set up branch plants in Canada to circumvent tariff walls. Simon Reisman, the future deputy minister of Finance, who was then a young man working for the director of the Canadian negotiating team, would come to regard the agreement as potentially the most important bilateral development of the post-war period.[8]

But even though it was embraced enthusiastically by the prime minister's men, it was not to come about. At the last moment Mackenzie King turned cold. He remembered 1911; he feared for the political ramifications; he thought the limited time before the 1948 presidential election would create problems; and he feared the American intent was still to annex Canada. He explained to his disappointed negotiators that it was too much of a gamble: "I pointed out that the issue was very large. That it unquestionably came back to what the future of Canada either in the British Commonwealth or as part of the U.S. will be. I said I felt sure that the long objective of the Americans was to control this continent. They would want to get Canada under their aegis. If I was an American, I would have the same view especially considering Russia's position etc. On the other hand I did not feel we would be as well off as a State of the Union as we will be possibly as the greatest of self governing portions of the British Commonwealth of Nations."

No public disclosure was made of the negotiation. The prime minister left no trace of having dealt personally with the president on the matter. Although Reisman was under the impression that the negotiations had the president's blessings, Truman left no evidence of personal involvement. The two leaders were clashing at the time, not over trade, but Korea. The country, under Japanese rule from 1910 to 1945, was divided into communist and non-communist areas and the issue was how to set free and fair elections. While King was out of the country, St. Laurent, his External Affairs minister, indicated that Canada would be willing to serve on a United Nations commission to supervise the campaign. But King, reflecting his new isolationist posture, returned angered, feeling that such a commission would only increase tensions between Moscow and Washington, and lead Canada into a faraway crisis he didn't need.

He sent Pearson to explain his views to Truman. Pearson, who regarded this assignment as one of his most difficult ever, was told by the president: "Don't worry. You won't get into any trouble over there. And if you do we are behind you." The latter part was just what King would not want to hear. "If I had repeated that comment," wrote Pearson, "our prime minister would have considered that his worst fears had been realized."

The Canadian ambassador wanted Truman to telephone King to allay his concerns and settle the matter but Truman wouldn't do it. He was afraid the prime minister would get the better of him. The reason, Jack Hickerson of the State Department told Pearson, was that Truman simply didn't know much about the Korean situation. The president chose instead to write a letter:

"I am deeply concerned over the possibility that Canada's failure to appoint a representative on the Korean Commission would be misunderstood and distorted out of all proportion to the modest importance of this temporary agency. I am fearful that it might be seized upon by persons in this country and elsewhere who are anxious to find grounds for opposing cooperative efforts to resolve urgent political and economic problems which confront the world and which must be solved if western civilization is to endure. I need hardly add that the U.S.S.R. would exploit Canada's absence to the fullest in its propaganda."

King was furious. He called Pearson away from a U.N. security council session, told him Truman was wrong, and instructed him to return to Ottawa. The prime minister then prepared a stiff reply to the president. "It is I think the first time I have quite emphatically declined to meet a wish expressed by any President of the United States," he said. His letter told the president that the commission idea was a mistake, that it would draw U.N. members into a position of "great future embarrassment."

St. Laurent, King's star cabinet member, was compromised. He told Jack Pickersgill: "I may not be in the government tomorrow."[9] Pearson, however, persuaded St. Laurent to have dinner with the prime minister. A solution was found. Canada would serve on the commission but would withdraw if it became apparent that Soviet cooperation in the elections was not forthcoming. King pulled back on the Truman letter and send a response of a different kind, a response which was still strong enough to please Pearson, who commented: "It will show the Americans that we are not going to be pushed around by them on security council matters."

The tempest did not seriously aggravate the King-Truman relationship, one which maintained much of the bilateral good will generated under FDR. They met for the last time at the beautiful William and Mary College in Williamsburg, in April 1948, to receive honourary degrees. With the crisis brewing in Berlin, Truman told King conditions were as serious as in 1939. King concluded: "if we escape war before this month is over or next at the latest, it will be a miracle." They spoke briefly about the upcoming presidential election. Truman, far behind in the polls, said that he was going to fight "for all he was worth." He would "lick those other fellows yet."[10]

When he did just that, stunning the pundits, Mackenzie King retired, leaving the reigns of power to Quebec's Louis St. Laurent, the urbane lawyer who said after the first meeting of the United Nations General Assembly: "We have advanced from barbarism to a sort of international feudalism." A brisk, direct man, he was respectful in his dealings with Truman, then Eisenhower, but never fawning and seldom deferential. He didn't believe in doing things for the sake of appearance. He didn't try to use the presidents for political capital back home. The relationship between Canadians and Americans struck him as something extraordinary. "Like farmers whose hands have a common concession line we think of ourselves as settling from day to day questions that arise between us without dignifying the process by the word 'policy.'" He had little to do with Truman, meeting with him only twice in four years. Their limited relationship was one of mutual respect. St. Laurent objected strongly to the notion of Canada being taken for granted and in Pearson he had a diplomat who was seldom hesitant to sound off on the subject. "There will be difficulties and frictions," Pearson said in 1951 in one of his most brusque appraisals. "These however will be easier to settle if the United States realizes that while we are most anxious to work with her and support her in the leadership she is giving the free world, we are not willing to be merely an echo of somebody else's voice.... It would also help if the United States took more notice of what we do and indeed of what we say. It is disconcerting for example that about the only time the American people seem to be aware of our existence, in contrast to say, the existence of a Latin American republic, is when we do something that they do not like, or do not do something they would like."

Multilaterally, the Korean War proved the toughest test to the Canada-U.S. relationship in the St. Laurent-Truman period. But while King and Roosevelt tended to handle state-to-state relations personally, the style of diplomacy changed with Truman and St. Laurent. The new president and prime minister had minimum contact on the war, leaving the weaving to the men from their respective inner circles.

Although Canada had been one of the staunchest proponents of U.N. collective action during the formation of the body, the St. Laurent government stirred resentment in Washington through its reluctance and procrastination to commit ground forces to the combat zone. Three weeks after the June 1950 invasion of South Korea by the North, Ottawa had provided only three destroyers for stand-by duty in Far East waters. To Pearson's assertion that they represented "no mere token" assistance, an American embassy official replied: "Okay, let's call it three tokens."[11]

The Canadian government had waited for years in World War I and in World War II for American participation and, reflecting the omnipresent Canadian sensitivity to the hint of being pushed around by the White House, the St. Laurent government was not prepared to jump into the Korean conflict when Truman said jump. It wasn't until August that a Canadian brigade was contributed and throughout the war the Canadian effort was to rein in the Americans. When the North Koreans retreated, the Pentagon advocated pursuing them into the North, but St. Laurent was more conciliatory, urging that the North Koreans be given the opportunity of entering into a cease-fire. The prime minister and his foreign policy establishment shuddered when Truman suggested at a press conference in November 1950 that General Douglas MacArthur had the authority to use nuclear weapons in the conflict if he so desired. Pearson was quickly to the podium with a stern warning that the consequences of such an action would be disastrous. The Canadians also fought Washington, in vain, to prevent a White House introduction of a resolution declaring the Chinese guilty of aggression. But because St. Laurent chose to place much more confidence and responsibility in his associates than King, because of his more detached, imperial style of operating, any acrimony over

Korea did not extend overtly to his relationship with Truman. The two leaders never found it necessary to meet to discuss the war.

Bilaterally, the issue of consequence between the president and the prime minister, an issue which compelled person-to-person work between them, was the three-decade-old St. Lawrence Seaway proposal. In the 1920s the Canadian government did the stalling on the project. But in the following years it was Washington and by St. Laurent's time, when power shortages in Ontario dramatically increased the importance of the project, the Truman administration was clearly anxious. Sensing continued congressional opposition, the State Department's James Webb issued a strong warning to Truman in a memo. Don't put the Canadians "in a box," he said. Don't give them the idea there is no hope. "If the Canadians were to gain this impression it would probably injure our relations with Canada more than any other single incident which has occurred during this century."

The Seaway figured prominently in the first meeting of the two men in February 1949, and was the sole reason for the second in September of 1951. At the first, only a few months after Truman's upset win, St. Laurent joked that he was in Washington to find out the secret of winning elections. Truman had told the U.S. press that no matters of substance would be discussed, but St. Laurent, according to a State Department memo on the meeting, banged away on the Seaway, Otta.va's balance-of-payments deficit, and wheat markets. He warned Truman that he had to give consideration to going ahead alone on the hydro phase of the St. Lawrence development because of the power shortages. Truman expressed sympathy with the prime minister's plight and promised to look into the possibility of purchasing more military equipment from Canada to ease the current account deficit. The visit ended, the memo noted, with "mutual expressions of esteem."

A month later, St. Laurent, who respected Truman, gave this glowing account of Washington's treatment of Canada. "We have been negotiating many times with our American neighbours. We have been agreeing to do a great many things and they have been agreeing to do a great many things. But never have we been made to feel that we were obliged to agree to something because they were bigger and stronger than we were."

In 1950 Congress again failed to approve a renewed St. Lawrence agreement, thus ending Ottawa's patience. Canadians, said Transport minister Lionel Chevrier, "cannot sit idly by and wait forever." The problem, as the Webb memo made clear to Truman, was also political. The Ontario Tories, led by Premier Leslie Frost, were helping their federal colleagues by shouting loudly that the central government was not pushing Washington hard enough. "It appears now," said Webb, "that the Canadians may try to force the problem to a head within the next few months."

He was right. St. Laurent, who telephoned the president asking to see him and arrived the next day, put the matter on the table. His government had waited long enough. If the administration couldn't secure immediate passage of the joint proposal, it was time for Ottawa to move alone. Truman said he was a great supporter of the Seaway, that he voted for it in the Senate as early as 1935. David Bell, one of his advisers making notes of the conversation, thought this was unlikely. "I do not believe," he wrote in parentheses, "there was a floor vote on the St. Lawrence in 1935."

"Since I've been President," Truman continued, "I've been doing everything possible to get Congress to take a broad view of the matter. But if there's no other way I'll go along with you."

St. Laurent was pleased. When "you and I have passed on, people will be grateful to us," for starting this project. He recalled that when the railroads were being built across Canada some people said they "wouldn't even earn their axle grease." Events proved how wrong they were and the same thing will happen in regard to the St. Lawrence project, St. Laurent predicted.

Truman rose from his chair and moved to a corner where he talked privately with St. Laurent for a few minutes. The prime minister then conferred with some of the president's officials on the draft of a public statement and he was warned of technicalities which might require Ottawa and Washington to ratify any agreements made on the project between the province of Ontario and New York State. But St. Laurent said not to worry about it. He cited the instance of the Rainbow Bridge at Niagara Falls, saying it probably should not have been built without the consent of Parliament. "But it was, and it's there now."[12]

The prime minister left happily. Jack Pickersgill, who accompanied him, was impressed. "St. Laurent just dominated the whole thing."

CHAPTER ELEVEN

Country Cousins:
Ike and Uncle Louis

BY THE TIME Dwight Eisenhower became president, Canada had already named a mountain after him. Castle Mountain in Alberta was renamed Mount Eisenhower in tribute to the general's leadership in the war. At the Ottawa announcement in 1946, tears filled Eisenhower's eyes as he spoke of Canada's marvellous expression of friendship. His subsequent ascendancy to the White House seemed to confirm the wisdom of the choice of such a majestic memorial. On a 1953 visit to Washington, Prime Minister St. Laurent referred to it, recalling that Eisenhower had found some significance in the mountain being bald. "It is, in fact, snow capped," St. Laurent said, "and we in Canada are proud that one of our highest peaks will always bear the name Eisenhower."

But the people of Alberta were not so proud. After Ike's death, they decided that Castle Mountain was too big an honour for him. They withdrew the designation. Mount Eisenhower was renamed Castle Mountain. Another far less significant peak was given the name of the president.

The peculiar development was fitting for what, in the continental context, was a peculiar presidency. Eisenhower was admired by Canadians. He was admired by St. Laurent. He was admired by Diefenbaker. With some exceptions, he managed the bilateral relationship, whenever he got around to it, in a cooperative, friendly spirit. But in an inadvertent kind of way, the Eisenhower presidency inspired Canadian hostility. In the late years of his stewardship, a wave of anti-American feeling, or at least what John Diefenbaker perceived to be a wave, would sweep Canada, spawning the bitter, inglorious struggles of the early 1960s. Well before Kennedy would come into power, Diefenbaker would be complaining behind closed doors that Canada was being pushed around by Washington. But he did not want to confront Eisenhower, his friend. Instead he chose to wait for the next president. John Kennedy was not a friend.

For Eisenhower, the north country was a member of the club, a place he could allude to as the "Republic" of Canada; a place where he could play golf, make ceremonial appearances, and look at his own mountain. Benign, avuncular, and sometimes remiss in his approach, Eisenhower was capable of stunning Canadian officials with his lack of information. When he told them he didn't read newspapers, they believed him. In the first half of the decade he had a prime minister in Louis St. Laurent who fit his style like an old shoe. They were both elderly, aloof statesmen, both cut from the chairman-of-the-board mould, both late and rather reluctant politicians. They didn't become close friends. They saw each other only four times in their five years together as heads of government. But Ike and Uncle Louis shared a distant respect. Their relationship was close to the relationship the president wanted for the two countries; they were like country-club cousins, the type of people who would send each other occasional notices of affection, such as shining red apples. St. Laurent had a son in Quebec who was an apple grower and it so happened that Senator Harry Byrd passed through his orchard, sampled a few and found the flavour extraordinary. The prime minister concluded that perhaps the president would find these Canadian apples delicious too, and sent off a batch. "I hope...that you also find that they do have an agreeable flavour," he wrote, spelling flavour with a "u" as all good Canadians do. Great applies, replied Ike. "They are unusual in flavor and quality."

That was Ike and Uncle Louis. Their relationship seldom surpassed that level of excitement even though St. Laurent could be a most prickly gent on occasion. When the focus switched from apples, to oats and groundfish fillet, the prime minister got so upset he sounded like his population was about to take up arms. The U.S. Tariff Commission threatened to set an import quota on these two Canadian products in

1953. Such an action, St. Laurent wrote the president "could not fail to create resentment and ill-will and consequential demands for action on our part." Oat cut-offs would contradict the American commitment to free trade, he said, and run against the spirit of the Canada-U.S. trade agreement of 1935. "The possibility of any action which would mar those harmonious relations [1935] is something our government would greatly deplore." Eisenhower basically told him not to get so excited.

But trade was a hot point for the prime minister and he upbraided the U.S. administration in a speech to the National Press Club in the same year: "Is your economy not too strong and are your industries not too productive to be in any serious danger from imports? American business has always proclaimed its faith in the wholesome effects of honest competition. Is it not then the part of wisdom to widen the area of competitive free trade and see if more nations cannot make their own way into prosperity and strength?

"...Unless the national economies of the free world can be made and kept healthy and productive, Communism could win a bloodless victory without any war, hot or cold....It is not very helpful to preach the abstract advantages of freedom to men and women who are suffering from misery and starvation."

The advice on communism, most prescient advice, was extraordinary. It was not the custom of the Canadian prime minister—nor would it be—to publicly criticize the White House on multilateral questions, particularly when visiting the country. Years later, Pearson would try it with Johnson and rue the day.

Usually the counsel was bilateral, St. Laurent's being—"Much as we like you Americans, we want to remain Canadians." To many observers, particularly those from the New York *Times*, the bilateral relationship was in distressing condition in 1953. James Reston and Walter Lippmann would gather at dinner parties with Canadian officials and discuss the problems—continental defence, trade, and the St. Lawrence again. Reston maintained a keen interest in Canadian affairs, one of the few great American journalists to do so. He went to the Canadian embassy one day to meet Lester Pearson for the first time and couldn't find him. A staff assistant said he might try the backyard. There was Pearson, playing baseball. The two men quickly became great friends, and through Reston's work, Canada received more notice in the capital than it otherwise would have.

But despite the concern of the *Times*, the problems of 1953 were not terribly different from most years. They were not substantive enough to stand in the way of celebration when Eisenhower made his first presidential visit to Ottawa that fall. Nor were they serious enough to even command his attention during that visit.

The train carrying him to Ottawa had barely reached the border on the morning of November 17 when loving Canadians demanded an appearance. Before 7:00 A.M., in Rousse Point, Quebec, the sleepy-eyed president was moved to roll out of bed and, in blue pyjamas and red robe, climb to the platform. "Good morning folks, I'm sorry I'm not dressed." He waved a few times and started back into his quarters, whereupon photographers called for just one more picture. "It's always one more," Ike grumbled and rejoined his wife Mamie for some more sleep.

Adulation pursued the president throughout the trip, the crowds shouting, "We like Ike. We like Ike." There were scores of reporters, rigid security, and so much pomp that the president concluded that one of the advantages of the Canadian system was having a governor-general to take care of much of the fluff for the prime minister. On visits to Washington at this stage of the relationship, however, prime ministers rarely had to worry about fluff. A few months earlier, St. Laurent's trip to the White House had been as casual as a walk to the barber shop.

While there were many issues confronting the two countries, Eisenhower had arranged that his trip not be marred by them; that it be ceremonial. And so, the highlights included such features as the executive tree-plant. "You're the superintendent," Ike called to his wife, Mamie, as he lofted his shovel. "This is the first time I've had some exercise in a long time," he said with a mock grunt. "I could do this for a living." President Kennedy would wrench his back while planting his tree in Ottawa. Nixon's tree would die. But this spading, like the Ike-St. Laurent period on the whole, was rather uneventful. "Look," said Mamie as she flung dirt with all the force a first lady could muster. "I'm getting the swing of it."

In their speeches, both the president and the prime minister took runs at the bilateral cliché record. In preparing Eisenhower's address it had actually become a source of debate in the State Department and White House whether to use the old bilateral colloquialism—the undefended border. A memo from the head of the

Canada section in the State Department complained to a presidential adviser: "The speech still contains a reference to 'undefended frontier.' Frankly, this was considered a 'corny' topic for after-dinner speeches when I went to Ottawa 23 years ago. I still think it is a mistake for the President to mention it."

A compromise was reached. Eisenhower would use it, but acknowledge that it was boring. The speech?—"We have a dramatic symbol of the partnership in the favored topic of every speaker addressing an audience made up of both our peoples—our unfortified frontier. But though this subject has become shopworn and well-nigh exhausted as a feature of after dinner oratory, it is still a fact that our common frontier grows stronger every year, defended only by friendship."

In a semifinal draft, the State Department included this optimistic assessment of Canada's future: "Today, a bulwark of the British Commonwealth, Canada is destined for international leadership. My country rejoices in that prospect." To the State Department's dismay, the White House dropped it.

Commenting on the visit in his memoirs, Eisenhower said: "Specifics were not so much on my mind at the time as was my desire to create an atmosphere in which difficulties could be discussed and composed. "In the parliament I began by attempting in my execrable French a few words of salutation... I knew that because of the comparative size of our two nations, our Canadian friends sometimes suspected us of arrogance. As I told my audience, our country made no claims to a monopoly on wisdom."

The only portion of the three-day visit devoted to issues was a ninety-minute Eisenhower session with the Canadian cabinet. There was some expectation that the ministers would challenge him. But about all they did was butter Ike's toast. Arnold Heeney, Canada's new ambassador to Washington, was disappointed. "I was struck once again by the reluctance of Canadian ministers to take issue with a celebrated guest or to raise embarrassing questions. I had no doubt that Eisenhower and his advisers left with the impression that Canada had no problems of any consequence with the United States."

There were times, however, when issue was taken, and one was in 1955 when the Eisenhower administration atempted to bully Canada into backing off on a resolution to admit sixteen new members to the United Nations, additions which would alter the power balance in the body. Secretary of State John Foster Dulles, a cold, imperious man thoroughly disliked by many Canadian officials, threatened Ottawa, saying there would be many options open to Washington if Canada supported the bid, including an embargo on Canadian oil imports. Cabot Lodge, the U.S. ambassador to the United Nations, approached Paul Martin, head of the Canadian delegation. "We know Pearson doesn't like the Eisenhower administration. There are things that we can do." Martin was incensed. "I've had enough of this kind of talk," he said and walked away. He was called in by Dag Hammarskjold, the secretary general. Hammarskjold had just received a call from Dulles. The United States was threatening to withdraw from the United Nations if the resolution wasn't pulled. Martin told him not to believe it, that Dulles was bluffing. "I'm sure that Eisenhower never authorized that kind of declaration," Martin recalled.[1] From Ottawa, St. Laurent instructed his delegation to stick to its position. It did, the resolution passed, and Eisenhower took no retaliatory action.

The president did not see the prime minister from November 1953 until March 1956 and only then, because Ike insisted. For a first in continental summitry, and for some favourable publicity heading into his re-election campaign, Eisenhower called a three-way meeting to include Mexican President Adolfo Ruiz Cortines. But there were no major issues to be settled. Pickersgill thought it "just a junket." Heeney thought it "cockeyed," and St. Laurent, age 74, didn't want to go. In the end he relented, but demonstrated his disdain for the event by rarely participating in discussions and showing complete disinterest. "It is almost a pathetic spectacle," ambassador Heeney said of his performance in a diary notation. "In long intervals he says nothing and is completely withdrawn. I now realize how difficult things are for Mike [Pearson]. Surely the PM will have to give up and LBP take over. It seems to me we are approaching a crisis...."

If the St. Laurent performance was the most languid ever given by a prime minister in the presence of a president, Eisenhower's was not much better. Golf was his preoccupation, and one of the most exciting developments the press could find to write about. On the way to the summit, which took place at White Sulphur Springs, West Virginia, Dulles had told Pearson that golf would be on the menu and used the occasion to needle the external affairs minister. "You Canadians," Dulles said almost sneeringly, "are always complaining that we never consult you about our policies. Ike as you know is a great golfer and, who knows, he may want us to play a few holes together on this visit. If we do and the score is all square on the eighteenth green, I'll wager that you will intervene just as I am about to make the deciding putt to demand that I consult you about it first."[2]

Pearson got the same rap from Acheson, the previous secretary of state. When Pearson complained about Ottawa not being consulted on a certain White House decision, Acheson exploded: "If you think, after the agonies of consultation we have gone through here to get agreement on this matter, that we are going to start all over again with our NATO allies, especially you moralistic, interfering Canadians, then you're crazy."[3]

As did Acheson, Secretary of State Dulles had Canadian ties, holidaying there almost every summer. But the connection brought no special advantage from Dulles. The point man for Ottawa in the administration became Sherman Adams, Eisenhower's all-powerful top adviser. A former governor of New Hampshire, Adams was well-acquainted with Canadian concerns, and Pickersgill established a relationship with him whereby he could pick up the phone and have instant access.[4] Adams was a frequent contact for Canadian embassy officials who, particularly following the controversy over the U.N. additions, were not wild about dealing with Dulles. Heeney was out of town during the affair, and Dulles called over his second-in-command, George Glazebrook. He ripped into Glazebrook in blistering school-master style. Canadian officials subsequently lodged complaints and Dulles eventually apologized for his behaviour.

Much warmer was the Canadian contact with the White House during the Suez crisis in the fall of 1956. The principals, the president and the prime minister, were in the background as Pearson's expert, well-documented diplomacy cleared the course for the adoption of the resolution establishing a peace-keeping force to bring calm among the French, British, Egyptians, and Israelis. It was a classic display of Ottawa's intermediary role between the British and the Americans and a heralding of the Canadian shift from support of British foreign policy to support of American. So close was the collaboration between Ottawa and Washington that the resolution submitted by Canada was actually written by the American officials at the United Nations. The American wording was tantamount to Pearson's and considered more likely to succeed because the Egyptians had already agreed to it. The United States didn't want to introduce a resolution itself because it would provoke a more polarized reaction. Canada, with its clean international reputation, had more chance of being successful.

On November 6, 1956, after the resolution establishing a U.N. command was accepted, after the Canadians had agreed to contribute to the emergency force and after it was announced that a cease-fire was to take place in the disputed canal zone area by midnight, President Eisenhower telephoned Prime Minister St. Laurent:

Eisenhower: "Things are pretty encouraging. Never have I seen action on the part of a government that excited me more than the rapid way that you and your government moved into the breach. You did a magnificent job and we admire it."

St. Laurent: "I very much appreciate that, and my colleagues will, too. But we happened to be in a position that no one had any misgivings about it. But you can't explain the vagaries of human nature. We have trouble up here, with people who look upon bigness as a sin."

Eisenhower: "I just really felt it necessary to say congratulations—I think you have done a wonderful thing."

St. Laurent: "We do our best. We have been trying to get our teeth in this thing since 1946, and I think this will be a permanent set that will serve as a pretty good example."

Eisenhower: "If we can get this settled today without complications, we will be a most fortunate people."

St. Laurent: "Have you seen the dispatch from the French and British?"

Eisenhower: "Yes, I have."

St. Laurent: "They want to be authorized to remove the obstacles from the Canal."

Eisenhower: "I don't think they should quibble now—should accept Mr. Hammarskjold's plan."

St. Laurent: "They are not making it a condition, you know. They are merely saying they have the equipment that would do the job if the UN feels..."

Eisenhower: "I can't tell you how sensible and logical their offer is. I don't want Egypt to get a chance to say they are getting Russian backing. So I think they should offer it to Hammarskjold and let him work it out."

St. Laurent: "I hope our General Burns will be over here soon and will be able to tell us how much he needs and then allocate his needs, and tell us who, under the resolution can take part."

Eisenhower: "In a message to Anthony [Eden], I told him I was glad he didn't insist on using any big five troops; because then the Russians would send 6 Army Corps."⁵

A month later, the work of their U.N. representatives successful, the groundwork laid for a Nobel Peace Prize for Lester Pearson, the two leaders ended their country club relationship with a final meeting on a golf course. Eisenhower was vacationing at the Augusta National in Georgia, his favourite club and the home of the Masters Tournament. Uncle Louis was on holiday in Florida and the president rang him up and invited him over to play a few holes. The interesting spectacle of the prime minister receiving full military honours before teeing up his golf ball ensued. On the links the leaders discussed tariffs on Canadian fish, balance of trade problems, and the Cold War policies of Indian Prime Minister Nehru. They travelled the picturesque Augusta fairways in an electric cart, a relative novelty in those days. "Well I found, in fact, you know," St. Laurent said, "that a game of golf in one of those electric go-carts was about the best way to have an international conference because you are getting off the go-cart quite frequently for only a couple of minutes, but for time enough to reflect on what had been said up to that moment and to reflect on what is going to be said when you get back on the seat of the go-cart."

Eisenhower was astounded when St. Laurent told him Canada would be importing one billion dollars more in goods in the current year from the United States than it would be exporting there. American capital was entering Canada in waves also. It was the 1950s and the American takeover of the Canadian economy was moving full force. But St. Laurent wasn't complaining to Ike, just explaining: "I also told him... that there was going to be, as a result of the investment of American capital in Canada, a very substantial increase in production and that we were buying more than we were selling at the present time just as it sometimes happens to a farmer that he buys more in the spring than he sells in the spring. But it is because he is going to use the fertilizer and seed, which occasion the additional buying, to have a crop that is going to be larger in the fall; and that we were going to have a crop of production in our country, a portion of which was going to be the crop resulting from the investment of his own fellow citizens in the industries of our country."

There was some advice, asserted with conviction, for the president on anti-communism. The fears were not the same in places like India, the prime minister told him. It should not be forgotten, he said, that the backdrop of the United States was not the only backdrop against which the attitudes of other people in the world should be appraised.

As for the golf scores, Eisenhower, a player with a respectable 15 handicap, was the clear winner. Uncle Louis played "no worse than usual." Quashing a rumour that he had cracked the important three-digit barrier, he said: "when I manage to break 100, I'll announce it myself."

When Diefenbaker broke the twenty-two-year Liberal dynasty in 1957, American officialdom was startled. The assumption had been that the Grits would win again. The U.S. embassy in Ottawa ran a pool on the election results and nobody came close. Officials there, desperate for information on members of the new Conservative cabinet, telephoned Eugene Griffin, a veteran Ottawa correspondent for the Chicago *Tribune,* asking for help. "To them," said Griffin, "it was like a bunch of guys from Mars had taken over."[6]

A harbinger of discontent when the Tories took control was the Herbert Norman affair. Norman, the Canadian ambassador to Egypt, committed suicide in the spring of 1957 following reckless disclosures by a U.S. Senate subcommittee linking him with communism. His death occasioned an outpouring of venom in Canada against the anti-communist excesses of the McCarthy period. The Eisenhower administration reacted with relative nonchalance, fueling the passions. St. Laurent and his officials had been perturbed by Ike's essentially timid response to the witch hunts in the first place. Now they were furious. Norman Robertson, beginning a term as Washington ambassador, saw the president, but received little satisfaction. Eisenhower, who had been so impressed with Canadian diplomatic efforts in the Suez crisis, told him that the American governmental structure was such that he could do little about congressional indiscretions. He could give no assurances that they wouldn't continue.

Diefenbaker, a fiercely proud Canadian, a man who cherished the British heritage, gave early notice of the new direction by campaigning to shift Canadian trade from the United States to Europe. When reporters inquired how much, the prime minister didn't seem to know. One scribe suggested that it may be something like 15 percent. Diefenbaker said that sounded about right, and his first anti-American policy was on the books.

The White House was somewhat anxious about Diefenbaker, the

prairie populist, but the fears were eased by the quick, friendly rapport Eisenhower established with him. Diefenbaker felt Eisenhower was a truly great man. He liked the non-Anglo name, he could talk to Ike about fishing. While Eisenhower and St. Laurent addressed each other by titles in correspondence and formally in person, Eisenhower requested not long into his relationship with Diefenbaker that it be "John" and "Ike." "I like Mr. Diefenbaker," he told the press, "and I think he is a very able man." The prime minister boasted to friends about the relationship. "Why, I can get Ike at any time, just by picking up the phone at my elbow."

They met briefly in October of 1957 when Diefenbaker accompanied the queen to Washington, and again in December at a NATO meeting in Paris. Four months later, Eisenhower telephoned to suggest the prime minister come down for a private visit. Diefenbaker persuaded him that it should be the other way around and although the president had already addressed the Canadian Parliament, he agreed to a repeat performance. He is, to date, the only president to have made one.

Suspicious of Diefenbaker's "tinge of neutralism," the State Department emphasized an anti-communist theme in briefing papers for the president. "The present is a time of great danger," said one outline. "Soviet communist imperialism aims to weaken and disrupt and to pick off the nations of the free world." In a later phone call to the prime minister, Eisenhower, after a few words about a plaque being dedicated at his mountain, recalled a Peking communiqué to the effect that the Russians and the red Chinese were going to "liberate" the peoples of Central America, South America, Africa and Asia. "Can you imagine!"

Communism was a theme in his second speech to the House of Commons, but a more surprising feature was Eisenhower's direct rebuttal of Canadian grievances on bilateral issues. A meaningless, ceremonial speech it wasn't. He ticked off the Canadian complaints one by one and shot them down. On American takeovers of Canadian business: "These investments have helped you to develop your resources and to expand your industrial plant at a far faster rate than would have been possible had you relied wholly on your own savings. They have thereby helped to provide employment, tax revenues, and other direct benefits. These funds have also helped Canada to finance with ease its recent surplus of imports from the United States." On restrictive policies against Canadian oil imports: "A healthy, domestic oil producing industry is vital to our national security." On Canada's imbalance of trade in manufactured goods: "I assume that Canada is as interested as we are in the expansion of world trade rather than in its artificial redirection.... To try to balance our books once a month or once a year with every nation with which we trade would stifle rather than expand trade."

Diefenbaker stuck mainly to pleasantries. He disclosed that a Canadian had been present on the platform at Lincoln's Gettysburg address: William McDougall, a future father of Confederation had immediately recognized the speech as being famous, and written home that the president's words would live through history.

With Ike present, there had to be the obligatory reference to golf, and Diefenbaker managed to combine that theme with the omni-present undefended border motif: "The intelligence service informs me after diligent inquiry that you come bearing no arms and carry no armour other than a brassie and a putter. May I, sir, as an aside, express the wish that under clear skies and fairways not too narrow you will be able, while here, to use this armour and add to your list of victories." The prime minister was puzzled by Ike's obsession with the game. He would flinch during White House visits at the sight of him swinging irons on parquet floors and chipping balls through the open back door of the mansion onto the lawn. Kennedy later showed the prime minister the damage Ike's hobby had wrought—chip marks and holes in the White House floors.

One of the supposed accomplishments of the Ottawa visit was the establishment of a joint cabinet committee on defence to supplement other combined efforts on defence cooperation. But it was this—the continental closeness demanded by Washington on defence matters—that was to trigger the rift with the Diefenbaker government. In External Affairs minister Howard Green, Diefenbaker had an intransigent nationalist and a close confidant. In letters from the public, which began to come in slowly in 1958 and faster in the ensuing two years, Diefenbaker had what he thought was evidence to support Green, evidence of a brewing anti-Americanism. Diefenbaker put disproportionate stock in the letters. He fancied himself as a man of the people, a man to represent the small, single voices. One of his models was Franklin Roosevelt, whose successes he considered the result of an ability to appeal directly to the people, to be one with them.

On June 30, 1959, Diefenbaker told ambassador Heeney that he was getting too much pressure from Washington for cooperation on military concerns. Requests were coming in for overflights of U.S. aircraft, for special alerts, for extended cooperation in respect to the newly created North American Air Defense Command. The prime minister said he was not prepared to meet them all. Heeney was surprised; Eisenhower and his men had been more cooperative recently, he felt, than ever. A conscious decision had been taken in the White House, he told Diefenbaker, to meet Canada wherever possible on all issues. That didn't assuage the prime minister. Heeney left feeling there would be trouble in the months ahead. He saw Green and told him that the U.S. requests were merely normal suggestions for the improvement of joint defence. Green replied that the prime minister had political considerations to keep in mind.[7]

Green's views and those of his boss hardened with time. But although Diefenbaker was not afraid to be blunt in dealing with Eisenhower, on issues such as Washington's threat to curb lead and zinc imports, he would not confront him personally on the large questions responsible for what he privately termed an anti-American "avalanche" in his country. Had he done so, some of the problems of the early 1960s could have been pre-empted.

In June 1960 as Diefenbaker prepared for a visit, the State Department informed the president that the question of locating nuclear warheads in Canada had sparked a domestic political controversy. But there was no suggestion that Eisenhower go slow on defence cooperation: "It is hoped that you may be able to influence the Prime Minister toward the desirability of maintaining strong and united defenses. It is suggested that you attempt to secure his assurance of Canada's approval of the planned joint exercise Sky Shield to test North American air defenses."[8]

The briefing papers contained a personal appraisal of the prime minister: "After three years in office, Mr. Diefenbaker has lost none of his self-confidence and vigor which are among his most striking characteristics. His reputation as a shrewd politician remains undiminished. He maintains a tight rein on his cabinet and reserves all important decisions for himself...

"Mr. Diefenbaker is a little deaf in his left ear and is somewhat sensitive about it. He is intelligent, shrewd, serious but also emotional and sentimental. He is a devout Baptist, a Freemason, and a teetotaler, although he does not mind others imbibing."

The meeting of the two leaders turned into a triumph. Notwithstanding the anti-American avalanche, the prime minister told the president that Canada-U.S. relations had never been so wonderful. Delighted with the appraisal, Eisenhower repeated it at a toast: "The one thing that I want to take the privilege of repeating to you that the Prime Minister said to me this afternoon is this: 'In the last two and a half years, Mr. President,' he said, 'the relations of Canada and the United States have reached a height of friendliness, cordiality and true cooperation that has never before been attained so far as I know.'"

Then the Chief chimed in: "I come into your country. You come into mine. We don't always agree. We sometimes have our differences but I will always look back on this day as one that represents, to me, the embodiment of those great and eternal principles of liberty. We get together. We discuss. We are not at all afraid.... We speak freely. We understand each other."

The nice words bore no resemblance to reality. Eleven weeks following the visit, Diefenbaker called in Heeney and laid out the real story. "In his judgment," Heeney observed in his diary, "anti-American sentiment was now worse than at any time in his lifetime or mine.... This was causing him the greatest concerns."

Heeney asked the reasons for the bad feelings and the prime minister gave him four: "the widespread impression that the U.S. was 'pushing other people around'; distrust of the U.S. military and anxiety over the Pentagon's real intentions; the economic aggressiveness of U.S. interests; and the adverse trading position." An alarmed Heeney said he didn't realize the feelings ran so deep, that he had regarded the Canada-U.S. alliance as "our most precious asset."

The next day Diefenbaker had him back for more. He pulled out a sheaf of letters and showed Heeney one from a young Conservative denouncing Eisenhower's nuclear policies and economic aggressiveness. "The letter had been read with care," noted the ambassador, "and marginal comments made by Mr. Diefenbaker. It was quite clear the letter had made a deep impression on him." Diefenbaker read Heeney several others, all promoting Canadian neutrality. The sampling was only a tiny portion of what he was getting, he said, and surely Heeney could now understand what he meant.

The question was what to do. The prime minister wasn't prepared himself to say anything but suggested that Heeney start telling the authorities in Washington. The word was put through to Secretary of State Christian Herter. In a few weeks, Green was in town personally to tell Herter that the heart of the problem was that Canadians "were not nearly so worried about the Russians." But he had no suggestions toward a possible solution and, in the end, tended to play down the split. A man who seemed to think most Americans were inherently evil, Green was amazed to find that Herter was actually a nice guy. A fine man, he told Heeney, "completely the opposite of what Canadians expect an American to be." A meeting with Vice-President Richard Nixon had also stunned Green. Even Nixon appeared to be nice and Green criticized Heeney for not warning him in advance that this was the case. "To this I could only reply," said Heeney, "that not all Americans had horns."

Diefenbaker and Eisenhower met for the last time on January 17, 1961, three days before John Kennedy moved into the White House. The meeting was a ceremony to mark the signing of the Columbia River Treaty, a pact giving joint control over hydro-electric power from the Columbia. It was Eisenhower's last major foreign responsibility as president, and he gave the royal treatment to his Canadian friend. He spoke of the glorious bilateral relationship, and Diefenbaker reciprocated: "My hope is that in the years ahead this day will be looked back on as one that represents the greatest advance that has ever been made in international relations between countries."

Any clash over the reality of the bilateral relationship would have to await the arrival of the "young pup," as Diefenbaker called him. As is normally the case, it was easier for Diefenbaker to get tough with someone he didn't like than with a close acquaintance.

"I felt that we were friends," he wrote Ike, "and as friends could speak with frankness regarding the problems of our two countries. Indeed whenever matters of disagreement, actual or potential, were brought to your attention they were acted upon by you to the last extent possible."

CHAPTER TWELVE

The Diefenbaker-Kennedy Schism

IN 1952 WHEN John F. Kennedy was just another New England senator, the Canadian issue, the St. Lawrence Seaway, was up for a vote again. Massachusetts lobbyists warned him that the Seaway would harm state railroad and port interests. Hundreds of people would lose their jobs. Others argued that national gain outweighed parochial pain. Kennedy was faced with the politician's classic dilemma: Should he back the interests of his constituency or the interests of the country? Without much hesitation he voted parochial. He voted against the Seaway.

In 1954 when he faced another vote on the project, the young senator asked his assistant, Theodore Sorensen, to do an objective study. New England, Sorensen reported, wouldn't be hurt as much as alleged and the nation would be better off with the Seaway. Kennedy had his aide write a speech in support of it and he said he would decide in the morning. That night, he was restless. "Years later he would make far more difficult and dangerous decisions without any loss of sleep," observed Sorensen, "but this was in many ways a turning point for the 36 year old senator. He had no obligation to vote for the seaway and endanger his political base. He was not required to speak on either side. A quiet vote of opposition would have received no attention."

The next day, said Sorensen, he hesitated. "Then with a shake of his head—a shake I would often see, meaning 'well this is what I must do for better or for worse' — he walked over to the senate floor and delivered the speech."

"I am unable to accept such a narrow view of my function as a United States senator," Kennedy announced and strongly endorsed cooperation with Canada. Sorensen was besieged by the press for copies, and although the Boston *Post* accused Kennedy of "ruining New England," his bold stand won him new respect in the Senate and in the country. In Sorensen's view, it was a significant step in Kennedy's march to the presidency.[1]

On Inauguration Day, January 20, 1961, Canadian ambassador Heeney had a seat among the dignitaries, from which he could see the "New Frontier" face of Kennedy juxtaposed against the tired 1950s visage of Dwight D. Eisenhower. It was an intensely cold day; the white snow was wind-blown, piled high, and the sunlight kissed it. Clean, pure, and shining, it was a day meant for departures. As he watched, Heeney marvelled at Kennedy: "Tall, serious, young and really very strong." For the ambassador there wouldn't be more memorable moments; there was the feeling that something was being born. To him, when the new president spoke, "it really seemed to rank with Lincoln."[2]

The ambassador, like so many others, was caught up in the idealism John Kennedy embodied. The first Catholic president was capturing the imagination of Canada as much as he was that of the United States. In Hamilton, Ontario, a precocious fifteen-year-old high school student was so moved that he formed a club to exalt Kennedy and to chase his dreams. Within a few days, dozens of youths had joined the group, which called itself "The Muckers," and soon there was a clamouring waiting list. The Muckers wore Kennedy sweatshirts to class, made a pilgrimage to Washington, went on a sixty-mile walk in his honour and became the dominant social force at the school. To Prime Minister John Diefenbaker, their own leader, they paid scant attention. Kennedy was their man and long after his death The Muckers lingered to cherish his memory.

For Diefenbaker, had he been informed of them, The Muckers would have been repugnant. A person could have diligently searched the Canadian landscape in 1960 and had trouble finding many who strongly disliked Kennedy, but the prime minister was the exception. John Diefenbaker developed a dislike for Kennedy well before he met him. He was suspicious of his wealth, youth, and arrogance. More importantly, he feared that his own star was being eclipsed by Kennedy's.

No politician had entranced the Canadian population like Diefenbaker in his record-smashing, landslide victory of 1958. He was the spellbinding orator, the champion of the little man, the great raconteur, and the outstanding parliamentarian. But suddenly it was Kennedy who was galvanizing the political world and reaching out to Diefenbaker's own countrymen, displacing him in their affections. Under the circumstances it was hard for a man like Diefenbaker, whose rancour was often rooted in the petty, not to be jealous. He told people that he had originated the "New Frontier" slogan in speaking of his vision of the north, and that Kennedy had stolen it. He told Heeney as the 1960 campaign opened that he preferred Nixon to Kennedy and after the Kennedy victory, it was apparent to many that there could be trouble. "For all the promise of the incoming team [US]," Basil Robinson of the Prime Minister's Office wrote Heeney, "there is no doubt that the absence of a personal relationship is going to introduce an incalculable factor into relations with the United States. It is disturbing that the Prime Minister seems to have formed some rather unfavourable early impressions. I just hope these can be erased."

Heeney met with Dean Rusk, the new secretary of state, prior to inauguration. Rusk, an old friend of the ambassador's, asked immediately why Canada felt it should have special status with the United States. Why shouldn't it be treated like any other foreign country? Heeney said that the status was a natural consequence of continental and historical association. Moving away from business, Rusk mentioned that he sometimes took his son fishing to Canada. In the future, Heeney suggested, stop by Ottawa for talks on such excursions. Rusk was enthusiastic and Heeney forwarded the news to the prime minister's office. The response was a sign of the times. Heeney's suggestion, in his own words, was "dismissed as one more indication that the Americans thought of Canada only as a place for fishing and hunting."

Canadian issues hadn't figured in the election campaign but Kennedy was mindful of the country's importance to him. In the selection of ambassadors he told Rusk he wanted no political hacks for Canada. For his choice of first foreign visitor, Kennedy selected Diefenbaker, and for his choice of first foreign visit he selected Canada.

For a president who had generated as much anticipation as Kennedy, they were not small compliments.

The new president could hardly have found a better way of tarnishing first-visitor honours however, than by getting the guest's name wrong. As Diefenbaker had spent three years as Canada's head of state, as he had an ego sometimes bordering on megalomania, and as he was a man who cherished his own status, his reaction to Kennedy's announcement that "Mr. Diefenbawker" was coming to town was one that did not require speculation. It was further evidence for him that the heralded chief executive was an arrogant upstart. It was the start of the road to disaster.

Three days before their first of only three meetings, the Washington view of the Diefenbaker government was set out for Kennedy by Secretary Rusk who reminded the president in his first sentence that it was "Deefen-BAKER." The appraisal was lucid and incisive, defining clearly the disparity between Canadian and American attitudes and lashing out at Howard Green as the bad guy.

"The primary problem the United States faces in its bilateral relations with Canada," Rusk told Kennedy, "lies in an evolving Canadian attitude of introspection and nationalism. The magnitude of neighboring U.S. wealth and power has long engendered a Canadian inferiority complex which is reflected in a sensitivity to any real or fancied slight to Canadian sovereignty. Thus the essential element in problems involving Canada tends to be psychological.

"On the one hand there is Canada's wish to be known as truly separate, independent and different. Many Canadians are persuaded at times that they somehow face the threat of being engulfed culturally, economically and ultimately politically by the United States. They wish to preserve and promote a Canadian national identity, an objective as old as Canadian confederation and still considerably unfulfilled. On the other hand the Canadians desire, and believe themselves entitled to, a privileged relationship with the United States."

Diefenbaker's appeal in 1957 and 1958, the memo said, was to "Canadianism," with some strong anti-American overtones. Now, "Canadian support cannot be taken for granted and there will most probably be a variety of Canadian suggestions and initiatives, some of which will be most annoying to the U.S., but which will probably not be fundamentally damaging. The fact remains that basically most of the Canadian people are favorably disposed toward the United States and believe that each country inescapably needs the other."[3]

But Diefenbaker was looking to bolster his waning popularity, Rusk warned, and therefore could place a renewed emphasis on nationalism. The major problem, Rusk asserted, was defence. Canadian cabinet splits, stagnant defence budgets and general indecision were producing the possibility of "a drift toward a kind of unconscious neutralism."

This, Rusk said, was something the United States could not afford: "The fact of Canadian military dependence upon the U.S. is admitted, no matter how much it may annoy, but Mr. Diefenbaker also knows this dependence is reciprocal. Loss or diminution of U.S. use of Canadian air space and real estate and the contributions of the Canadian military, particularly the RCAF and Royal Canadian Navy, would be intolerable in time of crisis."

For Howard Green, the British Columbia-born External Affairs minister, there was no mercy. "He has exhibited," Kennedy was told, "a naive and almost parochial approach to some international problems which was first attributed to his inexperience but which is now believed to be part of his basic personality."

Hitting out at his extreme sensitivity "to any implied interference with Canada's independence of action" Rusk called Green self-righteous, stubborn, less flexible than Diefenbaker and almost pacifist. He was suspicious, too, about Green's devotion to the United Church of Canada. Reflecting back on his experience with the tall, earnest man, Rusk mused, "When people start mixing politics with God, I get nervous."[4]

The president and the prime minister had never met. But the signs pointed to discord. Diefenbaker was suspicious and jealous of Kennedy. The anti-American letters were still landing on his desk. He was extremely sensitive to them. And in his trusted lieutenant, Mr. Green, the fires of nationalism raged.

Kennedy was a man of a different generation, a different sense of humour, a different style. He knew little more about Diefenbaker and his government than what the briefing papers told him. And what they told him was not complimentary. Kennedy wanted an expansive alliance with Canada and they told him he was not likely to get it.

The first meeting, one month after Kennedy took office, did not please the president. He found Diefenbaker insincere, and did not like or trust him. "Diefenbaker, who felt at home with Eisenhower," recalled Arthur Schlesinger Jr., a top Kennedy adviser, "had been uneasy with the new President."

But strangely the prime minister had an entirely different view. He thought the talks went splendidly. On the way to the airport he told Heeney how he was impressed by the informal and genuine atmosphere Kennedy created. Back in the House of Commons the same day, he was laudatory: "To me this was a revealing and exhilarating experience. The President of the United States has the kind of personality that leaves upon one the impression of a person dedicated to peace, to the raising of economic standards... and to the achievement in his day of disarmament among all nations of the world."

On substantive issues there were no fireworks. Diefenbaker gave assurances Canada would continue with negotiations for acquisitions of nuclear warheads for its weapons systems. The government has to be more than just "birdwatchers," he told reporters. Kennedy, interestingly, had personally ordered a report on Canadian civil defence progress shortly before the discussion. Canada was behind, he was informed, but could soon move ahead of the United States. During the talks, the matter received minor attention.

One thing that bothered Diefenbaker, one of the little things, was a Kennedy-installed White House portrait of the War of 1812 which suggested the Americans were the clear victors. This was intolerable for the prime minister and he tried to secure a picture illustrating the opposite to be sent to Kennedy. But perhaps a more foreboding footnote to the first meeting of Kennedy and Diefenbaker was the melancholy ending. That night, Diefenbaker's mother died.

Three months later Kennedy arrived in Ottawa for what would become the most controversial of all Canada-U.S. summits. Kennedy had no great cause for being in a cocky frame of mind when his plane touched down at Uplands Airport on that May 14. Only a month earlier he had been the architect of one of America's most humiliating foreign policy exercises. Washington-backed Cuban exiles attempting to overthrow the Castro regime were erased in a matter of hours at the Bay of Pigs.

It was a fiasco, but White House officials didn't really need Howard Green to rub their faces in it. Green fancied Canada, and therefore himself, as a leading middle-power mediator in the world. Leave this U.S.-Cuba problem to us, he publicly suggested in one of diplomacy's more gratuitous incursions, and everything will be fine. His statement, made in Geneva, came only a few days before the Ottawa meeting: "The more Cuba is pushed the greater becomes her reliance on the Soviet bloc. Of course Canada is farther away from Cuba than the United States and so it's easier for us to seem more dispassionate. But we would hope to be able to solve this problem when the situation slows down and eases a bit."

The best and the brightest were not pleased. The State Department cabled its consulates in Ottawa and in Geneva: "President is concerned over these statements which, assuming Green correctly quoted, reflect distressing lack of awareness of facts in Cuban situation. Therefore request that you speak with Green in effort [to] bring him to greater awareness of what is really going on in Cuba.... In the meantime we are calling in Canadian ambassador Heeney to inform him of planned approach to Green, express our unhappiness over Green's alleged statements and present facts in Cuban situation as we see them."

Heeney got nothing but cold wind. Schlesinger cornered him at a cocktail party and "with unrestrained sarcasm" asked whether Canada had "arrived at the position where we put Castro and Kennedy on the same footing."

The president, meanwhile, was receiving briefing papers for the Ottawa trip which were even more negative about John Diefenbaker than the notes for the first get-together. "His rhetorical gifts, which tend toward the emotional, enable him to promote his vision of Canada's national destiny with evangelical fervor. Since becoming Prime Minister however he has demonstrated a disappointing indecisiveness on important issues, such as the defense program, as well as a lack of political courage and undue sensitivity to public opinion." The State Department believed that Diefenbaker had no basic prejudice against the United States but would use anti-Americanism for political expediency: "His government's waning popularity... may lead him to continue to exploit issues which have a nationalistic political appeal."[5]

A low-key drama was brewing that May over whether Kennedy should pressure Canada to join the Organization of American States, the U.S.-Latin American alliance for hemispheric defence and economic cooperation. A clash of serious consequence, it started one month before the visit, when Livingston Merchant, reappointed as Ottawa ambassador by Kennedy after a successful stint in the 1950s, was asked to do an immediate draft of Kennedy's speech to Parliament. Merchant gave the job to Rufus Smith, one of his top men and a diplomat who would earn a distinguished reputation while working almost twenty years in capacities dealing with Canada-U.S. relations. "I drafted the speech," said Smith. "Stayed up all night to do it. Thought it was great stuff."[6]

A White House instruction had been to include a line calling on Canada to join the OAS. But Smith left it out. He and Merchant were certain the prime minister would take great offence to such a suggestion. They explained their reasons for the deletion in a separate note. In Washington, however, Heeney and embassy officials were meeting with Assistant Secretary of State Walt Rostow. They told him the opposite. Ottawa would not object to a discreet recommendation. Rostow then wrote a memo to Kennedy saying: "They would hope that you might tactfully encourage the growing sentiment within Canada to join the OAS and to assume increased responsibilities in the hemisphere." He added a harpoon shot at Green: "I take it they are prepared to join on grounds other than 'mediating' between the U.S. and Cuba."

Hearing of the developments, Merchant made a twelfth-hour bid to change Kennedy's mind. He went to Washington and then flew back to Ottawa with the president, warning him on OAS: Don't do it.[7]

But Kennedy was sold on his popularity in Canada. The Bay of Pigs had not disfigured his stardom. State briefing papers emboldened him, saying he had "stirred the imagination of Canadians" and must take advantage. "This particular time therefore affords the United States a superb opportunity to advance our objectives with the Canadian public and government because even those who resist American influence in Canada are now impressed by the new administration and their criticism is muted."

On the old Canadian complaint about not being consulted, Kennedy was told to go on the attack: "It is useful to remind Canadians that they sometimes do not consult us about matters of great importance to us and that their criticism of us... is often levelled from the position of bystander."

Kennedy heeded the advice. The controversies started as soon as he landed. Diefenbaker, in his introduction, went through the painful ritual of saying a few words in French. His French had always been awful. Once during a campaign stop in Quebec he was introduced to a gentleman to whom he said *"bonjour."* The gentleman then introduced the prime minister to his son or, as the gentleman said in French, *"mon fils."* Diefenbaker, happy to be introduced, said, *"Bonjour Monsieur Mon Fils."* At the airport he was typically abominable. Kennedy's wife Jacqueline was fluent in French, but the president himself a novice. When his turn came, Kennedy broke into a wide grin and said that "after having had a chance to listen to the prime minister," he was now encouraged to try French himself. The audience howled, Jackie leading the way. It was a typical example of Kennedy's sardonic sense of humour, a facet of him, Rusk remembered, which Diefenbaker couldn't understand.

But the ridicule of the French was just an opener, one of several Kennedy jabs which would have tested the forebearance of any host head of state. The second occurred in Diefenbaker's office. The prime minister, who had brought in a rocking chair for the visit because he knew the president liked them, was a proud fisherman. On the first visit he had told Kennedy about his finest catch—a 140-pound blue marlin. In the interim he had it mounted on his office wall and now he was expecting a glowing tribute from Kennedy. But the president wasn't impressed. Caught many larger ones myself, he so much as said. Diefenbaker did a slow burn. Of all the things that rankled him about Kennedy, the blue marlin mock was a leader. Long after he had left the prime minister's office he told and retold the story about what the "boastful young son of a bitch" had said about his fishing.

When the office discussion moved to the OAS, Diefenbaker made it clear that Canada was not interested in joining at this time. Kennedy had been warned by his ambassador. Now he was getting the word from the prime minister himself. The next day he addressed Parliament: "Your country and mine are partners in North American affairs; can we not become partners in inter-American affairs?...I believe that all the members of the Organization of American States would be both heartened and strengthened by any increase in your hemispheric role.... To be sure it would mean an added responsibility, but yours is not a nation that shrinks from responsibility."

Kennedy was ignoring the wishes of the host government and going over the head of the prime minister to the Canadian people. An act of gall, it shocked Canadian officials like senior diplomat Ed Ritchie, a future ambassador to Washington. "I shuddered when I heard him say that."

The president wasn't finished. He called for a larger Canadian contribution to foreign aid and NATO, instructions the prime minister could have done nicely without. He poked fun at the Canadian Senate: "There are many differences between this body (Parliament) and mine. The most noticeable to me is the lofty appearance of statesmanship which is on the faces of the members of the Senate who realize that they will never have to place their case before the public again."

The address contained some of the Kennedy word-magic. "Geography has made us neighbors. History has made us friends. Economics has made us partners. And necessity has made us allies. Those whom nature hath so joined together, let no man put asunder. What unites us is far greater than what divides us. . . . Our alliance is born not of fear but of hope."

But there was not a word of praise or even pleasant acknowledgement for the prime minister. Diefenbaker, despite his inner mistrust, had at least made some effort with Kennedy. He had publicly praised him after the first visit, he had brought in his favourite chair, and now in his own speech before Parliament, he lauded Kennedy as a scholar, author, and statesman. Citing an Irish poem, the prime minister gave it a Kennedy twist.

"When I was in Ireland a few weeks ago—and Ireland is the rock from whence you were hewn, sir—I was told something of your ancestry, shown the arms of the O'Kennedy's of Ormonde and of the Fitzgeralds, renowned in Irish history as the Geraldines. And I was shown a poem...

> These Geraldines! These Geraldines! Rain
> Wears away the rock
> And time may wear away the tribe
> That stood the battle's shock;
> But ever sure while one is left of all
> That honoured race,
> In front of freedom's chivalry is that
> Fitzgerald's place."

Then, picking up on "In front of freedom's chivalry," Diefenbaker said: "That is your place today, Mr. President."

In fact, however, Diefenbaker was seeing far less than chivalry in Kennedy's performance. His French ridiculed, his fishing ridiculed, his name wrong, his policy on the OAS brazenly repudiated, the prime minister was hard pressed to do so. Kennedy was also spending too much time at receptions, in Diefenbaker's view, with Opposition leader Pearson. The media didn't please the prime minister either because it was predictably lavish in its praise of the visitor. "Kennedy was a Smash Hit and His Lovely Young Wife a Wow" declared a Toronto *Star* headline.

All the insults were outdistanced, however, by the infamous missing-memo affair. A one-page document prepared by Rostow instructed Kennedy on what to "push for." Never intended for Canadian eyes, the memo contained phrasing less delicate than the average diplomatic note:

"WHAT WE WANT FROM OTTAWA TRIP"

1. To push the Canadians towards an increased commitment to the Alliance for Progress. Concretely, we would like them to have at least an observer at the July IA—ECOSOC.
2. To push them towards a decision to join the OAS.
3. To push them towards a larger contribution for the India consortium and for foreign aid generally. The figures are these: they have offered $36 million for India's Third-Year Plan, we would like $70 million from them. Over-all their aid now comes to $69 million a year; if they did 1% of GNP the figure would be $360 million. Like the rest of us, they have their political problems with foreign aid; but we might be able to push them in the right direction.
4. We want their active support at Geneva and beyond for a more effective monitoring of the borders of Laos and Vietnam.

Rufus Smith, for one, could understand how a prime minister, particularly one as sensitive about being bullied as Diefenbaker, could find it abrasive. The memo was left behind on the table in the cabinet room. Diefenbaker found it. And he did find it abrasive. At the time he chose not to make it public, not to return it or a copy of it to the White House, nor to inform the American officials they had left it behind. Instead he chose to use it as an excuse to seethe, then a year later, as a threat, and then, a year after that, as a real weapon.

The public was unaware of the problems developing between the president and the prime minister. From its perspective, from the limited perspective the press could provide, the summit was another splendid manifestation of bilateral bliss. But even something as innocent as the ceremonial presidential-tree plant turned out to be a disaster on this ill-fated tour. Kennedy was handed a gleaming silver shovel to plant two red oaks. Standing erect, with the spade at arm's length, he shovelled with great enthusiasm, unable to resist after about twelve throws the line—"I wonder if this is symbolic?" He handed the shovel to Diefenbaker who grinned and stood with it. Then it was Jackie's turn. Looking like the queen of a senior prom a shovel did not become her, and after three dainty, tablespoon scoops and a giggle, that was that. But for the president it was the beginning of months of pain. A few hours after his hard exercise, he felt a twinge in his back, and later, an acute ache. As a senator he had experienced severe back problems. Now, the tree plant reactivated them. For six months after the visit he would suffer, sometimes terribly. In the last month of the year, he would visit Bermuda where his schedule also included tree work. But this, as the Bermudan authorities described it, was a "modified tree planting." All the president had to do was snip a ribbon hanging from the bark. "A very good way of doing it," Kennedy remarked. "Much easier than in Canada."

The Ottawa visit failed to accomplish anything substantial. The points on the Rostow memo that Kennedy was to pursue were made in his speech and in private talks with the prime minister. A joint statement given to the press listed topics discussed but contained no hard conclusions. Despite this, despite the beginnings of new back problems, Kennedy, charged by the glowing reception of the Canadian press and public, left the city in upbeat spirits. On the flight home he invited Heeney to join him and his wife in the front cabin and immediately inquired as to the ambassador's opinion of his first foreign visit. Heeney said it was great. Delighted, Kennedy turned to a large stack of paperwork. Intermittently, he handed Heeney a memo or cable on a foreign affairs matter and asked his advice. "That's how it went all the way back to Washington," remembered Heeney. "No small talk. No pleasantries after the first almost perfunctory exchange. The President was addressing himself to his business and paying me the compliment of assuming I would understand that its importance transcended lesser conventions."

He didn't mention it to Heeney but Kennedy, with all his style and *savoir faire*, had decided that John Diefenbaker was boring. He informed his colleagues of this view and the word spread and soon it got to 24 Sussex Drive. The prime minister of Canada now had more reason to dislike the man and the bilateral relationship had more potential for plunging, as it would, into its worst state of disrepair in the century.

At a press conference after the visit, Diefenbaker decided to go on the attack. The United States took Canada for granted, he said. The president's suggestions on foreign aid were unacceptable. American press coverage of Canada was totally inadequate. "We know a great deal more about you than you know about us," the prime minister said to a U.S. reporter.

The next month a controversy arose over Canadian wheat sales to China. Eisenhower had made a strong point of telling the president-elect that one initiative he would staunchly oppose would be any accommodations with China. Rusk never felt that Kennedy was personally against rapprochement, but Ike's advice, combined with the fact that Kennedy was operating on the narrowest of election mandates, stopped him.[8] In the Canadian case, American loading equipment was being used for the wheat and the Kennedy administration wished to block purchases of the equipment. After consultations with Ottawa officials, however, the president decided not to do it. Diefenbaker, in later years, would use the case as a prime example of how he refused to be bullied. He and Kennedy engaged in an all-out shouting match, he told Southam's Charles Lynch. "When I tell Canada to do something I expect her to do it," Kennedy had thundered, according to the Diefenbaker version of the conversation. "I will not be talked to that way," the prime minister shot back. "You can't have the loaders," shouted Kennedy. "You release those loaders," cried the Chief in the winning volley, "or I'll... go on television and tell the Canadian people what you are doing to us." Unfortunately for the Canadian ego the only supporting evidence for the Diefenbaker version was his roomy imagination.

After the personality problems between the two men had been well-established, the issue problems quickly began to mount in the summer of 1961 with the nuclear weapons dispute in the forefront. Ambassador Merchant had asked Diefenbaker prior to the Ottawa trip if his government was prepared to take nuclear-equipped F-101Bs. Diefenbaker said caution was required because opposition in Canada was coming from more than just "Communists and bums" —those whom Douglas Harkness, the prime minister's Defence minister, had suggested. But the "intimation was clear his sympathies lie with us," Merchant cabled Rusk. "...I am certain we have a strong ally in Prime Minister as well as Harkness." This was significant news. It had been as recent as the end of February that Merchant had wired: "As you know the greatest single outstanding problem between us and Canada is Canadian failure to face up to question of nuclear warheads." Now Diefenbaker added a word of warning to Merchant to keep his new views quiet. Don't tell anyone in External Affairs, he said, because the initiative would then run the risk of "being flattened before it even got off the ground."[9] The fear was in keeping with Diefenbaker's near paranoia about the department being stocked with Liberals working against him.

But the conversation with Diefenbaker, who said his cabinet was about to make a final decision, took place before the Kennedy visit. After, his attitude had changed. On August 3, no news from Ottawa having arrived, Kennedy wrote to the prime minister suggesting that it would be nice if there was some movement. The purport of the letter was then carried in an article by Harold Morrison of the Canadian Press, the suggestion being that Diefenbaker was being pressured into an early decision. The idea of Kennedy forcing his hand was the last impression Diefenbaker would want given to anyone. The American embassy knew it. "Press story reported Embtel 316 cannot fail," it wired home, "to be quite disturbing to Prime Minister and others in Canadian Government who are seeking to arrive at decision we want.... In our opinion both decision [Canadian] and timing have obviously been considerably complicated by totally unnecessary publicity resulting from conversations by US government officials with Canadian reporters in Washington."

The U.S. embassy was fully aware of the sensitivities of not only Diefenbaker but their number one Canadian enemy—Howard Green. Shortly before the news of the letter broke, Green fired off another undiplomatic broadside in the Commons with the rallying cry—Nobody is going to tell us to jump through hoops. "One of the least effective ways of persuading Canada to adopt a policy," he said in reference to the OAS, "is for the President or the head of state of another country to come here and tell us what we should do.... I am rather surprised that the honourable member [Liberal Paul Martin] would suggest that we should at once have jumped through the hoop when the President of the United States made this suggestion."

On the nuclear warheads decision, the embassy conjecture was accurate: there was none. Despite mounting pressure, both domestic and from Washington, Diefenbaker delayed through the rest of the year and through 1962. In the spring of 1962, one of the least-known, but one of the most bitter elements in the Kennedy-Diefenbaker feud opened over the question of a nuclear test ban treaty with the Soviet Union. The Canadian position was that a treaty with only limited verification clauses was better than none at all. Kennedy, less trusting of the Soviets, didn't want an agreement unless the means for verifying were failsafe. "For some time I have had an uneasy feeling," he wrote the prime minister, "that perhaps the positions of our two countries were becoming increasingly disparate on the nuclear test question." He urged Diefenbaker to oppose a proposal before the United Nations because "there is no safety in it for any of us." The prime minister initially went along, but changed his position a few months later, promising support for a move toward an unverified moratorium on tests. Livid, Kennedy sent a word missile to Diefenbaker beginning, "To my distress...." He said that just like the Soviet Union, "with its complete lack of moral scruples," Canada would be voting in favour of a moratorium. Should Canada go ahead, "it will be tantamount to Canada's abandoning the western position at Geneva on this issue. This will be seen by the Soviet Union as a successful breach of the western position."

The hot prose poured forth: "I can assure you most strongly Mr. Prime Minister that the United States will not agree to end tests unless we have reasonably adequate assurance that the Soviet Union will not carry out such tests."[10]

Kennedy was presumptuous enough to feel that he knew what was good for the Canadian population. "A mere Soviet promise is not satisfactory either to me or to the Canadian public," he said.

The letter was written on October 19, 1962, when Kennedy was in the throes of perhaps the most difficult decision in his life. Soviet missile sites had been discovered on Cuba. Three days after writing the letter, he would announce to the world that he was embarking on a game of showdown with the Russians: Move your missile sites off the island or we'll move them off for you. In the context of the times, his letter to the prime minister could hardly have been expected to take anything but a hard line. The concluding paragraph? "Mr. Prime Minister, I cannot overemphasize my concern in this matter and, for the reasons I have advanced above and in the interest of a vital Western solidarity on this testing issue, I hope you will reconsider this decision to cast an affirmative vote for a resolution which can only damage and damage seriously the Western position on an essential issue of Western security."

Diefenbaker, in effect, told him to pound sand: "I am fully aware Mr. President that there remains a risk that low yield underground tests could be carried out in secret. Such a risk should not be judged in isolation and should be weighed against the graver dangers which will continue to exist as long as an agreement is not reached and the tests go on."

"In the opinion of the Government of Canada the resolution of the non-aligned nations represents a genuine effort to achieve a compromise position on the question of nuclear tests." There was no response from the White House. "I recommend against a reply," Carl Kaysen, a senior security official scribbled on a memo. "Why thank him for nothing."[11]

The autumn confrontations were preceded by the first of two Canadian election campaigns in which Diefenbaker was convinced he was fighting against three parties—the Liberals, the NDP, and the White House party. A few days into the spring campaign of 1962 Kennedy hosted a dinner for Nobel Prize winners at the White House. The star of the show was none other than Liberal Party leader Lester Pearson with whom Kennedy talked for forty minutes before the dinner began. The effect at Tory headquarters in Canada was the appearance of collusion. The popular president was putting Pearson in the spotlight for public relations bonus points. White House officials later claimed that the dinner had been arranged weeks earlier and that no thought had been given to any Canadian election at the time. A few days before the dinner, the possibility of a controversy was discussed by top Kennedy officials, but the decision had been made to go ahead. As for the long chat before dinner, the president had hoped to have seen Pearson in New York weeks earlier but their schedules failed to coincide. So he chose to spend time with him on Nobel night.

Kennedy genuinely liked Pearson, as did many in the Washington establishment. "A special relationship," said Dean Rusk "had developed between Mike Pearson and the United States." For Diefenbaker, it was far too special. The dinner, the one at which Kennedy made the crack—"Never has so much talent been gathered in one room since Thomas Jefferson dined alone" —stirred the fuels of vengeance in him. He didn't admire Pearson and was forever bothered by his winning the Nobel Prize. The day after Pearson's death in 1972, journalist Stu Macleod visited Diefenbaker in the hopes of evoking some fond words from the Liberal leader's chief adversary. Big snowflakes were falling in Ottawa and Diefenbaker was cozy in a large chair beside a crackling fireplace. When Macleod raised the subject of Pearson's most noted accomplishment, Diefenbaker paused for a few seconds, fixed his glare on the reporter, and pacing his well-weighted words in the dramatic cadence that only he could affect, said slowly: "That man should never have won the Nobel Prize." [12]

So angered was the Chief over the Nobel dinner that he decided to play his cheap card. Ambassador Merchant was leaving his Ottawa posting but before he could get out of town, the prime minister had something to show him — the Rostow memo. Threatening to make its contents public, Diefenbaker bore down on Merchant, accusing his country of trying to push Canada around. Because of the dinner and because the White House was working to help Pearson win, Diefenbaker said he had little choice but to release the document so that the Canadian public would know what had been going on. Merchant was shaken. Diefenbaker was almost out of his mind with rage, he reported to the White House. McGeorge Bundy, national security adviser and George Ball, Rusk's deputy, told Merchant to inform Diefenbaker that Kennedy was not going to be told of the threat; that out of respect for the dignity of Canada it would not be wise; that the United States would not tolerate blackmail.

Of course, the president had been informed and, furious at the prime minister's attempted intimidation, he told Sorensen: "Just let him try it!" The White House and the State Department had been stunned at the impropriety Diefenbaker had demonstrated by not returning the document when it was discovered. "The handling of that by Diefenbaker was scandalous," said Rusk. "An almost unbelievable discourtesy. That kind of thing you just don't do. You don't do that with the Russians." [13] Kennedy wondered why the prime minister "didn't do what any normal friendly government would do...make a photostatic copy and return the original." [14]

Merchant reported the Bundy-Ball reaction to the prime minister. He found him still fuming but correctly predicted to his superiors that he didn't think Diefenbaker would use the memo in the campaign.

Charles Ritchie had just been appointed the new Canadian ambassador in Washington. Rusk, a man respected by Canadians for the class with which he carried out his difficult duties, stepped out of character one evening, leaned into Ritchie, and with a four-letter-word flurry blasted the Diefenbaker government for its singularly uncooperative attitude. At the obligatory presentation of his letters to the president, Ritchie found Kennedy purposely cool and platitudinous. The subject of the memo was not raised. Kennedy was "far too canny" for that. Concluding fifteen minutes of discomfort, Ritchie headed for the door whereupon he heard the president shout, "Shoo!" Ritchie froze, thinking that he was being told to make haste for the streets. He turned and noticed that young Caroline Kennedy had entered through another door, bringing with her the family's pet donkey. Ritchie was relieved to discern that Kennedy's remark was aimed at the donkey, not at him.[15]

During the campaign Diefenbaker gained further evidence that Washington might be trying to help the Liberals. Merchant briefed a hand-picked group of Ottawa reporters at the home of one of the U.S. embassy officials. He explained the U.S. position on the nuclear issue, clearing up misconceptions. No dramatic revelations were made but many, including the prime minister, later considered the timing of the briefing inappropriate. Merchant, however, showed little evidence of being enamoured of the Liberals. He wired the State Department during the campaign, outlining the defence and nuclear policies of the Grits and concluded: "In short while Liberals justifiably charge GOC [Government of Canada] with confusion and indecision, their platform is no more decisive."

Kennedy replaced Merchant with the pompous Walton Butterworth after Diefenbaker was returned with a minority government. But Merchant, who was back at the State Department, soon had another Canadian assignment. Kennedy, well aware of the frigid relations between Merchant and the prime minister, sent him to Ottawa on October 22 to deliver this message:

"My Dear Prime Minister...I am asking Ambassador Merchant to deliver to you the text of a public statement I intend to make today at 1900 hours Washington time. It is occasioned by the fact that we are now in the possession of clear evidence which Ambassador Merchant will explain to you that the Soviets have secretly installed offensive nuclear weapons on Cuba, and that some of them may be operational....I am sending Chairman Khrushchev a personal message making it clear that these latest actions constitute an unacceptable threat to the security of this hemisphere."

Earlier in the day, Kennedy had telephoned Defence Minister Pierre Sevigny, informing him that Merchant was on his way and asking if the meeting with Diefenbaker could be set up. The president hadn't phoned Diefenbaker directly because the two men weren't speaking to one another.

Diefenbaker heard Merchant out and convened a cabinet meeting. "Then," Sevigny recalled, "something happened—one of these ridiculous little things which have such an effect. President Kennedy announced on his own that he had the full cooperation of the Canadian Government."

To the prime minister it was another blood-red example of presidential presumption. "That young man has got to learn that he is not running the Canadian Government," he told Sevigny and others. "What business has he got? There is no decision which has been made as yet. I am the one who is going to decide and I am the one who has to make the declaration. He is not the one."

Merchant had shown Diefenbaker aerial surveillance photographs of the missile sites to establish the legitimacy of the Kennedy charge. But after hearing the president's statement on cooperation, the prime minister, trading swipe for swipe with Kennedy, went before the House of Commons with an expression of doubt and suggested that further evidence was required.

The only western ally not to accept Kennedy's word at face value, Diefenbaker told the nation: "What people all over the world want tonight and will want is a full and complete understanding of what is taking place in Cuba.... The determination of Canadians will be that the United Nations should be charged at the earliest possible moment with this serious problem....As late as a week ago the U.S.S.R. contended that its activities in Cuba were of an entirely defensive nature....The only sure way that the world can secure the facts would be through an independent inspection."

Although long painted as a villain in this episode, Diefenbaker had the support of the opposition parties, neither of which were prepared to jump through hoops either. Pearson said that international verification was the best idea and New Democratic party leader Tommy Douglas was customarily blunt in putting the situation in fair perspective. "We have only the statements of the Americans.... Before we get too excited we should remember that for 15 years the Western powers have been ringing the Soviet Union with missile and air bases."

Much of the Diefenbaker strategy during the missile crisis was orchestrated by one of Canada's most heralded civil servants — Norman Robertson. "It seems," he told Howard Green, "that the United States took a deliberate decision not to consult any of its allies in order to achieve maximum surprise and impact on the Soviet Union. The question arises for Canada whether the existence of NORAD presupposes special obligations which entitle Canada to special treatment over and above that accorded the other allies of the United States."[16] For him and for Diefenbaker the answer was yes.

Following the rebuff to Kennedy in his speech, Diefenbaker stalled on putting Canadian forces at the level of alert Washington desired. His attitude, said Sevigny, was that "it is no use to alarm people unduly," and it was an attitude apparently shared by British Prime Minister Macmillan. During cabinet Diefenbaker received a call from Macmillan and returned to tell his colleagues his version of what Macmillan said. "Whatever you do don't do anything to encourage that hothead in Washington. Cool it. Because the more we make Kennedy provocative, the more difficult we make it for Khrushchev."[17] If the Soviet leader was forced into a corner, they feared, he might do anything. As it turned out, Kennedy was acutely aware of this possibility throughout the crisis. To try to leave Khrushchev in a position where he could save some face was a guiding imperative pushed hard on him by brother Bobby.

Nobody, Dean Rusk remembered, was more conscious of the horrors of a nuclear confrontation than the president. Rusk would never forget the time shortly after inauguration when he and the president were given a full day's briefing on the extent and destructive power of the American and Soviet nuclear arsenals. The news was that the bombs could turn the continent to rubble and make the rubble bounce. Kennedy, drained, wanted to see Rusk in the cabinet room. As Rusk entered the doorway, the president stopped him. His face covered in gloom, he looked at the secretary of state. "And they call this the human race," he said.[18]

Canada had no crucial role to play in the crisis, but it was important to the White House that the Dominion and the Western allies be uniformly supportive of the president's stance. "Had Khrushchev seen a lot of dissension," said Rusk in respect to Diefenbaker, "he could have misjudged the entire situation." From the other allies, the support was solid. Charles de Gaulle accepted the president's word on the existence of the missile bases without even asking to see the aerial photographs. Bobby Kennedy would tell that to Dalton Camp and others as a way of emphasizing how the White House viewed the effrontery of the wavering Diefenbaker.

The prime minister was still reading his anti-American mail and still listening to Howard Green. "If we go along with the Americans now," Green told the cabinet as it debated putting the forces on alert, "we will be their vassals forever."[19] Through the critical days of the crisis, however, the government presented a sputtering, confused picture to the public, many officials yelling yes, many yelling no with the overall impression one of indecision and chaos. When Kennedy won the showdown, emerging daring and gallant, he was vindicated and the doubting Diefenbaker made to look doubly bad in his non-support. Intensifying the defence debate in Canada, intensifying the question of whether Diefenbaker had mismanaged relations with the United States, the Cuban missile crisis sped the Tory government into a crisis of its own, a crisis from which it never escaped.

At this time Diefenbaker had yet to make a determination on equipping Canada's weapons systems with nuclear warheads. His Defence department had increased its stockpile of Bomarc missiles, Honest John rockets, and Voodoo fighters to the value of $685,000,000. The hardware was generally considered useless without nuclear warheads, meaning that Ottawa was outfitting itself with empty cannons. A compromise proposal was offered by Diefenbaker; Canada wouldn't accept the warheads on a permanent basis, but in emergencies would allow the Pentagon to ship them in. While studies showed this plan to be viable, the transportation and installation taking only a few hours, Washington balked for two reasons. One was its firm belief that Diefenbaker had committed himself to the permanent placing of nuclear weapons on Canadian soil in NORAD and other decisions shortly after he took power. The other was that the Cuban missile crisis demonstrated that his compromise plan would be ineffective. A last-minute movement of warheads would only tip the Soviets off to American intentions.

Kennedy and Diefenbaker hadn't met for a year and a half. There was no intention that they would ever meet again. They collided inadvertently, however, a week before Christmas in Nassau. Kennedy and Macmillan were meeting there, Kennedy giving the British leader the shocking news that the United States was cancelling development of the Skybolt missile, a nuclear weapon that was to be a staple of the British arsenal. Diefenbaker had arranged to see Macmillan after the president. But the Kennedy-Macmillan talks spilled over to the day Diefenbaker arrived and, out of courtesy, the prime minister was invited to join the other two leaders for lunch. Kennedy initially wanted to duck the meal. Macmillan argued for him to stay and enjoy some good shellfish. "I can get all the good shellfish I want in Cape Cod," the president shot back, "without having to stay here and eat with Diefenbaker."

The animosity between the Canadian and American leader was well known at this time, so well known that at Diefenbaker's pool side press conference in Nassau a reporter from Edmonton had no qualms about asking: "Is it true that the President hates your guts?" The prime minister was not categorical in his reply.

With Macmillan dejected by the Skybolt decision, and with Kennedy and Diefenbaker having a mutual loathe-in, it was a trilateral which wasn't exactly up to the mirth of the King-Roosevelt Quebec Conferences. Kennedy later described the atmosphere to friends: "And there we sat, like three whores at a christening."

The big Canadian news from Nassau would remain cloaked for a month—until such time as Diefenbaker was sufficiently riled by other events to defy Kennedy again. In Ottawa, on January 3, 1963, General Lauris Norstad, the recently retired supreme commander of NATO, held a press conference as part of his round of farewell courtesy calls. The courtesy he did Diefenbaker was to state unequivocally that the Canadian government had, in fact, committed itself to provide its NATO squadrons with nuclear weapons and that therefore the government was not fulfilling its obligations. The statement, believed by some to be orchestrated by Washington, completely undermined Diefenbaker's already shaky position. Norstad looked at Defence Minister Sevigny in a lounge afterward and said: "Now I am afraid I have embarrassed you a bit." Sevigny agreed and Norstad said, "I have deep regrets." But Sevigny thought he "couldn't care less."

A few days later there were more shock waves. Pearson, in a dramatic reversal, announced that a Liberal government would accept nuclear warheads until such time when new arrangements could be made. The decision drew the lines between the Grits and the Tories, and drew out the prime minister on Nassau. On January 25 in the Commons came his "I was in Nassau" and "I formed certain ideas" speech. The certain ideas were remarkably convenient because they were a vindication of his non-policy on nuclear weapons. Of the cancellation of Skybolt and a renewed emphasis on conventional forces, Diefenbaker said: "That is a tremendous step—a change in the philosophy of defence; a change in the views of NATO." There is, he said, "general recognition that the nuclear deterrent will not be strengthened by the expansion of the nuclear family." With the ever-changing defence needs of the west, "this is not a time for hardened decisions that cannot be altered."

The statements prompted concern in France, Germany, and elsewhere that a major revision of NATO defence had been plotted at Nassau without consultation. The White House phone lines were hot with angry diplomats. Reporters, particularly Canadian correspondents, pressured the State Department for a response. Peter Trueman of the Montreal *Star,* a young journalist who would play a major role in the Diefenbaker follies, wrote a strongly worded letter to the State Department detailing the confusion and recommending that a clarifying statement be issued. In Ottawa the acidic Walton Butterworth, feeling that "we had to set the record straight," drafted a response to the Diefenbaker declaration. The draft was sent to Washington where it was worked on by George McGhee, George Ball, McGeorge Bundy, and Secretary Rusk. President Kennedy was not shown the final version that would go to the press. But, as Rusk remembers, "I probably had a telephone call with Kennedy on it."[20]

It was the statement which, in the written words of Bundy, "knocked over" the Diefenbaker government. It baldly rejected several of the points in the prime minister's speech and castigated the Canadian defence performance. "The Canadian Government has not as yet proposed any arrangement sufficiently practical to contribute effectively to North American defense," the press release said. "The agreements made at Nassau have been fully published. They raise no question of the appropriateness of nuclear weapons for Canadian forces in fulfilling their NATO or NORAD obligations.... The provision of nuclear weapons to Canadian forces would not involve an expansion of independent nuclear capability or an increase in the 'nuclear club.'"

The repudiation sparked outrage in Ottawa and criticism in

Washington. The objections were not against the points made but the method of making them. Shock press releases kicking the other guy was not the Canada-U.S. way of doing things.

The NDP's Douglas Fisher said: "It is an insult to me as a Canadian. I see the next election between Diefenbaker and Kennedy and Kennedy's going to lose."

Pearson thought the release inappropriate. Tommy Douglas was more pungent: "I think the Government of the United States should know from this Parliament that they are not dealing with Guatemala."

Diefenbaker boiled. "Quite apart from the terms of the statement, this action by the Department of State of the United States is unprecedented and I weigh my words when I say that it constitutes an unwarranted intrusion in Canadian affairs.... The Government of Canada does not consider that open public pressures by way of press release or otherwise are appropriate methods of exchanging views between equal sovereign nations or allies."

The prime minister took the unprecedented and yet to be repeated action of recalling his ambassador. It was a signal that Canada was not going to put up with satellite treatment. A problem, however, was that ambassador Ritchie didn't want to come home. His absence wouldn't make any difference to White House officials, he argued. "I told him they probably wouldn't even notice."[21] He ultimately obeyed the order but after a few days in Ottawa was back at his Washington post.

Diefenbaker was convinced the press release was further evidence of White House collusion with Pearson. He glared at the Liberal leader in the Commons. "When are you going back for further instructions?"

In the raucous House, Defence Minister Harkness defended his government's approach to military matters, saying to a chorus of laughter that "we have followed a clear and responsible policy for the last five years." When Pearson challenged him, Harkness was splendidly derisive, explaining that no matter what is said, "the Leader of the Opposition will refuse to understand.... Only God will put sense in that head." Social Credit leader Robert Thompson advocated a somewhat softer approach to the Americans as he unleashed one of the classics of bilateral history: "The United States is our friend, whether we like it or not."

In Washington, Dean Rusk attempted to tranquillize tensions, issuing this half-apology: "There is a strong tradition of fair play in both our countries and our friendship is too close for a misunderstanding of this sort. I wish to say to all Canadians that we regret it if any words of ours have been so phrased as to give offense, but the need to make some clarifying statement arose from a situation not of our making."

President Kennedy had jumped into momentary rage on being apprised of the details of the press release and its full impact. But his concerns quickly abated as did those of others in the White House. Butterworth cabled from Ottawa on February 2. "Initial resentment at United States 'intrusion', as was to be expected, widespread but by no means universal. Strong swing now clearly appearing in direction [that]...this overridingly important matter had to be brought into open and United States had long been patient and forebearing.

"Man on street interviews carried by press and radio reflect strong sympathy for United States position....

"United States case has also had full and sympathetic presentation by most Canadian press representatives in Washington particularly stories by Creery of Southam News, Trueman of Montreal *Star*, and Bain of *Globe and Mail*. All stress long period United States patience with GOC indecision.

"Major political cartoonists concentrating their ridicule on Prime Minister Diefenbaker."

While other Americans were sorry, Butterworth had been in favour of the press release tactic all along: "We decided we had to set the record straight. There was too much at stake. We decided to do it that way because Canadian statements had not come in polite notes, through channels, but on the floor of the house. If you want to play rough then we'll play rough too." Bundy was privately apologetic, taking the responsibility for the action. It was a "case of stupidity," he said, "and the stupidity was mine." Years later, Rusk would be a bit surprised at all the uproar. "Re-reading it; it doesn't seem all that harsh to me."

It was harsh enough, however, to crush the Conservative government in Canada. As the Butterworth memo accurately surmised, sentiment soon began to shift behind the Americans. Diefenbaker's cabinet, already split on defence policy, split wider. Harkness resigned, non-confidence motions filled the air, and, in a series of well-documented events, the Diefenbaker government died on a House vote decrying its ineptitude in handling American relations. In one of his most remembered speeches, Diefenbaker got in some last lashes before the vote: "I cannot accept the fears of those who believe we must be subservient in order to be a good ally of any country in the world.... When I hear some saying that the fact that one dares to speak out will endanger Canada's economy, I wonder what the future of this country would be if those who have such fears and those who are of little faith held office in our country.... I believe in cooperation, in the closest cooperation, but not in the absorption of our viewpoint by any other nation. I believe in the maintenance in spirit and in fact of Canada's identity with the right to determine her own policy without extramural assistance in determining that policy." The speech was interrupted thirty-five times with applause but the confidence vote was lost 142-111. At the White House, they laughed and joked about Dief's demise.

The prime minister now had to face his second election campaign within a year. In 1962, the anti-American issue was present but not paramount. In 1963, it would dominate like it had in 1891 and 1911. Diefenbaker told his colleagues that the great Conservative Macdonald had been victorious with an anti-American campaign and that the good Tory Borden had won on the same and that now it was his turn.

The first salvo came from south of the border with the publication of a *Newsweek* magazine cover-story on Diefenbaker. It was a crucifixion, a hatchet job of astonishing proportions for a respectable publication. The cover picture of the prime minister made him look like he had no control over his face. It was frightening enough to make a baby cry. The first paragraph of the story quoted anonymous sources in the British House of Commons as saying: "It would be too flattering to dismiss him just as a superficial fellow—he's really much dimmer than that."

Announcing that he ran the country like a tantrum-prone county court judge, the article then ridiculed his appearance. "Diefenbaker in full oratorical flight is a sight not soon to be forgotten; then the Indian rubber features twist and contort in grotesque and gargoyle-like grimaces; beneath the electric gray V of the hairline, the eyebrows beat up and down like bats' wings; the agate-blue eyes blaze forth cold fire. Elderly female supporters find Diefenbaker's face rugged, kind, pleasant and even soothing; his enemies insist that it is sufficient grounds for barring Tory rallies to children under 16."

At his next press conference, the prime minister faced reporters carrying copies of the magazine. "We held them in front of our faces," said Southam's Charles Lynch. "Just for fun." Diefenbaker thought the story was just another facet of the White House plot to finish him. His suspicions were fueled further when, late in the campaign, he came into possession of a letter allegedly written by Butterworth to Pearson congratulating him on his switch to a pro-nuclear position. The U.S. embassy and the Liberal party declared the letter a forgery and the evidence seemed to be with them. But Diefenbaker never thought so, carrying the letter virtually everywhere in his suit-jacket pocket. He disliked Butterworth more than he had disliked Merchant. In private conversation he referred to him as "Butterballs." Sent in by Kennedy as a tough man to stand up to a tough prime minister, Butterworth was one of the most unpopular envoys to Canada. Almost everything he did was "offensive to somebody," said the Liberals' Pickersgill. Charles Ritchie was enjoying a ride to Uplands airport one day when Butterworth tore into Ottawa, declaring it "appallingly provincial" and adding that those "like Norman Robertson who think themselves the least provincial are the most provincial of all." Diefenbaker found him so suspicious that he always felt like asking him, "What's your racket?" In reports back to the State Department and the White House Butterworth demonstrated that the feelings were mutual. On March 27, he filed an update on Canadian defence developments, listing nine statements by the prime minister and concluded: "Every one of above statements made by Diefenbaker is inaccurate."

The Conservative campaign took on a feverishly nationalistic tone. "I say this to our friends across the border," Alvin Hamilton, the popular cabinet minister declared. "Don't push us around chum!" Picking on Central America, as had Douglas, he added: "They [Americans] don't even know we're a sovereign country up here. They think we're a Guatemala or something." Diefenbaker, an orator who could fire and brimstone with the best, cried out in Chatham, Ontario, "We are a power, not a puppet." His patriotic blood roared. "I want Canada to be in control of Canadian soil. Now if that's an offense I want the people of Canada to say so." Always there was the hint of the "invisible incognitos" working in Washington against him. "There are great interests against me—national and international." Then his favourite: "Everyone is against me—but the people."

He received what he hoped was a big break toward the end of

campaigning when the House of Representatives released secret testimony of Defense Secretary Robert McNamara. The testimony revealed that one of the purposes of Bomarc bases in Canada was to attract the fire of Soviet missiles which would normally be targeted at American locations. "This is what I've been saying all along," declared a jubilant prime minister. "This is a knockout blow.... Happy days are here." Lashing out at Pearson's support for the Bomarcs, he said that it was obvious now that the Liberal leader would make Canada "a decoy duck in a nuclear war." At Dorion, Quebec, he asked, "Are they going to make Canada into a burnt sacrifice?" The McNamara testimony embarrassed Washington. Looking back, Rusk observed that "it was unlikely there would be a nuclear attack that didn't involve both our countries." Defence cooperation from Canada was important, he said, but whether or not Canada had nuclear weapons as such was "not such a big deal."[22]

With the April 8 voting day approaching and prospects dim, Diefenbaker grew desperate. The case of President Kennedy's misplaced memorandum of May 1961 had not been made public. On a western swing two weeks before election day, Charles Lynch was leaked the guts of the story. "Secret Paper Discloses U.S. Pressuring Canada," the Ottawa *Citizen* headline shouted. "Prime Minister Diefenbaker is understood to have in his possession a document that is the root cause," the first paragraph said, "of much of his bitterness toward the United States and a number of his supporters think he proposes to make it public in the closing days of the election campaign."

The prime minister initially denied he had the paper but sources confirmed that it indeed was in his possession and he wished to disclose it. He was being blocked, the reports said, by cabinet members who, fearful the anti-American campaign was backfiring, were threatening to resign if he did.

In Washington, five days after the Lynch story, *Newsweek* reporter Ben Bradlee had dinner with Kennedy. The talk was about travel, Jackie saying she preferred a holiday in Morocco over Ireland. Kennedy switched suddenly to the subject of Diefenbaker. He told Bradlee that the story about the stolen document was at the root of all Canada-U.S. problems. Bradlee said he would love to hear the details. Wait until the election, said the president. If Diefenbaker lost, he said, Bradlee could have the exclusive. And if he won? asked the future editor of the Washington *Post*. "Well then," said Kennedy, "we'll just have to live with him."[23]

The matter stood until the night of April 4 when, at about 8:00, Peter Trueman got a new break on the story. On the controversial memo, he was told, there was a note in the margin written by the president. It called Diefenbaker an S.O.B. The full line supposedly was: "What do we do with the son of a bitch now?"

Trueman's source had not seen the memo himself. He had only talked to two people who said they had seen it.[24] Trueman's deadline was approaching. He faced the dilemma every reporter faces. Is the information solid enough to go with the story? Should the source be believed? In a decision he regrets to this day, Trueman decided to forego seeking further confirmation and write the story. The Montreal *Star* gave it dramatic display although leaving the quasi expletive out. That part was left to the reader's imagination. But the next day, the Washington *Post* chose to be less reverential. In a front page account reporter John Maffre wrote: "I learned that the expression deleted from The *Star's* published story was the famous S.O.B. once used with reverberating effect by former President Harry S. Truman."

In Hamilton Ontario, Diefenbaker neither confirmed nor denied the report, fudging forth with the response that he was "not getting mixed up in anything like that." Kennedy press secretary Pierre Salinger got on the phone to Trueman and hotly denied it. Other Canadian reporters scrambled to chase down more information. One, Max Freedman, stuck his head in Trueman's office door and said angrily: "That story is wrong. I've checked it out. It's a fabrication, Trueman."

Time magazine's Hugh Sidey had an appointment with Kennedy to get a photograph. It was shortly after the story appeared. "I remember he was very irritated, the President was, that morning and he said, 'Come on now, what do you want?' He was very gruff about it in his office. He said, 'Let's go over. Where do you want a picture?' I wanted it from Harry Truman's balcony. He said, 'Come on,' and then as he went out the door he said to Mrs. Lincoln, "tell one of our photographers to come over here in case Sidey doesn't have any film in his camera.'

"And as we got out there and walked along the arcade, I remember the first thing he said. 'Now I want you to get this damn thing about Diefenbaker correct. I've been in this damn business long enough to know better than that.' He said, 'there are a lot of stupid mistakes I make but that isn't one of them. I didn't do anything.' And then he kind of chuckled and said, 'Besides at the time I didn't know what kind of a guy Diefenbaker was.' The clear implication was that he felt he was an S.O.B. but he had not learned it at that time.... And then he also said, 'Some day, it can't be told now, but some day you'll know just all the difficulties we've had in dealing with this man.'"[25]

The alleged name-calling, the McNamara revelation, and the alleged Butterworth memo, could not help Diefenbaker. In 1891 and in 1911, when election campaigns had been won on anti-Americanism, a larger threat loomed over the Canadian electorate—the threat of annexation. In those years, no president was as popular in Canada as was John F. Kennedy. In those years, the Canadian party leaders running on anti-Americanism were not encumbered by their own records of indecision and ineptitude the way John George Diefenbaker was in 1963.

The Liberals won 129 seats and the Conservatives 95. As promised, Kennedy had Bradlee to the White House to tell him a few things about Mr. Diefenbaker. The president denied he had scribbled the nasty notation in the margin of the memo. "At that time," he told Bradlee, "I didn't think Diefenbaker was a son of a bitch. I thought he was a prick."

The S.O.B. story, though absolutely false would live through the years as one of the most notorious in bilateral relations. The public would come to believe it because it was a nice story to believe. Only the principals would know it wasn't true, Diefenbaker himself writing that it wasn't. Trueman would go on to become one of Canada's top journalists but the memory of the one story would bother him. He would keep hoping for evidence that Kennedy had done such a deed but none would appear.

He had not met the president personally before his memo story was published but was confronted with the moment of anxiety after the election. The president was hosting Lester Pearson and Canadian correspondents in Hyannis Port. The pleasure of working with a new prime minister however was such that even the sight of Peter Trueman didn't bother Kennedy greatly. It was a time when, with the Diefenbaker devil exorcised, joy was returning to the continental partnership.

"The advent of a new Government in Canada," McGeorge Bundy wrote in a memo, "has naturally stirred all branches of the government to new hope that progress can be made with this most important neighbor on all sorts of problems. It is the President's wish that these negotiations should be most carefully coordinated under his personal direction."

CHAPTER THIRTEEN

'Burlesque Circus':
LBJ and Lester Pearson

ON NOVEMBER 22, 1963, Air Force One landed in the dreariness of Andrews Air Force Base carrying a different president from the one with whom it had departed. Lyndon Baines Johnson descended the steps and tried to reassure a nation whose suffering was too deep to be reassured. After a few words, he moved slowly through the dignitaries, placing his huge hands softly on their shoulders, spreading what little comfort could be provided.

Charles Ritchie, the tall, lean, properly educated Canadian ambassador, waited. Like other politicians, diplomats, ordinary people, instinct had taken him to Andrews. Now the new president, his look that of a big, sad bear, was upon him. "Pearson," he said gently. "Your Prime Minister. My best friend. Of all the heads of Government, my best friend." He would be dependent on his best friend's help, Johnson said. Very dependent.[1]

In Ottawa, Prime Minister Pearson was preparing a eulogy for Kennedy, a president far closer to him than Johnson would ever be. In the evening, in an address viewed by millions of Americans as well as Canadians, he paid tribute to a man whose appeal was "not to the comfortable but the daring."

"Listen," said Pearson, "to these words from his inaugural address: 'Now the trumpet summons us again. Not as a call to bear arms, though arms we need. Not as a call to battle though embattled we are. But a call to bear the burden of a long twilight struggle year in and year out, "rejoicing in hope, patient in tribulation" —a struggle against the common enemies of man: tyranny, poverty, disease and war itself.'

"These words were the measure of that man," said Pearson. "For him the burden has now been lifted, but for us that trumpet still sounds."

The words produced hundreds of letters from thankful Americans, many of whom said they were brought to tears. But it might have been wise for Pearson to curtail his Kennedy tributes thereafter. Like Diefenbaker, Johnson was a man who harboured deep resentment of the Kennedy allure. John Kennedy's shadow stalked him. Robert Kennedy's person stalked him. And although he was politically judicious in keeping many from the former president's staff, Johnson desperately wanted to dispel the shadows. So when "best friend," Pearson visited him two months after the assassination, stood under the White House portico, and went on at length in his speech about John Kennedy's greatness, Johnson was not impressed.

Pearson was compelled to commit this, one of his lesser offences against LBJ, out of genuine respect and admiration for Kennedy. He was only in office eight months while Kennedy was president but his compatibility with Kennedy and the respect they shared for one another gave their relationship a promise that no others had.

Given time, their partnership could have engendered a continental harmony and cooperation comparable to, if not surpassing that of the King-Roosevelt period. That time denied, Pearson was left with an opposite, with a man whose hillbilly style, whose hawkishness and supersensitive ego were too hard to bear. Even Mike Pearson, one of the world's greatest diplomats, a man trained, tested, and victorious in the art of getting along, could not brook the excesses of LBJ. The crude, capable president would drive the prime minister to his most undiplomatic act ever. The president would reciprocate in kind, making any future constructive dialogue impossible, making Ottawa relieved by the arrival of a new president, even if it was Richard Nixon, and making Lester Pearson's memory of his few months with John Kennedy larger.

Kennedy admired men of accomplishment. Pearson had been a

world-class diplomat. He had won the Nobel Prize and he had defeated Diefenbaker. He would store nuclear weapons on Canadian soil. He had wit. He wasn't boring.

Kennedy had reviewed Pearson's 1959 book, *Diplomacy in the Nuclear Age*, delighting the author with wholehearted praise of the person and the content: "Mike Pearson has been the chief architect of the Canadian foreign service, probably unequalled by any other nation.... He has been a central figure in the growth of the Atlantic Community and NATO.... He has been a superb interlocutor between the realms of statesmanship and scholarship."

"It seemed to me," Pearson half-jokingly commented on the review, "that anyone who valued my literary efforts must possess some special quality." What he liked about Kennedy was his stimulating personality and the "toughness and clarity of his mind. When talking business with our advisers around the table he did not waste any time but went right to the heart of the problem....."[2]

He discovered this in Hyannis Port where, with Pearson staying in Bobby Kennedy's residence, the two leaders met only a few weeks after the prime minister took office to try and stabilize the destabilized relationship. In the late months of Diefenbaker's stewardship, meaningful Canada-U.S. dialogue had virtually halted. The bilateral cabinet committee on defence hadn't met since 1960, and the committee on economic affairs hadn't met in eighteen months. Canadian officials found no access in Washington, American officials found no access in Ottawa and a stack of issues awaited action: defence production sharing, the test ban treaty, balance of trade problems, Columbia River Treaty revisions, territorial jurisdiction in east coast waters, trans-border air travel, Great Lakes shipping, and Canadian acquisition of nuclear weapons.

Distinguishing himself from many predecessors and successors, Kennedy came prepared. Working with a man he liked, he showed none of the arrogance and one-upmanship he had with Diefenbaker. On the issues he and Pearson had a four-hour, heavily detailed session in front of a fireplace. It marked a welcome change for Pearson because Truman couldn't talk four hours on Canadian issues, nor could Eisenhower nor, in the future, could Johnson. The prime minister's further commitment to stationing nuclear warheads in Canada grabbed the headlines. Working groups were set up to solve other problems, including the question of an equitable air route agreement for trans-border flights. The problem here was in finding a non-partisan to do the job, and who better embodied the duality than the Canadian-bred Harvard man, John Kenneth Galbraith? "Recalling that I had frequently identified myself as a Canadian, Kennedy appointed me the Canadian representative. Recalling the same, Pearson, a friend of many years, said I would do as the Canadian representative."

What struck Dick O'Hagan, the Pearson press secretary, about the prime minister and the president at Hyannis Port was the genuine flavour of their relationship. "It made you feel," said O'Hagan, who saw many summits, "that nothing was unresolvable in Canadian-American relations because you had two compatible guys."

O'Hagan organized a reception for the Canadian media with Pearson, a move which led Bill Lawrence of the New York *Times* to complain about the Americans being overlooked. Asked by O'Hagan if they could attend, Pearson inquired, "Do we have enough booze?" Then President Kennedy got in on the crash-the-Canadian-party act and with Old Fitzgerald bourbon heading the roster, a delightful party followed, the feature act being a mock replay of Kennedy's missing memo. A document containing information on the Kennedy-Pearson talks was moving through the drinks toward the president when it slipped from someone's hand, getting momentarily lost among the wing tips. David Broder, a young reporter making a name for himself with the Washington *Star*, was quick to fire off an allusion to the S.O.B. memo. Kennedy, who gave reporter Peter Trueman a steely glance during the reception, was within earshot. Pearson then got hold of the missing document and cracked: "I'm just going to make some marginal notations on it." He handed it to a smiling president, adding, "I just happened to find this on the floor."

Proud of his knowledge of baseball, Pearson wanted to show Kennedy he had more than a political dimension. David Powers, a Kennedy adviser, an old friend and a baseball nut was on hand. "Dave, the Prime Minister claims to be an expert in baseball," said Kennedy. "Test his knowledge." Batting and earned run averages were tossed back and forth. A question arose about a pitcher who threw a no-hitter through seven innings but was pulled and his team lost the game. Powers wanted to know the name of the hurler. "Ken Mackenzie," snapped Pearson. Powers had someone look it up, Pearson was found to be correct and Powers and the president were impressed. They didn't know that the decisive question they put was distinctly advantageous to Pearson. Ken Mackenzie was one of the few Canadians to ever play in the big leagues. He was also from Pearson's riding.

At the close of the visit it began to rain hard while Kennedy, wearing neither hat nor coat, escorted Pearson to the helicopter. Pearson insisted that he return. "No, I want to give you something when we get to the helicopter," said the president. Earlier Pearson had presented Kennedy with a 120-year-old rocking chair from Lanark County which had the quintessential Canadian distinction of having occupied a room with a large beaver painted on its ceiling. At the end of the driveway, Kennedy, getting thoroughly wet, lowered the presidential flag, rolled it up, handed it to Pearson and asked him to keep it. In the few future months of the Kennedy presidency they would communicate frequently by phone and letter but the handing over of the flag was the last time they would see one another.

With Johnson, during his first visit, it was at the gift exchange where Pearson got the impression that the president wasn't in the best of humours, that maybe he wasn't happy with the prime minister's speech which had lauded Kennedy. When presented with an English saddle, a gift hard to explain given the fact that LBJ rode western, Johnson grumbled about it having no pommel and suggested somewhat ungraciously that maybe Lady Bird could use it. Lady Bird, in fact, thought it was great. "Just like the Royal Canadian Mounted Police use," she noted in her diary. "Those men who were always the symbol of romance and daring adventure in my childhood."

But if an English saddle for Johnson was inappropriate, a silver cigarette box for Pearson was the same. Ten days earlier the Surgeon General had issued a scathing report linking smoking to lung cancer. Johnson was not a president who cared much for gift-giving and the surrounding persiflage. Later in one of his more earthy moods, he presented Pearson with a box containing something like a chandelier. "I don't know what the f——k it is," he said, "or what the f——k you're going to do with it."

Whether it was the tribute to Kennedy or whether there was something more, Pearson found Johnson disturbed and distracted through most of their first two days together. Johnson didn't know much or care much about the bilateral issues and his speeches and toasts consisted primarily of knee-jerk undefended border pulp. Some in the media scorned his effort, the Toledo *Blade* saying he had used "a threadbare and irritating cliché that ought to be banned by law.... The famous unguarded border fogs our thinking about Canada."

Lady Bird had her own thoughts on the matter. "Thank God there's one border in the world that, as of now, we don't have to worry about," she wrote. "I gather they too in Canada have their difficulties with minority populations, with the French province actually talking of seceding from the Dominion. Certainly nothing could conceivably come of this, could it?"

When the time came to talk about the Canada-U.S. issues, the discussion in the cabinet room had just begun when Johnson announced that he preferred to let the experts deal with the problems. He escorted Pearson outside where, "using some rough and very profane words... treating me as if I were a friendly Congressional visitor," he talked about multilateral problems that he knew something about. De Gaulle had recently signalled that it was the intention of France to recognize the People's Republic of China. Pearson had recently visited the French leader and Johnson wanted to know if the action was being taken to specifically irritate the United States and what might be done about it. De Gaulle's mind wouldn't be changed, Pearson advised, and the action was not anti-American in purpose. Let it stand.

The Canadian leader told about de Gaulle asking him a question. "You are always boasting you Canadians that you know the Americans better than anyone else...." De Gaulle said, "What do you really think of them?"

"My feeling about the United States is this," replied Pearson. "To live alongside this great country is like living with your wife. At times it is difficult to live with her. At all times it is impossible to live without her."

Pearson was dismayed by Johnson's ignorance of his country. "Perhaps these were the only facts about Canada in the Texas school books," But at least, he wrote, "the President did not pretend. He admitted he knew nothing about us."[3] There was some satisfaction for Pearson in that he got to know Johnson better and there were no quarrels. The only thing disputed, he told reporters, was whether Sammy Baugh of Texas was a better quarterback than San Francisco's Y. A. Tittle. But the prime minister didn't leave without a prophetic word of warning. He recalled once being criticized for saying the days of easy and automatic bilateral relations were over. "But so they are," he told Johnson. "I don't know how easy or automatic they used to be, but I know that in the future we are going to have problems and difficulties."

In the fall the presidential election campaign began, and Bill Moyers, Johnson's highly influential adviser, received a memo. "It would of course be extremely effective," it said, "for the President to mix dedication ceremonies and other events that dramatize the action achievements of this administration wherever possible." Heading the suggestion list was a trip to Canada to do another dedication ceremony on the Columbia River project.

A memo went to the president: "Over the past several years since its Senate ratification, there have been several public ceremonies on the Columbia River Treaty.... However Mr. Bundy and I feel that the next step... is the most significant in making the enterprise a reality. It has a lot of political pluses and we believe you may want to give it a major build up."[4]

"... The political pluses," the memo continued, "include: 1. Generally a big day in US-Canada relations, with flood control and many benefits for Canada, the same plus power in the US Northwest. 2. Private utilities as well as Bonneville get big benefits in low cost power.... Benefits go to all four Northwest states and California as far south as Los Angeles. 3. Flood control benefits for entire Columbia basin."

Johnson was on his way. For him, like so many other presidents, Canada was a good place to visit during an election year. It was no coincidence that the number of general election visits and mid-term election visits to Canada far exceeded those in the off-years. In Canada, polls showed that LBJ was a ten-to-one favourite over super-hawk Republican challenger Barry Goldwater, whose name had become attached to such quotes as "Let's lob one into the men's room of the Kremlin." In Vancouver and at a border stop, Johnson took advantage, pumping every Canadian hand available, kissing babies, clutching cheering teenagers.

The partnership with Canada, he said at the International Peace Arch at the border, rested on four pillars—peace, freedom, respect, and cooperation. "Difficulties that divide others have united us... Woodrow Wilson said 'you cannot be friends upon any other basis than upon terms of equality.' We maintain with each other the relationship that we seek for all the world; cooperation amid diversity." Johnson poured on the praise: "Pericles said of a state that was much smaller than yours: 'We have forced every sea and land to be the highway of our daring.' In the founding of the United Nations, in the Middle East, in the Congo, in southeast Asia, the world has responded to Canadian daring. You have followed not the highway of empire which helped destroy Athens, but you have followed the more difficult path to peace which can save the world."

The campaign exuberance was followed by two of the most bizarre summits in Canada-U.S. history. Pearson would find himself being cursed with names that made Kennedy on Diefenbaker sound like birthday greetings. He would be called the wrong name before a national TV audience, he would have unwanted bourbons shoved at him, and unwanted dinner guests at the table. Johnson would be shocked and stung that his "best friend" from "little 'ole Canada" would come south and criticize him. Relations between the countries, as a result, would be thorny for another four years.

Nothing so illustrated the contrast in characters of the two leaders as the culture-shock conference at the LBJ ranch near Austin, Texas in January, 1965. The purpose was the signing of the auto pact, an enormously important trade agreement striking down barriers on automobiles and parts. Johnson signed, knowing practically nothing about it and would soon snap at ambassador Charles Ritchie: "You screwed us on the auto pact!" Secretary of State Dean Rusk, the other powerful presence at the signing, knew nothing about it either. It was part of his aversion to the world of trade and finance. "I still think economics is a dismal science." The result was that agreement, to Pearson's chagrin, became a sidelight to the wild weekend's other fare—booze, gossip, raucous ranch tours, pyjama talk. In Ritchie's phrase, it was a "burlesque circus."

Pearson might have arrived better prepared for the occasion. It was 70°F at the ranch and O'Hagan, knowing Johnson and figuring he could well show up on a horse with Marlboros, suggested that the prime minister change into something more comfortable. Pearson declined the advice, opting for black homburg, heavy three-piece suit, polka dot tie, and boutonniere. As predicted, Johnson showed up looking like he was headed for a rodeo, and Pearson was distinctly out of place. He was only there a minute when the president suggested he might want to change. The prime minister said he was fine, whereupon

Johnson introduced him to his dog. "Here's a man you've been waiting to meet," said the president. Recalling Johnson's habit of putting guests on horses, Pearson cracked, "I don't have to ride him, do I?" Johnson, in front of the whirring TV cameras then called Pearson "Mr. Wilson" and not realizing his mistake (British Prime Minister Harold Wilson had been a recent visitor), called for a convoy-style expedition of the ranch lands.

The cavalcade across the homely, dry country entailed golf carts, convertibles, jeeps, and helicopters. A helicopter for the leaders, a helicopter for the wives, a helicopter for the security people and, as Pearson remembered, "another helicopter for the liquor — The United States is a great power." Shortly after take-off, Johnson turned to Pearson and said: "It's four-thirty, we'll have a bourbon and branch water." Pearson accepted, but only to be polite. Johnson fired back helicopter bourbons and jeep bourbons every twenty minutes whereupon he would demand that everyone have another. After one unsettling shot on the chopper ride, Pearson begged off.

While Pearson thought the Texas landscape was bland, Johnson referred repeatedly to its unbelievable beauty. The president would gun his jeep over a hill and say, "Now there's a fine buck." In the next breath, it would be, "Now on the subject of Vietnam." Then he would be on the phone to Saigon, to the Congo, to Austin, and to wife Lady Bird who, in her own raging motorcade with Maryon Pearson, was delighted in "seeing at close hand three armadillos."

At six o'clock, still out on the plains, Johnson barked through his phone, "Lady Bird, let's have the Connallys to dinner with the Pearsons." With a whole list of bilateral topics to be covered and a historic agreement to be signed the next morning, the prime minister was not overly enthusiastic about the prospect of seeing Texas Governor John Connally. But there was no choice. Lady Bird initially protested: "Don't you think it's a little late dear?" But LBJ was on the phone to the governor's mansion. "John, I want you to meet the Pearsons. I'll have a helicopter there in 20 minutes. Bring the wife, Okay?" Immediate agreement wasn't forthcoming but the president soon settled the matter. "You've lots of time."

Amid the afternoon mayhem, something was accomplished, although inadvertently. On the golf carts someone mentioned the serious problem brewing over the Soviet Union's refusal to pay its U.N. dues. The Soviets were threatening withdrawal from the United

Nations and the issue would move to a head unless Washington took decisive action such as making an exceptional loan to the body. Johnson hadn't indicated his leanings, but in response to questioning from the Canadians, he declared: "Well hell we can't break up the United Nations just because the Russians won't pay a few million dollars." Rusk, who recalled seeing Paul Martin flinch, asked Johnson if he was serious. Johnson said he was damn serious, even though it was apparent it was an off-the-cuff remark. At the ranch house there was more discussion and the president eventually went ahead with the loan. "The talk on the golf cart was the turning point," Rusk remembered. "Sometimes that's the way policy is made." The power was there to be used and loved. Rusk used to enjoy dropping a casual remark and watching the aides jump. "But, Mr. Secretary, that's not our policy," they would say. "Well, it is now," Rusk would reply and relish telling the story years later.

It was dinner time, and for Pearson, "dining with Mr. and Mrs. Johnson at the ranch in Texas was like dining in the old farmhouse in Chinguacousy township north of Toronto.... It was all very homey and unpresidential, perhaps a little too much so, even for a ranch." So many were wandering around with telegrams and important messages that Pearson was never sure whether he was looking at a valet or an assistant secretary of state. The women, to the Prime Minister's surprise, were let in on all the secrets. Pearson and Martin were handed the hottest telegrams coming in from Vietnam and asked to comment. "Let's have a look at this," Johnson would say. "Let's have a look at this."

It was "quite unlike," said Pearson, "anything that could have happened at any other place in any other meeting between the leaders of government." In a way he found it a compliment to Canadians in that it was "a reflection of the special relationship we have with the United States." But it was also "very dangerous because there's always a possibility you are taken pretty much for granted because you are so close-treated."

Following a dinner of steak and catfish on the same plate, Johnson turned on several TV sets, one for each network. Unwisely he had decided he wanted to see the news reports of Pearson's arrival. When he saw himself pronouncing greetings upon Mr. Wilson he was baffled, bewildered, and painstakingly apologized. Pearson had his line ready. "Think nothing of it, Senator Goldwater." He called him senator for the remainder of the stay. Weeks later he received from the president a picture of the arrival with the inscription, "To my dear friend, Mr. Wilson."

At 5:45 the next morning, a restless Paul Martin ambled into the kitchen to check out the refrigerator. He was there only a minute when he turned and saw lumbering toward him a towering figure in voluminous white pyjamas and no socks. The president of the United States made coffee, put in calls on Vietnam, discovered that American planes had bombed some of their own people, and talked with Martin at the kitchen table about almost everything except the auto pact.

Despite the bad war news, which prompted a call to Defense Secretary McNamara, Johnson was in good spirits, pouring down coffee after coffee until Martin had had enough and Pearson arrived to take over.

At last it was time for the anticlimactic formal business. The dignitaries moved out to a picnic table in the yard and, in freezing temperatures with reporters looking on, signed the auto pact. A ground-breaking agreement, it was an experiment in one-industry continentalism which Pearson felt might be extended to embrace other industries in the future. For him it was the "beginning of something big and important," and he was doubly delighted in that he felt Canada was getting the better of the deal. But Pearson was discouraged in many respects by the two days. He had been unable to talk meaningfully with Johnson on Canadian concerns. He had been discomforted and sometimes shocked by the sheer coarseness of the man.

Fittingly, the strange visit ended on a strange note. It was Johnson's custom to have his guests sign their names in a wet concrete slab. Martin signed his slab 1964 instead of 1965. Then someone accidentally stepped on it anyway.[5]

At this time there were some Canadian rumblings over U.S. policy in Vietnam, but no open wounds. As early as 1954, a Canadian prime minister had stuck his head in the Vietnam business. St. Laurent at that time urged Eisenhower, privately, not to get involved militarily following the surrender of the French to the Communist-led Vietminh at Diên Biên Phu.[6] President Kennedy had asked Pearson what he would do about Vietnam were he the president, and Pearson replied, "I'd get out." "Any damn fool knows that," said Kennedy. "The question is, how?"

In May 1964, Pearson met Johnson briefly in New York and said some things about Vietnam that the Americans would not soon forget. "He stipulated," said the State Department's report on the conversation, "that he would have great reservations about the use of nuclear weapons, but indicated that the punitive striking of discriminate targets by careful iron bomb attacks would be a 'different thing.'" The Johnson administration had solicited assistance from Canadian diplomat Blair Seaborn who undertook six peace-seeking missions to Vietnam. The State memo continued: "He [Pearson] said he would personally understand our resort to such measures if the messages transmitted through the Canadian channel failed to produce any alleviation of North Vietnamese aggression."[7] By early 1965 the Seaborn missions had failed to produce any such alleviation.

At the end of February 1965, Johnson unveiled Operation Rolling Thunder, a heavy, continuous air campaign designed to bomb North Vietnam to the conference table. For Pearson, despite the previous words, this was the wrong way to go. He feared it could escalate the conflict to frightening proportions. He thought Washington should have been making a greater effort toward ceasefire and negotiation.

The views were made known to the White House through a variety of channels. Paul Martin had warned well before the Johnson announcement that Canada would oppose heavy bombing. Ambassador Ritchie saw Rusk frequently. Rusk would respectfully hear him out and, in effect, say 'well, that's nice.' "Nothing that we said was getting to anybody," Ritchie recalled. "If it did, it was ignored."

Canadian academics and journalists began ranting against Rolling Thunder and Pearson came under considerable pressure to take a strong public stance against the bombings. Several close to Pearson, including his External Affairs minister, were decidedly against any such move. Martin had diplomats still pressing for a ceasefire with Hanoi. Their credibility, he felt, rested on the supposition that Canada's influence in Washington was high.[8] If Pearson publicly attacked Johnson, the foundation for influence would crumble. "I told Pearson myself, 'what would be the point?'" Said Martin: "But Mike wanted to show that he was a man of great courage."

George Ball, the American undersecretary of state, had been invited to speak in Toronto to explain Southeast Asia policy. Because of the volatility of the issue in Canada, and because Canadian officials felt they understood the American stance, Ball was cut off. Martin advised him in a phone call not to come. The feeling, a feeling which the White House would soon find extremely ironic, was that a U.S. official should not come into Canada's backyard and try to make points on the sensitive war issue. Ball, oddly enough, was a behind-the-scenes dove on the war. The only prominent man in government along with Hubert Humphrey to offer dissent, he warned the president in a memo: "Once on the tiger's back, we cannot be sure of picking the place to dismount." He was probably closer to the Pearson position than anyone.

The prime minister prepared to speak on April 2, 1965 at Temple University in Philadelphia, where he was to receive the school's second World Peace Award. His last contact with President Johnson had been a positive one. On February 9, Johnson telephoned to say he was sending a message to Congress asserting the American need for Canada to avoid excessive borrowing from the United States. He told Pearson the wording that would be in the speech, asking if it was suitable. Pearson checked it with financial advisers and won Johnson's approval for a few changes. For the prime minister it was a wonderful example of the special Canada-U.S. cooperation. He had put "credit in the bank" with Johnson the year before by way of the quick deployment of Canadian forces to serve on a U.N. peace-keeping mission in Cyprus. "You'll never know what this has meant, having those Canadians off to Cyprus and being there tomorrow," Johnson had told him. "Now, what can I do for you?" Pearson thought the balance-of-payments phone call was part of the pay-back. But in memos exchanged between Johnson and his men prior to the call there was no impression that he was seeking to do Canada any favours. "You might point out to him," said Treasury Secretary Douglas Dillon, "that unless you can make such a statement the pressures to fix a dollar limit for Canadian borrowings might prove irresistible.... Such a conversation may well produce the results we desire. If not, it will certainly pave the way for any future action we may feel compelled to take."9

Feeling deeply worried about the bombing attacks and feeling the domestic political winds, Pearson decided to use the Temple speech to call for a halt to Rolling Thunder. Ritchie asked him if he would at least observe the tradition of giving the White House a copy of the speech in advance. "Of course not," Pearson replied. "He knew," said Ritchie, "that if Johnson saw it early, he would go into one of his fabled arm-twisting routines to foil it. It was quite deliberately held up. It was Mike's own doing. He knew there would be a blow-up."

The day before the speech, the prime minister received a letter from the president. It congratulated Pearson on the award he was about to receive. "Your long record in the struggle for peace needs no repetition from me, but I want to bear witness to the wisdom and courage that you have brought to bear on every question affecting world peace that you and I have worked on together in sixteen months of the closest cooperation."

The night of the speech, the wisdom and the courage took on an entirely different aspect: "The dilemma is acute and it seems to be intractable," said Pearson. "On the one hand, no nation—particularly no newly-independent nation—could ever feel secure if capitulation in Vietnam led to the sanctification of aggression through subversion or spurious 'wars of national liberation,' which are really wars of Communist domination.

"On the other hand, the progressive application of military sanctions can encourage stubborn resistance rather than a willingness to negotiate. So continued and stepped-up intensification of hostilities in Vietnam could lead to uncontrollable escalation. Things would get out of hand.

"A settlement is very hard to envisage in the heat of the battle, but as the battle grows fiercer, it becomes even more imperative to seek and find one."

The first condition for a settlement, Pearson said, was a ceasefire. "Only then can there be negotiation with any chance of success. In this connection continued bombing against North Vietnam beyond a certain point may not have the desired result. Instead of inducing authorities in Hanoi to halt their attacks on the South, it may only harden their determination to pursue and even intensify their present course of action. Modern history has shown that this is often the result and one that we don't intend when we take massive retaliatory action."

Lyndon Johnson had a rule, a "kind of code of conduct" for political leaders, Dean Rusk remembered: "He would never let us criticize a foreign political leader by name—De Gaulle, Khrushchev or anyone else. He also felt that one political leader should not make trouble for another political leader in that other fellow's backyard."[10]

The code of conduct being broken by an act which Pearson realized was audacious, Johnson called the prime minister to Camp David and proceeded to administer the whipping. Ambassador Charles Ritchie, having viewed the spectacle with shock and amazement, wanted something done about it. While Johnson bellowed at Pearson on the porch, Ritchie had engaged in a spat with McGeorge Bundy. With their leaders at war the two of them stepped into the surrounding trees and, circling the cabin many times, contested the merits of the Pearson speech. Ritchie, becoming exasperated with the "my best friend" and "my own backyard" stuff told Bundy that the prime minister had every right to make the Canadian policy statement, that a distinguished awards dinner was the appropriate place to do it and that if the president couldn't get along with Mike Pearson, who could he get along with? Back at the cottage, he saw Johnson grab Pearson by the shirt and became "outraged at seeing such a tone adopted against a Canadian Prime Minister." Ritchie flew back to Ottawa that evening with Pearson but couldn't relax, feeling Johnson's behaviour was insufferable and asking himself—"Who the hell do they think they are?" Finally he decided to telephone Pearson. He congratulated him for having the conviction to make the speech in the first place but suggested that it would be wrong to sit back and absorb the treatment Johnson had doled out. On the surface Pearson sounded calm but Ritchie got the feeling he was "quite shaken."[11] Pearson rejected his advice however, deciding against escalating the matter further and choosing instead to defuse it with a conciliatory letter to the president.

"I assure you that my proposal, carefully guarded, was meant to be helpful; neither critical nor obstructive...I want you to know that I appreciate, as much as any person could, the crushing nature of the problem, domestic and international, that you are facing with such courage and wisdom.... But Canada is a political democracy too, with an active and often divided public opinion, sensitive that its leaders do not appear to be merely echoes of the United States but anxious, I believe, to back up their neighbour when required to do so, as an independent friend should."

The prime minister realized, as is noted in his memoirs, that "we would have been pretty angry, I suppose, if any member of the American Government had spoken in Canada on Canadian Government policy as I had spoken in Philadelphia."

This perhaps explains why Pearson went so far as to thank Johnson in the letter. "May I add that your exposition of the American case for planned and limited air retaliation, designed to do the job intended, with a minimum of loss of life and without provocation to China and Russia was reassuring and impressive. I am grateful to you for it as I am for your kindness and for your consideration in speaking to me so frankly last Saturday."

"Thank you for your thoughtful letter," Johnson replied in a business-like note. "I was glad to have your full account of your thinking."

The president was not about to let the incident fade in the memory. "LBJ's view," Rusk recalled, "was that if Pearson had made that speech in Canada, it wouldn't have mattered so much." He said that neither he nor the president ever "expected Canada to fight with us in Vietnam. But we expected understanding and support. To put it mildly, we did not have major political support from Canada. That made it more difficult for us."

Weeks after the storm at Camp David, Johnson had Ritchie and the West German ambassador to the White House for lunch. Barely into the main course, he began heaping praise on West Germany for the cooperation it was according the United States. Then the president turned to Ritchie. "But Ohhhh, those Canadians. They're so clever. They can come into your own backyard and tell us how to run the war. They're so clever." His voice was booming, Ritchie was dumbfounded. "Ohhhh, those Canadians," LBJ continued, ticking off areas in which they tried to outdo the United States. "They got an auto pact and they're screwing us on that. They're so clever. Ohhhh, those Canadians." Ritchie attempted rebuttals but they were scattered in the wind by the president's power and bluster.[12]

Extraordinarily sensitive to the media and public opinion, Johnson kept close track of his standing with the Canadian public. Lengthy White House memos detailed shifts in the north country's views. From the spring of 1964 to the spring of 1965, his standing dropped eight points. "We would think this is almost certainly caused by stepped up U.S. action in Vietnam," a memo reported. "Of course, President Johnson is not the Canadian leader. Nonetheless, Canada is a close ally and neighbor. He wants their friendship and support. He wants that support from Canada's leaders and Canada's people. Quite frankly, we expected a greater loss of support in Canada on Vietnamese policy."

Having first-hand evidence of how Vietnam was beginning to eat away at the man, Pearson felt as early as 1965 that the war could doom him. "The crisis over Vietnam is going to be a great test for LBJ," he recorded in his diary. "I'm not now certain that he is going to be successful in meeting it.... There is no doubt that the President is tired, under great and continuous pressure and that he is beginning to show it. He is more willing about U.S. policy in Vietnam than he is willing to show. His irritation at any indication of lack of full support for his policy; his impatience with criticism and his insistence that everything is working out in accord with a well conceived plan: All these really indicate a feeling of insecurity about the situation, rather than the reverse. As the President said: 'It's hard to sleep these days. I'm beginning to feel like a martyr; misunderstood, misjudged by friends at home and abroad.'"

Canadian prime ministers naturally wanted to have as much influence as possible at the White House. Pearson, clearly losing his, sought to regain it. Ambassador Ritchie was sent in to give a sales pitch to Jack Valenti over lunch in late July. He stressed Pearson's contacts throughout the world, his Nobel Peace Prize status, his personal affection for Johnson. Valenti forwarded a memo to the president:

"The Ambassador voiced his concern over the fact that the President may still be a bit unhappy with Prime Minister Pearson.

"....It is the hope and desire of the Prime Minister that he can be useful to the President in behind-the-scenes talks, probings and searchings which have as their objective unconditional discussions."

Pearson's status in the world, Valenti reported Ritchie as saying, "would allow him, if the President determined it wise, to quietly seek out ways to bring the matter off the battlefield and into a meeting hall.

"It was the desire of the Ambassador that the President know that the Prime Minister is at his service in any way or in any form that can be beneficial to the President and to the objectives of the United States."

Johnson had sent letters to Pearson and other leaders on the Vietnam situation. Pearson wanted to release the texts in order to clear confusion in the House of Commons where he was being attacked, strangely enough, for insufficient opposition to the president on the war. But Johnson turned down the request. Valenti, closely following Canadian developments, gloatingly told his boss a few days later: "Pearson is getting beat over the head from the opposition who have accused him of lying about what he told the President."

Early in 1966, Albert Edgar Ritchie, undersecretary of state for External Affairs, took over from Charles Ritchie as Washington ambassador. He hadn't been seated a moment in the Oval Office to present his letters of credence when Johnson instructed: "Now would you tell your Prime Minister that we're not bombing any civilians in Vietnam?"[13] The president had been to Vietnam and wanted Pearson to understand that he had checked out the facts with "my own God-given eyes." He used the phrase repeatedly as he did "my own backyard" again in referring to Pearson's unforgettable transgression.

Johnson was given the latest opinion survey results from Canada on his handling of the war: 35 percent approved, 34 percent didn't, and 29 percent had no opinion. Defense Secretary McNamara, preparing to speak in Canada, was provided some tips on what to say from Rostow, an irrepressible hawk. "Despite its violence and difficulties, our commitment to see it through in Vietnam is essentially a stabilizing factor in the world," said Rostow. "Should we fail," he added simplistically, "the world would become much less — not more — stable with the fate of Southeast Asia and the flank of the Indian subcontinent immediately endangered, and the Chinese Communist doctrine of 'wars of national liberation' vindicated for application everywhere."

Edgar Ritchie knew Rostow well, having gone to Oxford with him. He would meet with Rostow frequently in an office in the White House basement. Rostow, who informed Johnson daily on developments in the war, would be sitting, legs tucked under him on the sofa, doing the latest body count. "What does it mean, Walt?" Ritchie would ask. Rostow would point to the figures and say they meant that North Vietnam was losing.[14]

The president and the prime minister finally got together again in August 1966, a year and a half after the Camp David debacle. Johnson's primary motivation was political. The mid-term elections were in November. The public reason was the less-than-urgent necessity for a cornerstone to be laid at a partially built public washroom and office unit at the Visitors' Centre at FDR's old home in Campobello International Park.

Franklin Roosevelt being the theme, the prime minister quoted him to support his argument against the war and the president quoted him to support his argument in favour of the war. Pearson, who deleted a line from his speech expressing the Temple-type hope that "the bombs may cease to fall," said he hoped that discussion, negotiation, and agreement, "the processes in which FDR, the captain of Campobello so passionately believed and skilfully practiced...may soon replace the fighting and killing."

Johnson countered: "No man loved peace more than Franklin D. Roosevelt. It was in the marrow of his soul and I never saw him more grieved than when reports came from the War Department of American casualties in a major battle. But he led my nation and he led it courageously in conflict—not for war's sake, but because he knew that beyond war lay the larger hopes of man." Then the clincher: "And so it is today."

He indirectly asked for more Canadian help. "The day is coming when those men will realize that aggression against their neighbors does not pay. It will be hastened if every nation that abhors war will apply all the influence at their command to persuade the aggressors from their chosen course."

The two leaders had a blunt one-hundred-minute talk that failed to narrow their differences, but the visit ended with good cheer. After lunch in St. Andrews, New Brunswick, Johnson went into the kitchen to congratulate the women bakers on the Canadian pie—the best pie he ever had, he told them. "Mr. President, you're the most adorable man in the world," one of the women said. Pearson stepped outside to meet the press: "I have a very important announcement to make. The President had two pieces of pie for dessert."

Johnson raised a personal problem—the deer on his ranch. They were ill, and since they were from Alberta, the president asked Pearson for medical advice from Canadian authorities. "I'd sure appreciate it, Lester."[15] (Despite frequent reminders from State officials that he didn't like "Lester," that the name was Mike, LBJ almost always called him Lester.) Pearson agreed, and for weeks State and External Affairs exchanged expertise on the deer problem.

At the State Department, Canada was finally gaining more bureaucratic status. A report on bilateral affairs by former ambassadors Heeney and Merchant, which recommended Canada-U.S. problems be settled out of the public view in quiet corridors, also called for the establishment of an office of Canadian affairs in the department. Canada had previously been part of an archaic grouping with Scandinavian countries in the department's administration. The new office, under Rufus Smith, brought it only a step closer as Canada was now placed under the jurisdiction of the assistant secretary of state for European Affairs, a situation which remains today. Johnson would have liked an assistant secretary for Canadian Affairs alone but because congressional ratification was required, and because the White House was already burdened with complaints that the bureaucracy was oversized, the idea was scrapped.

Johnson's willingness, however, reflected an interest in Canada which, had the dialogue not been poisoned by Vietnam, could have produced an unusual closeness. His appetite for information was voracious, his prodigious intellectual capacity amazed the likes of Rusk and, although he started from almost nothing with respect to information on Canada, his performance demonstrated that it was not due to a lack of concern. Personal memos from his staff members informed him of all the significant developments in the neighbouring country in considerable detail. The controversial Walter Gordon budgets, for example, warranted three or four page memos from the chairman of the Council of Economic Advisers Gardner Ackley. "The economic and budget outlook all had a familiar ring," he wrote Johnson on Gordon's 1965 effort. "Only the words 'Canada' and 'Canadian' give away the fact that he was talking about Canada and not the United States!"

There was admiration among the president's economists for Ottawa's willingness in 1967 to battle inflation with higher taxes and cutbacks in government expenditure. Finance Minister Mitchell Sharp and Canadian politicians generally were more impressive than congressional counterparts in dealing with the problem, economist Arthur Okun told Johnson:

"While Canadians haven't earned a perfect score for managing fiscal policy, they deserve credit for their willingness to raise taxes when necessary. Of course, the parliamentary system makes a difference: once the cabinet decides to raise taxes, there is no serious problem of legislative resistance. But political attitudes also seem to be more enlightened: the Canadians apparently recognize that tax medicine may be a necessary antidote to the poison of inflation and tight money."

The White House wasn't impressed, however, with Canadian economic policy as it affected American banking. Pearson's resistance to Citibank of New York's bid to control the small Canadian Mercantile Bank touched off one of the sharpest quarrels of the Johnson-Pearson period. After Citibank's James Rockefeller ignored Ottawa warnings and acquired Mercantile, the Liberals brought in legislation calling for Citibank to sell at least 75 percent of its shares in Mercantile to Canadians. The action sparked strong-arm tactics by Rockefeller and the State Department to prevent the move. After what Pearson termed almost offensive representations from officials, Rockefeller visited him personally and was told there would be no change in policy. Walton Butterworth, still the American ambassador and still one of Canada's least favourite people, entered the fray, firing off one of the toughest diplomatic notes Ottawa had received. His message was straightforward—either back down or face retaliation. "For its part," the note stipulated, "USA Govt. continues to hold view that it is not, repeat, not reasonable to expect that privileged position now enjoyed by Cdn. banks in USA would continue unimpaired if only USA-owned bank in Cda. is subjected to retroactive and discriminatory treatment... USA Govt. has under exam. a number of other courses of action consistent with very serious view it takes of issue."

A half-compromise, one which did not please Citibank, was reached, with Mercantile getting a temporary five-year exemption from the Canadian ownership provisions of the Bank Act.

With President Johnson, Pearson had to get used to the heavy-fisted attempts to push Ottawa into subservience. Another clash came over Canada's move toward a bilateral air agreement with the Soviet Union, which would allow Soviet airlines to make stops in Newfoundland on the way to Cuba. Johnson sent Averell Harriman, the renowned diplomat, to Ottawa to tell Paul Martin and Jack Pickersgill that the United States would not tolerate such an agreement. The Harriman message, delivered in a Chateau Laurier suite, was so stern and uncompromising that it disgusted Pickersgill. "That sounds to me," he shot back, "like the type of message that goes from Moscow to its eastern satellites!" Harriman courteously explained that the words used were not his own. He had been ordered to use them by the White House.[16]

Even American journalists got in on the shoving, or the attempted shoving, of Canada. After the Canadian move to recognize the People's Republic of China, ambassador Ed Ritchie was startled at receiving a stinging telephone rebuke from columnist Joseph Alsop. "What are you doing crawling on your bellies to Peking?" Alsop demanded. "It will get you nowhere." Ritchie told him that his own government would be the judge of that.

In Canada's centennial year, an unhappy one for bilateral relations, Ritchie got the cocktail party treatment from Rusk, who unloaded on him at a Nepalese reception. The relationship was headed toward more trouble, Rusk said hotly. On the secretary's order, a meeting was called to air the grievances. A wave of anti-Americanism had hit Canada, Rusk complained. Canada was acting like a neutral power on the International Control Commission in Vietnam. The United States was "shaken," he said, by indications that a U.N. proposal for a bombing halt in Vietnam with nothing in return for Washington would be supported by Canada. Canadian officials were not backing the president's foreign policy speeches the way they should. Rusk continued. Canadian complaints that they were not being consulted on major questions were inaccurate. Ritchie fought off the barrage as best he could but noted in a memo to Martin that the meeting had been essentially a one-man show — Rusk's.[17]

In the less-than-promising climate, Johnson and Pearson met for the last time during the president's whirlwind, disinterested tour of Expo '67. Johnson had promised to go, but kept putting it off. Ottawa badgered him with little success. Rostow complained to Rufus Smith, saying Johnson had more important things to do. "Why does he have to go at all?" Because, said Smith, he has made a commitment to the Government of Canada and it's an important commitment. Rumours kept flying about a possible quickie trip and finally on May 24, Smith was told by the White House that Johnson would likely be going to Ottawa the very next day. Smith, the man responsible for all the preparations, said it was crazy to think that a presidential visit could be arranged on such short notice. "You don't know this President," he was told.[18]

Smith had invited ambassador Ritchie to dinner that evening. Finally, getting confirmation in the early evening that the visit was on, he phoned home to say that he would be a little late because of some last minute business. The Ritchies and Mrs. Smith went ahead with the meal. Smith finally arrived at 10:30 P.M. whereupon he casually dropped the news to Ritchie that the president would be going to Canada in the morning. The ambassador immediately telephoned Pearson, who had heard only that the visit was a possibility.

Hastily prepared, the visit was just as hastily executed. At the flag-raising ceremony officially declaring U.S. day at the American pavilion, a star-spangled banner was hoisted with about ten missing stars. Somehow, a large hole had been made in it. As hundreds of dignitaries along with the president and the prime minister looked on in embarrassment, the forty-star flag was lowered and a new one raised. With war demonstrators plaguing him, shouting "hey, hey, LBJ, how many kids did you kill today?" and other slogans, the ill-prepared Johnson stumbled through his speech. Montreal mayor Jean Drapeau was pronounced "Drape-O" and Expo commissioner Pierre Dupuy became "Doo-Pee."

The president rushed through the American pavilion without pausing for the obligatory words of high praise for the exhibits. He flew to Pearson's cottage at Harrington Lake, telling Pearson that if he withdrew the United States from the war it would create domestic tumult worse than in the McCarthy era. After his helicopter tore down a few tree branches on landing at the cottage, he stepped out and told Pearson: "I hope I didn't tear up your trees."

The talks featured Vietnam again. Pearson pushed Johnson to stop the bombing unilaterally, but the president said that if he did that, the Communists would just go on killing "our boys." He was polite to the prime minister in the response which was made in private. But when they rejoined the other officials, he vigorously denounced the idea. Pearson then suggested that the United States stop all fighting and allow the pope or the U.N. secretary-general to try and set up peace talks. That was rejected also and the day left Pearson depressed about prospects for the war and prospects for Lyndon Johnson.

He noticed that the president had "an intense human emotionalism about the conflict." This "does him credit as a man," Pearson wrote, "but could be a great handicap in dealing with international political strategy. He is emotional and warm but tough and obstinate. He seemed to take an intense satisfaction in the steps taken...to ensure that the bombing was so directed as to do the minimum damage to civilians: spare the people even if it meant sacrificing some effectiveness and planes. This is highly laudable but has helped hardly at all in reducing criticism of the bombing as cruel and heartless. All it has meant is that the Americans are getting the worst of both worlds. The President won't stop bombing but he wants it to be humane bombing."

He was concerned about whether the president was able to make independent decisions: "I wonder whether he really has control over these matters or whether—to keep the military from going full speed ahead and damn the torpedoes from China or anywhere else—he has decided not to interfere in any of their existing military tactics."

In the spring of 1968, three weeks before Pearson would step down as prime minister, Johnson shocked the country by announcing that he was going to step down as well. With the president's announcement came some long-awaited good news for the prime minister. Johnson also revealed that, in an attempt to stop the war, he was calling for a halt to all bombing north of the twenty-ninth parallel.

Pearson wrote a farewell letter to him. It contained both commiseration and congratulation.

CHAPTER FOURTEEN

Nixon and Trudeau: Ending Something Special

A WANDERING, PART-TIME lawyer in the 1950s, Pierre Trudeau, seeking to educate himself, travelled to China and the Soviet Union to talk to their peoples. To American authorities of the time, a time of McCarthyist, anti-communist hysteria, this was perverse behaviour. This was mixing with communists and did not the young man realize that the communist hordes were bent on world conquest, that the dominoes were starting to fall, that these people were repressive and evil? It may have been fine for Americans of the time to repress their own people by forcing blacks to the backs of the buses, by barring them from white restaurants, white washrooms, white voting booths. But did not Pierre Trudeau understand the true nature of the enemy?

For his travelling sins, the wealthy, young, well-bred Trudeau was barred from entering the United States. In the early 1960s, when he became politically active, it was not surprising then that his attitude toward the country was not overburdened with love and respect. Although a Liberal, he sided with the anti-Americanism of John Diefenbaker on nuclear weapons and shared the Tory leader's suspicions that the White House plotted his government's downfall. In the Canada-U.S. relationship, he did not find too much that was special.

By 1968, when he became prime minister, the banning experience was further behind him and he could admire some of the progress Washington had made on civil rights in recent years. His contrariness had softened somewhat but a detachment remained. His attitude toward the United States was that of a distant pragmatist. He understood and was sensitive to the overwhelming power of the neighbour and appreciated the restrictions it placed on his elbow room. But it was imperative for him that the Canadian sense of identity endure, and if possible, strengthen.

In respect to U.S. relations the situation Trudeau inherited in 1968 was as ominous as any prime minister faced in the century. He inherited eight years of strained and frequently acrimonious relations between the countries and between the presidents and the prime ministers themselves. He inherited a nationalistic storm over U.S. economic domination which demanded that he confront the White House. He inherited the continuing Vietnam War with its corrosive effect on the bilateral climate. He inherited a situation which would see the United States, already emotionally torn over the war, hurled into a series of other crises—balance of payments, Watergate, OPEC—crises which would push Canadian issues further into the realm of the abstract. Lastly, Trudeau inherited Richard Nixon, an antagonistic opposite.

Trudeau was a Harvard man, an intellectual, an internationalist, an athletic, cultured man with a playboy aspect. For John Kennedy he would have been splendid—shining intellect matching shining intellect, *savoir vivre* matching *savoir vivre*. But it was Trudeau's misfortune to face a streak of incompatibles and near-incompatibles—LBJ, Nixon, Ford, Carter, Reagan. Among them Nixon held out the most potential for disaster because not only were he and Trudeau a dreadful blend of personalities but, as in the case of Diefenbaker and Kennedy, their personality differences converged with issue differences.

Luckily there was one thing Trudeau and Nixon had in common. It was a proclivity to be direct, realistic, blunt in appraising the Canada-U.S. relationship. What each saw was a situation in which the gushing bilateral rhetoric of the past had created overblown expectations. What they decided was that rhetoric and expectations should be wiped away. They decided, in effect, that the countries could become more distant friends, that it might be in the best interest of each to start liking one another less. Disagreeable acquaintances that Trudeau and Nixon were, they were able to agree to disagree. It was about the only thing on which they concurred, but it was a non-accord of significance.

Of significance also was a trait in the Canadian prime minister few would have expected. The early images pictured him as gamesome, unconventional, nervy, a man who didn't suffer fools gladly. When he went to the White House for the first time a pretty newswoman asked, "When are you going to slide down a bannister or stand on your head?" But with the presidents of the United States, Trudeau was usually the opposite of the pictures. He was respectful, orthodox, pro forma. Although it was evident that, had he wished, he could have run cerebral circles around Ford and particularly Reagan, one-upmanship was not a game Trudeau frequently played with presidents. "One thing about Trudeau," said Don Jamieson, "he's not contemptuous of ordinary mortals." With Indira Gandhi, he once had to get testy. She had a habit of staking out an overly partisan position in negotiations and waiting in dead silence, the strategy being that the other side would tend to be more accommodating for want of something to say. Well aware of the tactic, Trudeau let her state her case and chose not to respond. The duel of silence lasted five minutes, Gandhi impatiently waiting for the prime minister to talk. Finally it was Gandhi who said something.[1] But she was not a U.S. president. With them, the key word for Trudeau in negotiations, although Reagan would put great strain on his patience, was respect, no matter what the personal feelings. In keeping, there was in Trudeau, unlike Pearson at Temple University and Diefenbaker everywhere, a great reticence to publicly criticize a president's foreign policy. Trudeau chose most often the quiet, diplomatic channel. It was a policy of non-escalation and in the Nixon years, it was needed.

For his first nine months in office, Trudeau dealt with the outgoing, lame-duck Johnson administration. To say he dealt with it is perhaps an overstatement because the contacts were minimal. "We got the impression Trudeau didn't want to have anything to do with us," said Dean Rusk. "The attitude was hell, those guys are on the way out anyway."

While those guys moved out, Trudeau set in motion a re-examination of Canadian foreign policy from which emerged a new internationalism. Increased foreign aid, closer contacts with the Soviet Union and Latin America, recognition of communist China, and a relaxation of military commitments to NATO: they were the harbingers of his third option—the move toward less reliance on the United States.

With Washington, the first major issue facing Trudeau was the American decision to deploy an anti-ballistic missile system. The

ABMs, defensive missiles designed to knock out incoming Soviet rockets, captured Canadian concern because the Soviet missiles would enter the United States via Canada. The explosions caused by the ABMs could conceivably take place over Canadian cities. Ottawa had not been consulted to any meaningful degree on the move to build the system. "We were notified of the decision," said Trudeau two months after Nixon came to power, "but there was no consideration in the sense that we might have been in a position to change the decision." NDP leader Tommy Douglas was moved to protest that Canada was again being treated like "a hunk of geography." American Defense Secretary Melvin Laird argued that the Pentagon briefed Ottawa officials in 1967 but acknowledged that Canadian objections may not have been meaningful. "In other words," said the irrepressible Senator William Fulbright, "If they don't like it, they can lump it."

The ABM problem topped a broad agenda of bilateral questions when Trudeau visited Nixon on a wet March 24, 1969. Briefing documents for Nixon prepared by the State Department informed the president that Trudeau was "worried about what is happening in the major cities of the United States because of the potential spill-over effect into Canada." Nixon was provided with a quotation from the prime minister saying "...in my scale of values, I am perhaps less worried now about what might happen over the Berlin Wall than what might happen in Chicago, New York and perhaps in our own great cities in Canada." Nixon was advised simply to respond to Trudeau's concerns by giving "a candid, realistic acknowledgement of the seriousness and urgency of these problems."

The president would later slap a huge tariff on Canadian imports but in 1969 he was instructed to say that "we wish to increase and further liberalize trade with Canada...we take a dim view of the tendency to move toward quotas and other methods [of protectionism]." Nixon would later forget but he was also told in 1969 that "Canada is also our largest trading partner."

On the 1965 auto pact, there was a glowing assessment of the benefits derived by Canada and a mistakenly optimistic forecast. "We believe the Canadian industry is now able to stand alone and will continue to grow and prosper. We believe there have also been economic benefits for the U.S. but they are more difficult to identify because of the much larger size of our industry and our market compared with that of Canada."[2]

Trudeau was the first foreign leader to be greeted by the new president, Canada again getting the honour, and on the first day, meeting his first president, Trudeau was reserved and timid, not daring to follow the advice of the Toronto *Star's* Stephen Clarkson: "Pierre baby, you've got to sock it to him. Drop the passive I'm here to learn pose and come on talking. You've got two days to penetrate those Republican gray cells with a single, simple message. 'Canada thinks differently. Therefore Canada is different.'"

Trudeau had to wear an identity pin with a number on it. "Can you imagine De Gaulle putting up with that?" a newsman cracked. While a tanned, confident Nixon trotted out all the right colloquialisms in a four-minute introduction, a pale, unrelaxed prime minister read fawningly from a script, emphasizing how he was looking forward to receiving "the information and the wisdom that you will want to impart upon me in your talks."

Senator Fulbright, who couldn't imagine Canada "becoming powerful enough to become unfriendly," waved a forefinger at the prime minister at a follow-up reception at the State Department. "All the wise men in the country aren't here in the State Department," he said. "Come over and see us on Capitol Hill. We know a lot about ABMs over there." At a boring White House dinner featuring Robert Goulet, a Canada-U.S. hybrid, Trudeau threw out some rare praise for Richard Nixon, calling him an honest man. "We are the kind of friends who do tell the truth to each other. We told the truth this morning and we will in the future." Days later in the Commons, he said Nixon was a "warm and understanding friend of Canada, a man with whom I shall be able to speak on behalf of Canadians in a frank yet genial fashion."

On the second day of the summit, Trudeau became Trudeau—self-contained, epigrammatic, pungent, philosophical, dashing. "At times in our history," he said at the National Press Building, "we have paused to wonder whether your friendly invitations to 'come and stay a while' have not been aimed at Canada as a political unit rather than at Canadians as individuals." He alluded to article IV of the 1781 American Articles of Confederation which was an exclusive invitation to Canada to join the Union. Any other territories would have to obtain the agreement of nine of the original states to become a member. All Canada had to do, the article said, was say yes. "So," said the prime minister in a deft touch, "we have always had a favoured position."

The reputed wit was on display when he was asked when De Gaulle, who had stunned Canada with *vive le Québec libre,* was returning for a visit. "I believe you have invited him to visit your country," Trudeau said. "We will see what he does if he goes to Louisiana and then we will report."

But the line to be remembered from the press-club speech was the elephant analogy. "Living next to you is in some ways like sleeping with an elephant: No matter how friendly and even-tempered the beast, one is affected by every twitch and grunt."

A newspaper cartoonist took the comparison a step further, making it an elephant and a mouse and much to the dismay of Ivan Head, the author of the Trudeau line, the cartoonist's exaggerated version is the one that has lived.

Head, Trudeau's foreign policy advisor, came to overshadow External Affairs Minister Mitchell Sharp on American policy the way Henry Kissinger overshadowed Secretary of State William Rogers on all foreign policy. Unlike some other people in External, Sharp reacted nobly to Head's ascendance. Sharp's role was to deal with Rogers. "You never kidded yourself," said ambassador Ed Ritchie, "that Rogers was going to change the world." Head bargained with Kissinger and when the president and the prime minister sat down, they were usually the only two other people in the room. They didn't interject often because in Trudeau and Nixon, they had two pros.

Canadian officials wondered from the beginning if Nixon, as Sharp put it, "had any principles" but one thing they didn't doubt was the man's ability. He was well briefed, crafty, and extraordinarily bright. He didn't have Carter's mastery of detail but was more incisive and better schooled in foreign policy. He didn't have Ford's degree of good common sense but dominated him in insight. He towered over Reagan in depth, perspicacity, and knowledge.

In the first summit Nixon was ingratiating to Trudeau and his White House demonstrated a courtly deference. What impressed Head and Kissinger at this and future meetings was the skill with which the two men camouflaged any personal animosities. "It cannot be said," Kissinger remarked with considerable understatement, "that Trudeau and Nixon were ideally suited for one another." However, "when they were together Trudeau treated Nixon without any hint of condescension and Nixon accorded Trudeau both respect and attention. They worked together without visible strain. They settled the issues before them and did not revert to their less charitable comments until each was back in his own capital."[3]

On the first visit, although both men spoke of the wonderful rapport established, they didn't settle many issues. Nixon gave Trudeau more information on how the ABM system could impact on Canada but Trudeau did not pose a stiff challenge on the issue, believing it would be fruitless. With the pragmatism that marked his relations with Washington, the prime minister told the Commons in May: "We are not enthusiastic about the system but this is a defense system being built in another country.... It is not likely that any moral judgment we enunciate will have a great deal of effect on the United States position.... If the Canadian Government had power to make decisions in this area I think we would suggest that the ABM system should not be proceeded with."

But had Trudeau lodged a vociferous protest on the ABM in the first meeting, would it have affected events in the fall? In September, again without prior consultation with Ottawa, the Nixon Administration announced that a one-megaton nuclear device would be exploded near Canada in a 4,000-foot hole on the Aleutian Island of Amchitka. Radioactivity could vent, so the scientists said, and spread over Canada. Worse, an earthquake or tidal wave was possible from the test.

The Canadian protestations were vehement, from the government, from the media, from the population. Insane risk, the newspapers cried. Thousands of students marched and at the British Columbia border, booed American cars. But the president didn't listen. The test went ahead and fortunately for Canadians and for relations with the United States, harmful side-effects did not result.

Sandwiched between the ABM and Amchitka episodes was a ceremonial meeting of the president and the prime minister in Massena, New York, and Montreal to mark the tenth anniversary of the St. Lawrence Seaway. The occasion did not include discussion of substantive issues but Nixon marred it nonetheless by absent-mindedness. Trudeau at the time was one of the world's most celebrated and eligible bachelors. As he looked on in amazement in Massena, Nixon, throwing out obligatory bilateral praises, said with great sincerity that he particularly wanted to thank "the Prime Minister and his lovely wife." Trudeau appeared on the podium and, as nimbly as possible, explained that he wasn't married.

It was another example of the slights and oversights which all Canadian prime ministers had to get used to in their dealings with the Oval Office. The ignorance of Canadian issues and the ignorance about Canadian people was particularly prevalent in a new president's first year and it particularly bothered Head, who found that as each new president entered office, the information process had to start from ground zero. In the Canadian system, the top political figures changed with elections but the bureaucratic forces remained essentially intact, meaning there was some degree of continuity. In Washington a change in government meant a change in thousands of the major public service positions. By 1981, the Trudeau government had viewed five such changeovers, the degree of frustration varying with each.

But while the prime minister's office had a right to be irritated with some of the developments in the early Nixon years, so too was the White House understandably affronted by some of the Trudeau thrusts. The threat to withdraw from NATO was a sore point. The eventual major reduction in the Canadian forces commitment to the organization was a symbolic setback. The ease with which draft dodgers and deserters spilled into Canada irritated Nixon. Trudeau's push for sovereignty in the Arctic was unwelcome as was his adoption of the Diefenbaker script in two areas: first, the removal of virtually all nuclear armaments from Canadian soil, and second, the effort to redirect trade away from the United States.

After Trudeau and Nixon's first two years, it was apparent that neither side was looking to do favours for the other, that good-neighbour policies were nostalgia, that the chemistry was wrong.

Nonetheless Canadians were not prepared for August 15, 1971. Moving to arrest a balance of payments crisis, Nixon startled the economic world by moving the United States off the gold standard and imposing a 10 percent across-the-board import surcharge. Historically, Canada had come to expect immunity or partial immunity from such sweeping trade strokes. Historically, ample advance consultation would preceed such a bold bilateral move. This time, there was neither. Canada was the largest trading partner of the United States. Close to 70 percent of Canadian exports went to Americans. The import surcharge stood to hurt Canadian interests more than those of any other country. Yet Canada, a member of the family, was not even forewarned, much less exempted.

Trudeau and Finance Minister Edgar Benson were out of the

country, leaving the attack to the lead of Mitchell Sharp. In the American embassy, Rufus Smith fired off a telegram to the secretary of state. "Subject: President's Economic Program: GOC to ask exemption from import surcharge." Canadians were hot and on their way to the capital, the telegram said. The reason? "Canada's floating exchange rate, determined only by market forces cannot be labelled 'unfair'. Neither, Sharp said, can GOC trade policy provoke complaint, since Canada raises no obstructions to US exports."

A delegation led by Benson arrived in Washington and was told to go home. Trudeau, indignant, grouched before a nation-wide TV audience that the American trade problems were not Canada's, that the surcharge would cost the country thousands of jobs. With estimates saying Canada would lose $300 million in export sales, he developed an $80 million patchwork program to help companies maintain existing employment levels. "It was a very big blow," Sharp recalled. "About as unhappy a period [with the Americans] as we've had."[4]

A month after his announcement, Nixon stung Canadians further at a press conference in Washington. "This is a time for our friends around the world—and they are all competitors—to build a new system with which we can live so that we don't have another crisis in a year. With regard to the Japanese incidentally, I think I can best summarize our dilemma in this way: After the Japanese were here I found that, both from the information they gave and the information we had ourselves, that Japan is our biggest customer in the world."

The error was egregious. Japan ranked nowhere near Canada as best customer to the United States. American sales to Canada exceeded sales to Japan, West Germany, and Britain combined. But making the mistake far worse was the timing. It was now apparent that Nixon made his major trade policy statement without even knowing the volume of trading with Canada, or how seriously his measure would impact in Canada. The press conference statement amounted to "total ignorance," said Head. "It was just stupidity. He didn't know."

Trudeau was hot. "When the Americans look at what they're doing, they say: 'well, you know, we're doing this to the Japanese and we're doing this to the Europeans,' but they don't seem to realize what they are doing to Canadians. If they do realize what they're doing and if it becomes apparent that they just want us to be sellers of natural resources to them and buyers of their manufactured products...we will have to reassess fundamentally our relations with them — trading, political and otherwise."

The special relationship with the United States, declared Conservative leader Robert Stanfield, was past history. "Far from being given special consideration it is obvious now that Canada is out in the cold as far as the special privileged relationship...is concerned."

Declaring the Nixon people insensitive and uninformed, Sharp announced in a New York speech that the government was undertaking a fundamental review of economic policies because of the U.S. actions.

In Washington, the Canadian outcry was viewed with composure. "The assumption here," remembered Rufus Smith, "was that it [surcharge] wouldn't have much effect in Canada. And our assumption was correct....It was something of a shock in the Canadian Government more so than anywhere else."[5] Smith and the other officials at the American embassy had not been asked for prior information by the White House on the possible effect on Canada of the surcharge or the anticipated reaction. They weren't informed of the measure until the day it was announced. They were disappointed that it came on a day when the prime minister was out of the country. "Had Trudeau been in Ottawa," said Smith, "the Government's reaction wouldn't have been as sharp."

Briefing papers given to Nixon a few months after his announcement alleged that the Canadian reaction was excessive. "As Canadians realized that no exemption was forthcoming, a wave of shock and uncertainty took hold. In a round of speeches in September and October, high Canadian officials did rather little to explain why the U.S. had to redress its balance of payments and the consequent need for cooperation, but played up the theme that the U.S. was treating Canada unfairly."[6]

As an indication of why concern should be limited, the memos told Nixon that the Canadian government estimated job losses owing to the surcharge at up to 90,000 for one year. "It has recently revised its estimate to about half that figure."

But a rather prescient warning for the president was included. The Trudeau government was not to establish the Foreign Investment Review Agency for more than a year. The Nixon briefers told him it was on the way. "A new and more restrictive policy may take the form of screening new foreign investments, particularly those involving 'takeovers' of Canadian firms."

A Trudeau-Nixon meeting had been scheduled for the spring of 1972 but events demanded an earlier summit. Canadians, the prime minister said, wanted to know, a few things: "Have the Americans stopped loving us? What are they going to do? Are they going to gobble us up? Are they going to leave us out in the cold? There certainly have been a lack of reassurances as to the American disposition toward Canada, and I think this is particularly accentuated since mid-August when President Nixon announced his new economic policy."

A lack of reassurances about the Canadian disposition to the Americans existed as well. One of Nixon's major problems with Trudeau was his feeling that the prime minister was soft on communism. Trudeau fortified the impression in Moscow during his 1971 trip to the Soviet Union. Sidestepping tact, the prime minister declared: "Canada has increasingly found it important to diversify its channels of communication because of the overpowering presence of the United States of America, and that is reflected in a growing consciousness among Canadians of the danger [to] our national identity from a cultural, economic and perhaps even military point of view." The words amounted to an indirect criticism of the United States by its supposed best friend in the land of America's worst enemy.

Nixon demonstrated his considerable hostility to the prime minister in this period in preparing his plans to open a dialogue with communist China—a development which would be a landmark achievement of his administration. In some ways the Canadian recognition of China helped open the door for the Nixon initiative. Several countries followed the Canadian lead, making a United States move more palatable to more people. Ottawa also provided important early information to the White House on the climate of opinion of the Chinese leadership to the possibility of a breakthrough. But Nixon, suspected by some Ottawa officials as being annoyed with the idea of Trudeau sharing in any credit, made certain the Canadian role did not broaden. Kissinger acted as Nixon's secret go-between in setting the plans for the Peking trip but a third party intermediary was also required. Choose anyone you want, the president told Kissinger, with one exception—Pierre Trudeau.

When the two leaders met in Washington on December 7, Trudeau, following discussions of multilateral topics, explained the ramifications of the import surcharge on Canada. He wondered if the new protectionism was a signal that the Americans wanted a permanent surplus trade balance with Canada so that they could always export capital to Canada. The details on the table, Nixon "just about dropped his upper plate," said Ivan Head who attended the meeting. "He'd never seen the issue in those terms."

His response to the capital export question, as Trudeau remembered it: "No. We, the Americans, we were in that position before the First World War. We depended on European capital and we wanted to free ourselves of that dependence, and we understand perfectly that Canadians are in the same position, and we will do nothing to prevent them from not feeling in any way that they are a colony of the United States."

Trudeau and Head were almost euphoric. "This to me was a fantastically new statement in the mouth of the President of the United States," Trudeau declared, "and it was said with utmost simplicity and not at all in a grudging way...."

"He said, 'Just take what you want [of our capital], and if we can help, we will. If you want less, take less.'

"For Canadians, I think this is the ideal position."

Trudeau placed a grand interpretation on the statement, viewing it as a bestowal of economic freedom on Canada, a grant of maneuverability without fear of reprisal from Washington. Nixon, presaging an announcement that he would make in a few months, was saying the countries should feel free to move further apart, to become more independent. Throughout the century, the presidents had pulled in the opposite direction—toward further integration. The Nixon reversal was therefore extraordinary to Trudeau, even if the rhetoric amounted to more than the reality.

A more immediate concern for Trudeau was the 10 percent surcharge. While he and Nixon talked, high government officials from both sides, including John Connally and Simon Reisman, the Canadian deputy finance minister, engaged nearby in crackling verbal combat. Connally, in Rufus Smith's description, was Canada's "bête noire." To Canadians, including many of the officials who dealt with him, he typified the horn-headed, ugly American. At the meeting, his uncompromising stance on the surtax lit tempers. "The blood in there was knee-deep," said Head. Reisman, not renowned for being low key, pressed the Canadian side with vigour. "It was a case of saying, 'Mr. Secretary, I think you haven't got the whole picture'... We simply had to tell them what the facts were and in a situation of that kind, that's tough." But unlike his colleagues, Reisman was the type who could respect Connally. Equally arrogant, equally obstinate, they became friends after the boardroom battles and went fishing together.[7]

At their meeting, the surcharge clash was inconclusive and the Canadians went away unsatisfied. But in the meeting of the big two, Nixon informed Trudeau that he was planning a phase-out of the measure and assured him that Canada wouldn't have to suffer for long. The catch was that it couldn't be announced yet. Trudeau and Head appeared before the press overjoyed but couldn't explain the full reason. They touted the part about the assurance of economic independence but it was not such a big seller, being effectively zapped by NDP leader David Lewis. "I suggest it is humiliating for Canada and Canadians that the leaders of their country should have to go to Washington to be reassured about Canada's independence, to be reassured by the President of the United States that he does not intend to treat us like a colony... I say to the Prime Minister that Canadians do not need assurance from the President... regarding the independence of Canada. They need to be assured by this government that it will not continue to sell Canada out to the multinational corporations and so destroy our independence."

Nixon gave no indication to the media that anything unusual had occurred. His big event with the press was the dispensing of presidential pens in the Oval Office. Showing a rare bit of wit, he aimed a barb at the hyper-sensitivity of Canadians. "Did I get everybody? I want to make sure I have so that I don't discriminate against our neighbor to the north. You will all get the Presidential pen. But with it, you can write anything you want."

Trudeau's excitement with the results of the December visit did not mean bilateral relations had suddenly become harmonious. On the contrary the list of disagreements grew. Ottawa was blocking the U.S. wish to have oil from Prudhoe Bay, Alaska, transported down the coast by tanker. Washington was angering the Canadian government with the proposal to establish the Domestic International Sales Corporation. Canada was holding back on uranium sales to its neighbour. There were problems with defence production sharing arrangements, the auto pact, U.S. policy in Vietnam and Trudeau's accommodation of the Soviets.

As his April 1972 state visit to Ottawa approached, Nixon was unusually blunt about the prospects. "I would have to say quite candidly," he told a press conference, "that we have had very little success to date in our negotiations with our Canadian friends, which shows, incidentally, that sometimes you have more problems negotiating with your friends than you do with your adversaries.... We will find that we have some very basic disagreements probably after the meeting as before."

Trudeau and Head anxiously awaited the visit, however, because Nixon had agreed to state publicly what he had told them privately regarding Canada's economic independence. The word leaked in Ottawa about a pending watershed event in Canada-U.S. relations, but in Washington, where the president and the media were preoccupied with a new offensive in South Vietnam, there was barely a mention of relations with Canada. Fear of mass protests over the war led to a cancellation of the Toronto leg of Nixon's visit. Although economic matters were high on the agenda, Treasury Secretary Connally decided against joining the party. Trudeau had suggested he would not be welcome. "With friends like Secretary Connally," the prime minister said, "who needs enemies?"

Nixon arrived in Ottawa April 13, 1972 in an evening rain. On the way to the podium to say some words of welcome, he took a piece of paper from his pocket and glanced at it briefly. Without notes, he then spoke flawlessly for five minutes, Mitchell Sharp looking on with admiration at such ability. At the governor-general's mansion the same evening, he was expected to say only a couple of minutes worth of post-dinner pulp. But Nixon riveted his audience for twenty minutes. Again no notes. Again not a misplaced word. "A brilliant performance," said Sharp. "Remarkable," remembered Rufus Smith. "I've seldom seen anyone hold the audience in the palm of his hand like Nixon did in that speech in Ottawa. It wasn't just platitudes. It was remarkable."

In his talk, Nixon recalled a time in 1957 when, as vice-president, he had visited Picton, Ontario. A local bartender thought he recognized the face and bet someone that he was the vice-president. On his way out, Nixon heard the bartender, five dollars richer, say: "Nixon doesn't look nearly as bad in person as he does in his pictures." Perhaps recalling the story because of the damage he felt that television did to his career, the president told the Ottawa audience that everyone looks better in real life than in pictures.

Sharp remembered well the time when he sat next to Nixon at a dinner for NATO foreign ministers in Washington. The president was about to give a major speech and Sharp, realizing how difficult Nixon found small talk, scratched his head for aimless chit-chat. Finally he began telling him about Gordon Sinclair's celebrated radio broadcast heaping praise on the Americans. Nixon reacted as though he hadn't heard of it but took a place-card on the table and wrote a note of thanks to Sinclair. "The perfect thing for a politician to do," said Sharp. The president then stood, said "I'm not going to say very much tonight," and delivered a perfect full-length foreign policy speech, without a script, without a scrap of paper. "I don't think there is any politician in this country who could match that," said Sharp.[8]

The president surprised most Canadian onlookers in Ottawa with his sense of humour. He wasn't supposed to have one. He was supposed to be a man whose spirit was only one colour — dark.

But the top prize for wit and repartee undoubtedly belonged to his secretary of state. When Watergate was in full storm, Kissinger shared a dinner table with Trudeau and Gérard Pelletier, cabinet member and friend. President Nixon was speaking, throwing out some obligatory mush about the behind-the-scenes workers who had made some important agreement possible. The analogy was to builders. Some of the background people, said Nixon, could be compared to carpenters as they had set the framework. Some were the electricians for providing the spark. "Yes," said Kissinger in an aside to Trudeau, "and we're the plumbers."

The main act of the April summit, the Nixon speech, was the most extraordinary address of a president in Canada. The presidents were not always trite and colloquial in Canada. Franklin Roosevelt committed the United States to protect Canada from invasion. Dwight Eisenhower gave a bare-knuckle defence of the American position on several bilateral sore points. John Kennedy did things his way, stomping Diefenbaker into the ground. But Richard Nixon took all the clothes off the bilateral relationship and held it up under a spotlight for inspection. Since Warren Harding's first eloquent oration in Vancouver in 1923, forty-nine years of clichés had gathered, virtually unchallenged, even when the circumstances called for challenge. Even through the bad times of Kennedy-Diefenbaker and Johnson-

Pearson, the leaders paid lip service during their visits to the special relationship. Now Nixon, while still laudatory in part, was telling Canadians that most of what the other presidents said was erroneous, that the special nature of the relationship was essentially rhetoric, that it was time to recognize a new reality.

In discussing that relationship today, I wish to do so in a way that has not always been customary when leaders of our two countries have met. Through the years our speeches on such occasions have often centered on the decades of unbroken friendship we have enjoyed and our four thousand miles of unfortified frontier. In focusing on our peaceful borders and our peaceful history, they have tended to gloss over the fact that there are real problems between us. They have tended to create the false impression that our countries are essentially alike. It is time for Canadians and Americans to move beyond the sentimental rhetoric of the past. It is time for us to recognize that we have very separate identities; that we have significant differences; and that nobody's interests are furthered when these realities are obscured.

Our peaceful borders and our peaceful history are important symbols, to be sure. What they symbolize, however, is the spirit of respect and restraint which allows us to cooperate despite our differences in ways which help us both. American policy toward Canada is rooted in that spirit. Our policy toward Canada reflects the new approach we are taking in all our foreign relations, an approach which has been called the Nixon Doctrine. The doctrine rests on the premise that mature partners must have autonomous independent policies; each nation must define the nature of its own interests; each nation must decide the requirements of its own security; each nation must determine the path of its own progress. What we seek is a policy which enables us to share international responsibilities in a spirit of international partnership. We believe that the spirit of partnership is strongest when partners are self-reliant. For among nations, as within nations, the soundest unity is that which respects diversity, and the strongest cohesion is that which rejects coercion....

As we continue together our common quest for a better world order, let us apply the lessons we have learned so well on this continent: that we can walk our own road in our own way without moving farther apart; that we can grow closer together without growing more alike; that peaceful competition can produce winners without producing losers; that success for some need not mean setbacks for the rest; that a rising tide will lift all our boats...

The president, as the prime minister had hoped, repeated the pledge of December on economic independence. "No self-respecting nation can or should accept the proposition that it should always be economically dependent upon any other nation. Let us recognize for once and for all that the only basis for a sound and healthy relationship between our two proud peoples is to find a pattern of economic interaction which is beneficial to both our countries and which respects Canada's right to chart its own economic course."

To laughter from the Parliamentary benches Nixon corrected a previous error. "Canada is the largest trading partner of the United States. It is very important that that be noted in Japan, too!"

The speech read as if it had been written in Canada, designed to appease the economic nationalists, designed to give the Liberal government leeway to carve out the direction it chose. Because of the interdependence of the two countries, it was usually impossible for one to make a strikingly new departure, economic or otherwise, without creating shock waves in the other, if not in the initiating country as well. In effectively calling for the closing down of the special relationship, Nixon was suggesting that Canada could climb out from under the wraps, could move in whatever direction it wanted without fear of being called traitor to a friend. If you don't want to be a satellite, the Nixon rhetoric proclaimed, don't be a satellite. Given the new freedom, the search of the Trudeau Liberals for the remainder of the decade and into the eighties would be for the alternative, for a way of shedding to whatever degree was realistic the satellite status, for a way of creating a society more distinctively Canadian.

The licence to get out from under the yoke was what Trudeau and Ivan Head, his brainy foreign affairs adviser, had sought. In fact parts of the Nixon speech were written by Head and approved for incorporation into the main draft weeks before delivery. Trudeau knew most everything Nixon would be saying. He had discussed it with Head. The White House and the prime minister's office agreed entirely on its thrust.

This unusually collaborative form of cooperation owed itself in part to the relationship Head had developed with Henry Kissinger. He could telephone Kissinger most any time and get him. It was something the Canadian ambassador couldn't do and something Mitchell Sharp didn't try often. Jealous of Head's power, ambassador Cadieux mockingly called him "The Professor" and other External Affairs career officials derided his ability. Head's strategy, one they did not wish to follow, was to make a greater effort to ingratiate Canada at the White House so that Canadian issues could gain a higher profile, so that benign neglect would be limited, so that there could be the type of cooperation that existed in Nixon's landmark speech on Canada.

On Canadian concerns, Kissinger possessed the pivotal power but for the most part he didn't have the time or inclination to deal with them. "He didn't take Canada seriously," said Dick O'Hagan, echoing the views of many. "I could understand it.... He felt, 'I'm a big league guy and I can settle big league problems.'" Canada was arguably the most important country economically and strategically to the United States but it was not a big-league problem. Kissinger backed the Canadian cause on some occasions however. He moderated the excesses of Connally. He worked to get Canadian participation in the western economic summits. And while many in the Nixon White House were prepared to treat Canadians like minions, Kissinger, a diplomat who admired the Trudeau intellect, showed respect. On the Nixon visit to Ottawa, he took the Canadian side against Bob Haldeman, the president's chief of staff and the most powerful figure next to Nixon in the executive mansion. After a gruesome gala at the National Arts Centre featuring unknowns from every region of the country, Haldeman had scheduled a meeting on the Vietnam war and other issues that dwarfed Canadian ones. The Trudeau party had scheduled a fancy buffet dinner in an adjoining salon. Haldeman, the White House tough guy, was a man who usually got his way. His cold drill-sergeant demeanor did not hide a warm heart. Once he had received a memo urging that the president be instructed to place a sympathetic phone call to the family of a Republican senator who was on death's doorstep. Seeing more political value in a later call, Haldeman scribbled on the memo: "Wait until he dies."

But as Ed Ritchie looked on in admiration, Kissinger challenged Haldeman, arguing stiffly that whether the president and the chief of staff like it or not they were guests of the Canadian prime minister and they must show respect for the host's wishes. Nixon reluctantly decided to go to the buffet and Haldeman was furious. He stood in the doorway of the salon like a storm cloud. He glared at his watch, made faces at Kissinger and, with most of the dignitaries aware of what was transpiring, motioned repeatedly that it was time to leave. "My friend isn't very happy, is he?" Kissinger said to his table guests. He repeatedly conferred with Haldeman to calm him down but with the chief of staff growing more obnoxious by the minute, Kissinger began to get anxious. "This is very serious," he said to Ivan Head. "Haldeman can make trouble for me."

Nixon, at least on the surface, appeared to be enjoying himself and his lobster. He had telephoned the prime minister on Christmas Day to congratulate him on the birth of his first son Justin and now he raised his glass and said: "Tonight we'll dispense with the formalities. I'd like to toast the future Prime Minister of Canada—Justin Trudeau." Should Justin ever become prime minister, Trudeau replied, "I hope he has the grace and skill of the President."

Charlotte Gobeil, Kissinger's Canadian date, was enjoying her champagne and with it, her conversation became uninhibited. She lashed out at Kissinger on his war policies, and noticing that his finger nails were bitten to the point of bleeding, inquired, "Why do you do that?" "If you had to send in the B-52s," replied Kissinger, "you'd be biting your nails too."

Haldeman, still fuming, had at last succeeded in getting the president to leave, and in the parking lot, Nixon was brisk with Trudeau, saying that he had done him a favour and would expect one back. Kissinger, continuing to be courteous to Canadians, followed Miss Gobeil's noisy insistence that he drive her home, only to find a nude man in her bedroom.[9]

Kissinger's considerateness toward Canada was complemented by a comprehension of the Canadian situation that was not without insight. "Canada," he wrote, "was beset by ambivalences which, while different from those of Europe, created their own complexities. It required both close economic relations with the United States and an occasional gesture of strident independence. Concretely this meant that its need for American markets was in constant tension with its temptation to impose discriminatory economic measures; its instinct in favor of common defense conflicted with the temptation to stay above the battle as a kind of international arbiter. Convinced of the necessity of cooperation, impelled by domestic imperatives toward confrontation, Canadian leaders had a narrow margin for maneuver that they utilized with extraordinary skill."[10]

Nixon had said it was in the clear interests of the United States for Canada to seek greater independence in the relationship. Now the

Trudeau government, taking advantage of the infusion of continental liberty, came forward with two bold initiatives: the third option and the Foreign Investment Review Agency. In relations with the United States, three avenues were possible: the status quo, a closer union, or a move away from dependency. In choosing the third, Trudeau wanted increased trade with western Europe and Japan, stronger diplomatic relations with countries other than the United States, and a more visible Canadian cultural identity. The question was whether a shift was viable. Diefenbaker had called for a dramatic trade shift in the late 1950s. His officials, including Simon Reisman, did a study and determined it was a non-starter—disruptive, extremely expensive, unwise. The advantages to the already established trade patterns on the continent were too great to alter. Now, fifteen years later, the same top financial mandarin looked at the idea again and concluded the same—that it was garbage. "Theatrical, mystical, idealistic.... You know, we're a north American country."[11]

In Washington the third option was not greeted with enthusiasm. Nixon had said go ahead but when Trudeau did just that, Rufus Smith, still running Canadian affairs at the State Department, found many unhappy people. The third option was viewed as retaliation for the import surcharge. "But I didn't see anything new in it," said Smith. "Diefenbaker had been saying the same thing."

As a component of the third option parcel, Trudeau established FIRA to act as a check against American investment and takeovers. "When I discovered Booth Fisheries in Newfoundland was owned by Wonder Bra," said Don Jamieson, "I began to get a little upset."[12]

FIRA, though largely ineffective, came to anger the White House more than the third option's intended trade thrust. But the low point of the Trudeau-Nixon relationship had nothing to do with Canadian economics. Nixon and his men, preoccupied with Vietnam, Watergate, and the actions of the Organization of Petroleum Exporting Countries, never got around to thinking much about or caring much about establishing a new relationship with Canada to replace Nixon's announced demise of the old special relationship. What rankled them most in their six years of dealing with the Trudeau government was the approval of a resolution in the Parliament condemning the December 1972 bombing raids in Cambodia. Kissinger thought Parliament's action reprehensible. Nixon ranted and raved about Trudeau. Not much had changed since Johnson's days in respect to Oval Office sensitivity over Canadian statements on Vietnam policy. The irony was that Trudeau, unlike some predecessors, had made a conscious effort to refrain from public criticism of American foreign policy in Vietnam and elsewhere. But if his behaviour had been considerate, there was no appreciation in the White House. When the word on the resolution, a motion that was not Trudeau's making, came in, the orders went out: Cut Canada off. For months, the doors were closed to ambassador Cadieux. Phone calls from Ottawa were not returned. The administration sent low-level officials to Canadian functions which clearly warranted top people.[13]

Oval Office anger increased when Canada announced—earlier than the president wished—withdrawal from its role in the International Commission of Control and Supervision in Vietnam. "They were trying to do all they could to create the impression they had not been defeated," said Sharp. "We knew it would be a farce in the long run." Rogers unsuccessfully put pressure on Sharp for a delay on the announcement. Annoyed, Kissinger said he would talk to Sharp. Rogers told him not to bother because the Canadians were not about to change their minds. Kissinger telephoned anyway and Sharp told him there would be no reconsideration.

It was at this time, the beginning of spring 1973, that Nixon pinned an unfortunate label on the prime minister. The president was in his office at the Executive Office Building which sits next to the White House and, with Bob Haldeman, John Ehrlichman, and John Mitchell present, was preparing to phone the prime minister on the question of the supervisory commission. "I'll take care of Trudeau," Nixon declared at one point in the taped conversation. Then, in reference to a previous action of the prime minister's, he said: "That asshole Trudeau was something else."

A tape was provided to the jury in the Watergate cover-up trial and because of the poor sound quality, a dispute occurred over what had actually been said. Haldeman lawyer Frank Strickler told Judge John Sirica: "It was the President speaking and the statement made was 'asshole Trudeau' and that's the way it should read." After more debate it was decided that the official version should include "was something else."

Pinned by reporters during a recess, Ehrlichman said of the president's remark: "I'm not aware of any problem between them. It was rather more a figure of speech." Trudeau, on the spot for a comment said that he'd been called worse things by worse people. He and Head were not surprised at Nixon's words. The president had used profanity in their company before. It was Nixon's way of trying to show that he was one of the boys.

As the Watergate scandal heated through late 1973 and 1974, contacts with the Canadian government dwindled as they did with others. Ottawa secured more hostility in the capital with the announcement that it was cutting back on oil exports to its oil-short neighbour. Additional strain came with the imposition of a special export tax on oil.

The moves infuriated many congressmen and though the Administration was less exercised, there was considerable pressure to force a change of position. Julius Katz, the deputy assistant secretary of state, put up an agreeable public front. "We cannot expect Canada to play the major role in the resolution of our oil problem," he told legislators. But in private, in dealing with Jack Austin, Trudeau's principal secretary, he was dogged and harsh. "If they think they can bully you off a position," said Austin, "they'll try."

In the final months of Richard Nixon, Trudeau had no contact with him. But as he watched the man collapse, there was a touch of compassion. "I wasn't Nixon's kind of guy," he would say later. "Nor was he mine."[14] But he was genuinely impressed with Nixon's foreign policy, saying in respect to it on the day before Nixon's resignation, that he "led his country in a direction which I thought was, by and large, good for the world." And he still thought that the Nixon pledge of more independence for Canada was marvellous. "President Nixon's policies and our bilateral relations have always been, I think, fair and just for Canada."

Following the president's resignation, the prime minister wrote a letter of sympathy to him. Nixon, who had been impressed by few things about Trudeau aside from the War Measures Act, responded warmly. Seven years and three presidents later, Pierre Trudeau would still speak highly of Richard Nixon. "The record will show that Nixon was, from the Canadian point of view, a good President."[15] Nixon remembered another prime minister more fondly. After the death of John Diefenbaker, he was one of the first contributors ($500) to a memorial fund to turn the former conservative leader's house into a Diefenbaker museum.

The Oval Office successor, Gerald Ford, became vice-president because Spiro Agnew resigned in disgrace and president because

Nixon resigned in disgrace. His ascendancy was attributable to fortune only and one of the prices was vulnerability to the charge that he was unfit for the job. Canadians, with their intellectual prime minister, quickly gathered around the conventional wisdom of Ford as light-weight. Unhappily, the former Michigan football lineman was to nourish the image. He asserted that eastern Europe was not dominated by communism. On hearing of some extraordinary statement, he made a rather extraordinary one himself: "If Abe Lincoln were alive today," said Ford, "he'd roll over in his grave." Although physically adept he managed to compound his image problems by shanking golf balls which injured spectators, by tumbling down stairways, by ram-ming his head into door frames. Cartoonists soon took to ridicule, one picturing Ford strapping on a football helmet while getting set to dive into a swimming pool.

Still, his incompatibility with Pierre Trudeau did not obstruct a friendly relationship from developing between them during Ford's two and half years in the Oval Office. Although intellectually distant, the two men had something in common—skiing, and other athletics—which gave them something to talk about besides the frequently boring bilateral spats, and something to make them feel easy in one another's company. Measured against the absence of bonds of com-monality between other presidents and prime ministers, the small link was noteworthy.

When presidents and prime ministers get along, as did Ford and Trudeau, as did Diefenbaker and Eisenhower, and King and Roose-velt, it takes the edge off controversy. With Ford and Trudeau, bilateral problems, though there and though serious, were left most often to the care of lower-level officials. The president and the prime minister managed to keep a happy face on the bilateral relationship even though the end of the special relationship was being proclaimed again—this time by Canada.

"The fact is that in both Canada and the United States," External Affairs Minister Allan MacEachen declared in 1975, "there has been a growing awareness that the special relationship no longer serves either of our best interests. What is being developed is a more mature relationship. It is one which permits us to maintain close ties, to cooperate fully on bilateral and multilateral matters, is of mutual benefit and yet leaves each country free to pursue its national interest.

"It is plain that Canada and the United States have entered on a new period of bilateral relations....Each government will have to make hard decisions in line with its own perception of the national interest—decisions with which the other may find it difficult to concur."

Ford wrote Trudeau shortly after Nixon's resignation promising to continue the "close consultation and cooperation" that was supposedly existent under Nixon. They met first in December 1974 when West German Chancellor Helmut Schmidt was also in Washington. The question as to which leader would get the plush Blair House accommodations and which would be relegated to a hotel was settled when Schmidt took Blair House. The Canadian decision to phase out oil exports to the United States was the hot topic but Trudeau immersed it, asking Ford what he would do if the shoe were on the other foot and getting no reply. Trudeau encapsulated the meeting and the casual tone he had established with Ford, telling the press, "we had a great visit. They make good coffee here."

Kissinger, still on the throne at the State Department following Nixon's demise, had the misfortune to make another trip to Ottawa. He didn't encounter Charlotte Gobeil this time but the trouble was elsewhere. Microphones left on the table at a banquet picked up his gossipy private chatter, transmitting it to reporters in another room. "What I never understood," Kissinger was caught saying, "is how he [Nixon] became a politician. He really dislikes people. He hated to meet new people." Nixon had "barely governed" during his final eighteen months, said Kissinger. He was an "artificial," "unpleasant," and "odd" man. Jacqueline Kennedy Onassis was "sexy" according to the secretary of state. "A hard woman who knows what she wants."

The embarrassment was ill-timed because Kissinger had been working behind the scenes to augment Canada's international stature. The first of the western economic summits was soon to open in France and Kissinger was lobbying to get Canada a seat. "Canada is no longer a minor partner," he said in Ottawa, "but a country which rightfully takes it place in the economic and political councils of the world." The country's presence at the summit was "crucial" he said. "We have closer consultation with Canada than with any other nation. We share more common problems and we share the need for parallel solutions on a whole range of issues." Canada was not admitted to the first summit but with the help of Ford and Kissinger became a participant in year two. The subject of intense media focus, membership was a boon to Canada's prestige.

With Ford casual and above the fray, the polemic on Canadian relations was left to ambassador William Porter who did the heavy spadework in protesting Canadian energy policy and who made an altogether inglorious exit from the lovely mansion that is the Ottawa envoy's. Common practice entails that the ambassador have a final audience with the head of state and leave quietly. With three phone calls Porter failed to get a response from Trudeau's office. Finally he chose to leave via a Saturday night on-the-record cocktail party for Canadian reporters. It was a parting-shot party, Porter condemning deteriorating Canada-U.S. relations and pinning most of the blame on Canada: gas and oil policies, FIRA, the provincial takeover of the potash industry in Saskatchewan, Ottawa legislation effectively blocking U.S.-border TV stations from obtaining Canadian advertising. To many observers, the outburst was largely unfounded, the laundry list of bilateral irritants not terribly unusual or provocative, particularly in light of the new un-special character of the Canada-U.S. relationship. "We ran the story," said Washington *Post* editor Ben Bradlee. "But I don't think most people down here have changed their perceptions of Canada. I for one don't really care if Buffalo TV stations continue to get Canadian ads. I don't use potash so nationalization doesn't bother me much; and you've raised your prices for gas and oil but then so has everybody else."

Trudeau told a buzzing Commons that Porter's views were not the views of Ford and Kissinger, that he was out of line. In Europe Kissinger, to Porter's lasting annoyance, said that he felt bilateral relations were "excellent." "My friend Kissinger noted which way the wind was blowing," Porter later recalled, "and said I had spoken without State Department clearance which of course was not true. I am not a fool." Trudeau chose not to have his farewell audience for Porter and most cabinet ministers snubbed him by refusing to show up for his farewell reception. Although MacEachen said relations were better than ever before, the State Department later endorsed Porter's remarks and an official added they had been cleared through the White House. Expecting and arguing for a reprimand for Porter from Kissinger and a demotion in his next assignment, Ottawa didn't get it. Porter was appointed ambassador to the oil-rich hot spot, Saudi Arabia.

The uproar did not uproot the Trudeau-Ford entente. Consultation and cooperation with the Ford White House remained better for Trudeau than with the other presidents he had faced and would soon face. One reason was National Security Adviser Brent Skowcroft who made a determined effort to erase a chronic Canadian complaint — lack of advance consultation with Ottawa on major developments.[16] Skowcroft set the National Security adviser record for long-distance calls to Ottawa.

In June of the American bicentennial year, four months before Ford's defeat, Trudeau and the president had a happy meeting on the Potomac, preferring to sidestep prickly bilateral matters in favour of aimless chatter. Despite Porter's outburst, it was Trudeau's view that bilateral problems at this time were not of major consequence. With Ford, who would invite the prime minister on ski trips long after his presidency ended, he wanted to relax. For the bicentennial, he presented Ford with a picture book of the great undefended Canada-U.S. border. Clichés were in abundance and for a while, it was like the old times of "special" relationship. Trudeau was introduced to the skipper of the Canadian schooner *Bluenose*. "Had the pleasure," said the skipper, "of entertaining Bryce Mackasey [Postmaster General] for two hours some months ago." "Oh," said the prime minister. "Was he able to walk off by himself?"

On the *Sequoia*, standing beside Ford and Kissinger, Trudeau waved a white handkerchief to reporters. "Surely not surrender already," someone shouted. "No," said the prime minister, raising a glass to his hosts. "It's the colour of my soul."

CHAPTER FIFTEEN

Jimmy Carter and Shattered Expectations

IN THE BACK of his long limousine, festooned with Canadian bunting, sat Don Jamieson, the portly cigar-smoking External Affairs minister of Canada. He was attending the 1977 London economic summit and waiting for his driver to take him from his hotel to 10 Downing Street. Just as the chauffeur touched the gas pedal, Jamieson heard a tap on his window and that sincere southern voice: "Can I hitch a ride?" Jamieson looked. "Jesus, it's the President!" An aide practically somersaulted into the front seat to make room for Jimmy Carter. As the limousine made its way, spectators lining the streets saw a big Georgian smile in the car of Canada.

Car pooling was not out of character for Jimmy Carter, the non-imperial president and in Canadian eyes his modest plain style was rather endearing, something Canadians didn't see often in presidents but something with which they could identify. Those were, after all, Canadian characteristics and there had rarely been a president who had shown them. The low-key, unassuming style of Jimmy Carter was one of the reasons the Canadian hopes for his presidency and for the bilateral relationship were unbounded.

He arrived at a favourable time. Watergate had passed, Vietnam had passed. The dark spirit of Richard Nixon had been exorcised. In the bilateral context there was a feeling that Pierre Trudeau and Jimmy Carter would be in harmony, that despite the obvious differences in the men, the respect for intellect, values, and vision would be mutual. In Canada, a separatist government in Quebec had been elected in the same season as Carter, the victory sapping any tendency toward moral and political superiority among Canadians. It was a more insecure Canada as 1977 opened, a country more willing to be closer to the United States. Following the distressing years of Kennedy-Diefenbaker, Johnson-Pearson and the distant co-existence ratified under Trudeau-Nixon, hope was considerable in the 110th year of Canadian Confederation that a new era of understanding and cooperation would begin.

On a cold February day, only a month after Carter moved into the White House but a few days after Mexican President Lopez Portillo made his first visit, the optimism increased as Trudeau and the Georgia Democrat met for the first time. With a Canadian cheering section on the White House lawn, with a national TV audience back home, with Margaret Trudeau resplendent in a blue coat with fur trim, with a green-caped Amy Carter waving a Canadian flag, Trudeau, the veteran statesman, cut a strong figure in the crisp air while Carter, the rookie, was deferential. "He was genuinely saying, 'Look, I want to learn,'" remembered Jamieson. "He respected Trudeau." The External Affairs minister had been whisked away on arrival for a secret session with top administration officials to clear up last-minute trouble spots on the bilateral agenda. "They wanted to make sure that nothing spoiled the party." The Carter people discovered Trudeau liked Harry Belafonte, so Belafonte was brought in to entertain. They thought he might enjoy meeting Elizabeth Taylor, so she was brought in. They worried lest not enough congressmen greet the prime minister on the hill and worked hard to get them out. Carter himself prepared for the meeting like no other predecessor. A president who would gain the reputation of being waist-deep in detail, Carter assimilated facts on complex bilateral matters that dazzled Canadian officials. He studied the background history of Trudeau's advisers so that when he met Ivan Head he could talk knowingly about Head's family and his education and leave Trudeau's foreign policy adviser feeling even more important than he already did.[1]

Two developments set the summit apart, giving it a look of importance few others attained. The election of René Levesque vaulted Canada in the American perspective to the level of a quasi-crisis country. Canada couldn't be taken for granted to quite the same extent as before. It was in the clear interest of the United States to have a united Canada on its northern border. Should Quebec split, it could fall under foreign interests inimicable to the United States. The Levesque victory, wrote James Reston, "is regarded by officials here as the worst proposition put to the U.S. Government since Nikita Khrushchev invited it to accept the emplacement of Soviet nuclear missiles in Cuba."

Unique also to the summit was the first invitation in U.S. history to a prime minister of Canada to address the United States Congress. While presidents since FDR had spoken before the Canadian Parliament, it was not an established custom for foreign leaders to address the Congress. On this occasion doubts surfaced as to its advisability. A few days before Trudeau's arrival Mexican leader Lopez Portillo, given the same opportunity, found the chamber three-quarters empty. Tip O'Neill, the crusty old Irishman who was speaker of the House of Representatives, warned that such speeches were a waste of time. Jamieson, fearing a disaster, took Trudeau aside. "I don't know how this thing is going to work out."[2] But the Canadian embassy found many guests, the Oval Office made a better effort than for the Mexican, Congress was no longer in recess, and with the help of page boys, the House was almost full for one of Trudeau's greatest speeches.

"I say to you with all the certainty I can command that Canada's unity will not be fractured," he said. "Revisions will take place: accommodations will be made. We shall succeed." Although a domestic matter, the prime minister, prompting glances of surprise from senators, devoted the heart of his speech to the Quebec issue. Specific Canada-U.S. disputes were ignored totally, Trudeau using the unprecedented occasion to address larger concerns. "Most Canadians understand that the rupture of their country would be an aberrant departure from the norms they themselves have set, a crime against the history of mankind: for I am modest enough to suggest that a failure of this always-varied, often illustrious Canadian social experiment would create shock waves of disbelief among those all over the world who are committed to the proposition that among men's noblest endeavours are those communities in which persons of diverse origins live, love, work and find mutual benefit."

His high regard for the civil rights legislation in the United States prompted Trudeau to make a special tribute to Americans, the message obvious for English Canada. "You have chosen to declare your belief in the protection of minorities, in the richness of diversity, in the necessity of accommodation.... We in Canada, facing internal tensions with roots extending back to the 17th century, have much to gain from the wisdom and discipline and patience which you, in this country, in this generation, have brought to bear to reduce racial tensions, to broaden legal rights, to provide opportunity to all.

"A touch of Churchill," said Hawaii senator Matsunaga. "The most eloquent speech I have ever heard," declared Michigan senator Griffin. To George McGovern it was the best speech in twenty years. Speaker O'Neill reversed his claims on such speeches being a waste of time and Congressman Clement Zablocki confirmed some of the worst Canadian suspicions with his assessment that many of his colleagues didn't believe Canadians could speak such good English.

The show moved back to the White House for a rare event, or at least what the press would come to consider as a rare event, at the Carter White House—an evening of elegance. "My, oh my," proclaimed First Lady Rosalynn Carter, surveying the opulence, "this is really the high cotton, isn't it?" But the high cotton was exactly what the Carters were supposed to lack. One of the major criticisms against them would be their lack of style, their inability to bring the majesty and aura of power to the presidency. It was one of the criticisms which hurt them the most. As they prepared to leave the White House, *Time* magazine's Hugh Sidey bit them: "This time around, let's have a little class," he wrote. Have someone carry the president's suit bag so that "he does not look like the Caterpillar salesman in search of the Holiday Inn." If Willie Nelson is going to sing at the mansion, make him wear "some clothes that dignify the place." When the president goes to New York, have him eat at some place with more status than "Mamma Leone's." Carter did play the role of commoner-in-chief instead of commander-in-chief, in many respects. He temporarily banned the playing of "Hail to the Chief," he banned cocktails at the White House, he sold the *Sequoia*, he carried his own bags, and as a complement to Hamilton Jordan's plough boots, preferred gunboats to wingtips.

But the low-brow presidency was not in evidence during the Trudeau visit. Liz Taylor glittered, dazzling the likes of John Evans, the president of the University of Toronto. "I have met the President but Presidents are transient," he told her. "You are a permanent cultural symbol." She paused: "I've never been called that before."

Margaret Trudeau glittered, turning heads with a knee-length frock that sparked controversial headlines. "They said I wore a short skirt to the President's dinner last night because I had great legs," she said. "Well, why not?" Margaret and Liz got as many column inches as the main players. The president, drawing an analogy to the Trudeau statement that living next to the United States was like sleeping with an elephant, toasted the prime minister. Elephants being the symbol of the Republican party, donkeys the symbol of the Democrats, Carter said, "well, the elephants are gone, the donkeys are here and the donkeys are much more companionable beasts, I think." Don Jamieson, circulating merrily, enjoying his martinis, taking in the beautiful people, was impressed. "Ah, I like this kind of thing,"[3] he said. "Had talk with Vance [Cyrus] today about maritime boundaries. I said, 'look, why don't we settle things this way?' He said, 'okay'. So we did, easy as that."

It was that type of a visit, successful in almost every respect. Carter stickhandled nicely the Quebec question, saying he didn't want to interfere but leaving no doubt as to the U.S. position. "I am not going to make a prediction about that but... if I were making my own preference, it would be that the Confederation continue. A stability in Canada is of crucial importance to us." The only marginal disagreement involved Trudeau's reluctance to support Carter's sweeping attack against the Soviets on human rights, the difference representing Canada's traditional, less paranoiac view of the Soviets. The prime minister returned home to rave reviews and 117 Liberal MPs wore red roses to mark his triumph.

As the personal relationship between Carter and Trudeau opened with promise, so generally did bilateral relations. The two countries signed an agreement to undertake the continent's largest private project in history — the construction of the multi-billion dollar Alaska natural gas pipeline, a plan which would move the energy resource from Alaska through the Yukon, British Columbia, and Alberta to the lower forty eight states. In the unusually cold winter of 1977, Ottawa approved the emergency export of oil and gas to help the United States through severe shortages. "I am all the more appreciative," Carter wrote Trudeau, "because I know that Canada too has been experiencing a particularly hard winter." The United States agreed to stall construction on the Garrison Diversion project, an irrigation scheme in North Dakota which, Manitobans feared, would pollute the rivers of their province. The two sides reached an interim agreement to ease territorial disputes in the east-coast fisheries.

Not since the 1950s had the bilateral relationship and the relationship between president and prime minister been so comfortable and so promising. The so-called "special relationship" had not been resurrected in official terms but for all practical purposes it was in effect. The third option remained on the Trudeau policy books but with the Washington relationship so much better, the pressure to try to implement a third option waned.

As a favour to Carter, Trudeau journeyed to Washington to be present for the signing of the Panama Canal treaty. The ratification of the treaty in Congress marked a major victory for the president and he wanted as much pomp and power lent to the occasion as possible. Trudeau however would remember the day for another reason. In his limousine on the way to the Mayflower Hotel, he was seated next to a man who had one hand in his coat pocket and another on an ear plug. To Trudeau's astonishment, the man, who the prime minister assumed was a security guard, kept attempting to enter into a heavily detailed discussion on Panama and other Central American issues. In the hotel elevator, Trudeau related the story to Jamieson, commenting on the man's wealth of expertise. "He was the strangest damn secret service agent I've ever run across." Jamieson finally interrupted. "I hate to tell you this, Prime Minister. But that was no security guard. That was our ambassador to Latin America."

One of Canada's more colourful ambassadors, so to speak, was Agriculture Minister Eugene Whelan. A Falstaff of Canadian politics, Whelan's barrel-belly protrudes happily over his belt buckle and his head is so large, someone said, that if the rest of his body was in proportion, he'd be eight feet tall. Whelan came to a seminar on world hunger in Washington in 1978 and, following some unsatisfactory grazing at the breakfast buffet, had the gall among the hunger panelists to publicly denounce the offering. "Lousy," he blurted. "They had no scrambled eggs or sausages. Just some old buns. I thought it was going to be like the MPs' breakfast in Ottawa. We get in the cafeteria there and you get to pick out your scrambled eggs or whatever you want." When the Agriculture minister's complaints received front-page treatment in a major Canadian newspaper, Whelan sent the reporter a note complimenting the accuracy of the story.

He sparked another flap when Tom Enders, the American ambassador to Ottawa, began promoting the ageless idea of a free-trade agreement with Canada. Whelan cried that he was "sick and tired" of hearing about it and that it was about time the Americans dropped it. Trudeau had to issue a statement in Enders' defence in the Commons, saying the ambassador had every right to express his views. The towering Enders, like most everyone else, was enjoying the early enthusiasm of Canada-U.S. relations in the Carter years. He was detecting a massive shift in Canadian public opinion toward the Americans.

But as the popularity of Jimmy Carter evaporated, as his effectiveness diminished, as crisis upon crisis manhandled him, the Canadian optimism rapidly faded. It soon became apparent that Jimmy Carter could not translate his good will into good deeds, that the piety of his pronouncements bore no resemblance to actual results. He became a president lurching from crisis to crisis with only a loose grip on the wheel. Energy shortages led to gas lines. Inflation roared on, unemployment plagued him, SALT II was lost, the Soviets encroached without an American response, mini scandals involving his family and friends stained his image, Afghanistan was invaded, Iranians took Americans hostage, Congress rebuked him time after time.

Lost amid the mass of more urgent problems were Canadian questions and promises he had made. Relations with Canada soon fell into their rightful historical state at the White House — the obscure. Consultation with Ottawa on major multilateral developments became minimal. Bilateral issues were handled by the White House in an ad hoc fashion. Accomplishments Ottawa had expected to make in the Carter years were not made.

Carter didn't lose his good will toward Canada or toward Pierre Trudeau nor did the prime minister lose the same toward Carter. Trudeau became sympathetic toward the president, respectful of his integrity, his motivations, his mind, but disappointed with the lack of results. Others would be less charitable. Ivan Head would find dealing with the Carter White House an utterly futile exercise, more futile than with Nixon or Ford. Peter Towe, the urbane Canadian ambassador to Washington, would be found standing in his ornate living-room office before a young group of students from Toronto engaged in the unlikely pursuit of practically cheering the arrival of Ronald Reagan — a right wing, Republican hard-liner, an antithesis of Pierre

Trudeau in almost every respect, a man to whom Canadians felt no affinity. But such was the disappointment with Carter. He had created such high expectations and with high expectations comes the risk of deeper wounds.

The essence of the Carter problem was in his inability to exercise the levers of power with any authority, a problem that was brought about by his inexperience in Washington, his lack of an overall sense of direction, his mediocrity with the television medium, and his feeble relations with a Congress that was becoming increasingly vulnerable to the pressures of special interest groups.

The latter problem, the president and Congress, emerged in the 1970s as a major obstruction to healthy Canada-U.S. relations. In previous decades the presidents exercised stronger authority over Congress meaning that if a treaty was negotiated with Canada, the Canadian government could be reasonably confident that the treaty would clear the Senate and enter into the law books. But during the late sixties and early seventies, changes in the operations on the hill, changes in election financing, the proliferation of election primaries, and the rise of single-issue groups all contributed to a breakdown in political party discipline. Parties no longer possessed the clout to sway their members to vote the party line with the regularity they did in the past. They could no longer finance members' campaigns, control key committee appointments to the same degree or select the nominee for president in the backrooms. Getting legislation passed, even for a president who had his party in majority in Congress, was becoming doubly difficult. Single issue groups such as the anti-abortionists, the environmentalists, the gun owners, were gaining sometimes more control of the elected party representatives than the president. This dispersion of power meant that the Canadian case in Washington had to be sold not just to the White House but to the congressmen individually and to other groups in the capital. Compounding the problem was the tradition in Washington which held that foreign diplomats were to do their lobbying at the Executive Mansion, not on the hill.

For Canada, the new problems with Congress and the problems with the Carter administration were symbolized by the case of the east coast fisheries follies. The dispute over the rich fishing area began after the American revolution in 1776, continued with the Grant-Macdonald dispute following the birth of Canada in 1867, and was still a thorny problem in the 1970s. Though not an issue of national ramifications for Canada in the Trudeau years, though certainly not an issue which galvanized public opinion in Canada, it nonetheless stirred the rancour of Canadian officialdom, encapsulating for Ottawa the frustration with the Carter years and occasioning pronouncements from the likes of Peter Towe that the pendulum of Canada-U.S. relations was swinging again in the wrong direction.

The two sides signed a treaty early in 1979 establishing a management commission to set quotas for Canadian and American fishermen in the waters and sending the question of the ultimate boundary line to international arbitration. For the treaty to take effect senate ratification was needed, meaning that the treaty first had to be approved by the Senate Foreign Relations Committee. But local New England interests, feeling that Canadian diplomats had out-negotiated their own, vigorously protested the pact to the senators representing their region, in particular Claiborne Pell of Rhode Island and Edward Kennedy of Massachusetts.

The Foreign Relations Committee took its time in taking up the treaty. Issues such as SALT II had more priority than Canadian scallop quotas in the Georges Bank and despite complaints from Towe who declared that Canada could not "cry loud enough to be heard" the committee didn't look at the treaty until a year after it had been signed. It became obvious when it did reach the panel that the Carter White House had signed the treaty without ascertaining how it might stand with the committee members. Kennedy, Pell and others indicated they wouldn't pass it without significant changes. Pell wondered what the Canadian fuss about delays and objections was all about. "It's a completely parochial matter on both sides.... This is not of national concern to Canada.... We've got along for many years without a treaty and life is going on."[4] Because of the chemistry of congressional committee politics, the New England senators controlled the foreign relations panel on the fisheries question. Deals were worked out whereby in exchange for helping defeat the Canadian treaty, the east-coast senators would give promise of support to other members on their constituency imperatives. A Canadian diplomat discovered how the system worked when he tried lobbying a committee member on the fish pact. "Listen," said the senator, "I don't bother him [Pell] on the fish and he doesn't bother me on the corn." End of lobbying effort.

Trudeau's office, aware of the outlook, pressed Carter to put some weight behind the treaty, first just to get the committee to look at it, second, to get it to pass it. Bundled under his pile of crises, Carter had little time for a big effort on the fish. To argue the case for the treaty one of the people he put before the panel was Warren Christopher, the usually adroit deputy secretary of state. But either Christopher had lost his usual adroitness or hadn't found the time to prepare his argument. His sole thrust was that the treaty had to be passed to preserve the wonderful relationship between Canada and the United States. Jacob Javits, the veteran New York senator, sawed his case in half, saying that the United States does not go about signing treaties that are not in the best interests of the United States just because it is a good friend of the other country.

With the lobbying effort of the local interests, with the New England senators holding the sway, with the White House effort unconvincing, the fisheries treaty was swept aside by the committee, never getting to the full Senate floor for a vote. Mark MacGuigan, Trudeau's new External Affairs minister, complained bitterly, saying that in future Canada would require prior assurance from the White House of senate support before signing a treaty. Such an assurance, American officials pointed out, was difficult since it would run counter to the intent of the United States constitution.

By 1979, seven years had passed since a president had visited Canada, the last trip being Nixon's. The absence was the longest since the presidents began coming to Canada. In the context of the new, nothing-special arrangement, it was only in keeping. But given the high expectations with Carter, it was a significant slight that he hadn't found the time to visit Canada. Repeated feelers from the prime minister's office were turned back because bilateral problems weren't deemed urgent enough and because Carter was too busy. In the past, issue disputes were not the major motivating factor for bilateral summits. It was not intended that real friends should only get together when there were differences to settle. The summits were displays of friendship, reassurances of friendship.

Finally, as he entered the last year of his stewardship and, without coincidence, as the election campaign opened, Carter decided he would visit Ottawa. His advance people were sent into the capital with instructions to be scrupulously polite. They were told by senior State Department officials about the bully treatment of Haldeman's henchmen in preparing for Nixon's 1972 visit and how it had insulted the prime minister's officials. In the bowels of the State Department the memory had lingered.

But five days before the scheduled November 1979 visit, Iranians stormed the American embassy in Tehran and held Americans captive. Carter cancelled the one-day Canadian excursion and, never willing to reschedule it, became the first president since Hoover to serve a full term without visiting the northern neighbour.

In the hostage crisis, on the response to the invasion of Afghanistan, on other major developments and on bilateral matters there came to be what Ottawa never expected from the Carter administration: in Towe's words, "a marked lack of consultation." It was difficult for Canada, said the ambassador, to support American policies which were never explained. Zbigniew Brzezinski, Carter's National Security Adviser, was schooled in Canada, extremely bright, and the most articulate man in the administration. But he alienated Ottawa. Hawkish in style and statement, he usually led talks with "a jab to the nose" as Head put it and his unsubtle, tough-line approach—a Connally of foreign policy—was unwelcome. Ottawa officials were eventually convinced that Brzezinski had no great love for Canada or its prime minister. Pierre Trudeau's upper-class upbringing in Montreal contrasted with Brzezinski's youth in the same city, setting the two men apart in style and outlook. Secretary of State Cyrus Vance was viewed differently in the Canadian capital. Reliable, understated, without arrogance, he was, in the Canadian perspective, the class person on the Carter team. Jamieson, who felt he had a better relationship with Vance than any Canadian had with any secretary of state in modern times, particularly enjoyed his no-frills nature. During negotiations in Africa on the Namibian question, Jamieson called a late-night meeting and Vance appeared at his door in pyjamas, overcoat, and no socks. In his few dealings with Trudeau, Vance found a depth of mind he was not used to finding in others. Leaving the prime minister's residence one day following talks on arms limitation, he remarked to Jamieson: "I wish European leaders and other heads of state had as strong an understanding of what's involved."

The value of the warm rapport with Vance was offset however by the Brzezinski cold front. "Big Z," as he was nicknamed, was hard-line, Vance soft-line, and Carter somewhere in between. The ambivalent foreign policy which resulted added further to the discouragement of the Trudeau government which, by the time it was temporarily replaced in the spring of 1979 by Joe Clark's Conservatives, had experienced enough in the way of exasperation with the Carter gang and was gaining a renewed interest in the third option.

On the night Joe Clark was elected prime minister, the Canadian embassy in Washington held a $12,000 reception for officials and journalists from both countries. Although the election results were being piped in via a closed television feed from the CBC, ambassador Towe decided that CBC reporters would not be allowed to file live reports from the reception. He reasoned that the reactions of partying diplomats to the election result might not serve as appropriate viewing material. He was right. As the Clark victory became obvious, a gloomy atmosphere gripped the salons. Clark jokes, ridicule of his speaking style, and mocking references to his world tour increased with the drinking, and by the time of his victory speech, some of the lingerers were whistling abuse.

The image of Clark in Washington was little different from that in Canada. Because he was new, because he had a background that was not illustrious, because he had been elected due to dissatisfaction with Trudeau and not satisfaction with himself, and because of his shallow grip of issues as displayed on his world tour, he was regarded as a lightweight. Some, such as Senator Moynihan, professed the belief openly. The Americans had come, slowly at first, to respect the intellect and style of Trudeau. The impressive image he had carved out, despite his marital difficulties, made him a difficult prime minister to follow in the foreign affairs arena.

Clark didn't receive the customary quick invitation to see the president after his victory, the need lessened by the pending Tokyo economic summit where they would see one another along with the other leaders. At the summit the fear that the new prime minister would make a fool of himself was not realized, Carter officials reporting that he held up well. At this time the president was in the throes of another energy crisis and political opponents such as Connally, Kennedy, and California Governor Jerry Brown were proposing a North American common market for the pooling of energy resources. The idea envisaged the United States getting more Canadian and Mexican oil and natural gas in exchange for other benefits. The Carter people realized the idea was a non-starter in both countries,

Canadians feeling it was an energy grab, Mexicans the same. The president was also under attack because the pipeline project with Canada was faltering due to lack of confidence among private financiers. In a speech in Kansas City, Missouri, before four thousand, the president, mentioning Canada for one of the few times out of his many hundred speeches, scolded the critics of his energy relations with Canada and challenged the pipeline companies. Oil producers, he said, "have dragged their feet in helping to finance the pipeline. I have instructed the Secretary of Energy to drag them in and get them going." His voice rising in intensity: "And I will insist personally that this gas pipeline be built." The weak relations with Canada amounted to "misinformation being spread among the American people." But the jaw-boning of oil producers by a president as enfeebled as Carter was to have minimal effect, the case of the pipeline becoming another example, in the view of the Canadian government, of a president failing to live up to his promises.

Clark was the first Tory prime minister to pursue closer relations with the United States. Macdonald, Borden, Meighen, Bennett, and Diefenbaker had all favoured maintaining or strengthening the link with Britain. The Clark government was essentially continentalist in its approach. Free trade became a hot topic. The Clark planners adopted the American idea of mortgage interest deductibility on income taxes. J. Duncan Edmonds, an influential Clark consultant, proposed a treaty of North America embracing further integration. James Gillies, a key Clark adviser and a former professor at UCLA, was examining the American model for more ideas. But Clark lasted less than a year and it was a year in which Carter was caught up entirely in crisis management — energy shortages, SALT II, Iran, Afghanistan and his own re-election prospects. There was no time for new departures.

The Iranian hostage drama, blown many times out of proportion to its real importance by an ABC television soap opera entitled *America Held Hostage*, featured the only major involvement of the Clark government with the Carter White House and witnessed a short revival of the Canada-U.S. kindred spirit. While the embassy was overtaken, six American diplomats escaped and eventually sought refuge in Tehran at the Canadian embassy which then hid the escapees until they could be spirited out of the country via phoney Canadian passports. With the Americans destitute at the door in a time of crisis, the Canadian assistance was less an act of great, altruistic friendship than one of natural, humane response to people in trouble. It could hardly have been expected that Canada or any western country would have thrown the diplomats to the wolves when they came calling for help. But given the stressful American emotional climate, the Canadian deed produced an unprecedented outpouring of thanks from Americans to Canadians. "Thank You Canada" signs were the order of the day. There were take-a-Canadian-to-lunch days, Canada appreciation weeks, free tows for any Canadian who got stranded on highway 81 in West Virginia, motions of gratitude introduced in most legislatures in the country, and thousands upon thousands of letters to the Canadian embassy and consulates.

Carter telephoned Joe Clark, who was in an election campaign, his government defeated on a non-confidence motion. "I want to call... publicly and on behalf of all the American people Joe to thank you and Ambassador Taylor and the Canadian Government and people for a tremendous exhibition of friendship and support and personal and political courage. You've probably seen the tremendous outpouring that has come from the American people on their own volition and it is typical of the way we feel." The Trudeau Liberals feared that the sagging Tories would get a tremendous boost from the story but although the episode proved of some help to him, it was too late for Joe Clark to be saved.

The Liberals were back and so was the third option. There was initial hope that the Canadian caper would produce something in the way of a quid pro quo. Trudeau supported Carter on the Olympic boycott in response to the invasion of Afghanistan and provided reluctant assistance on the grain embargo. But nothing was forthcoming from the White House on the major Canadian concerns—fish treaty, auto pact alterations, pipeline, Garrison Diversion, consultation on multilateral developments. About all Ottawa received in response for its hostage rescue was an embarrassing cover story in *Maclean's*, Canada's national magazine, entitled "Losing to the Yanks" and impugning the government for submitting to domineering treatment at the hands of the Americans. There was, in the last few weeks before Carter's humiliating defeat, a bilateral accord reached. It was in the form of a memorandum of intent to curb the trans-border problem of acid rain, or as some Americans preferred to call it, drifting pollution. The two countries agreed to enforce existing pollution standards with greater vigour while putting working groups to the task of working out details of a treaty. John Roberts, the Canadian environment minister, hailed the agreement as "an extraordinarily important step forward." Ottawa could at last boast of some cooperation with Washington. Ed Muskie, the new secretary of state, was there, smiling, and Douglas Costle, the highly effective head of the Environmental Protection Agency praised the accord as a significant first step in tackling a problem of dramatically increasing importance. Then, as if the Carter years hadn't been frustrating enough for Canadian interests, he declared in an aside: "Of course all this goes to hell if Reagan gets in."

Before Reagan got in, and while the Carter White House was preoccupied with losing the election, the Trudeau government chose the perfect time to quietly take another new and most important advance in the growth of the third option. FIRA, the first step, which limited American investment, had been followed by Bill C-58 which limited the American cultural invasion by making it more difficult for publications like *Time* magazine and *Reader's Digest* to do business in Canada. Now, the National Energy Program proposed the reduction in the American control and ownership of Canadian energy resources from 75 percent to 50 percent. As well as limiting new investment in Canada through FIRA, the Canadian government was now proposing to remove existing American investment. The move toward less dependence on the United States, the move away from the special relationship with the United States, was continuing in significant stride. The Carter-Trudeau period, so auspicious in its beginning, had turned into another in a long series of relationships that corroded the Canadian government's desire to be close to the United States.

CHAPTER SIXTEEN

Moving Backward

THE RELATIONSHIP BEGAN in 1867 with the president, the prime minister, and their countries remote and threatening. Slowly, very slowly, the distance shortened, Canada's fear of annexation disappearing, the belief in the wisdom of continental closeness strengthening. In the late 1930s, the president, Roosevelt, and the prime minister, King, two men in harmony, brought their two countries together in spirit and outlook, forging a psychological bond and shaping a Canada-U.S. relationship which was held up to be the best in the world.

But after a honeymoon which witnessed the American adoption of the Canadian economy, the entire process began to reverse itself. Slowly, very slowly, the relationship cooled, Canadians doubting the advisability of economic and cultural partnership with a domineering giant whose leaders treated them like givens. In the early 1960s, the president, Kennedy, and the prime minister, Diefenbaker, discordant men, split the bond. By the early 1970s the differences were such that the special relationship was declared dead and by the 1980s the Canadian search for another option was quickening. The countries, though welded by forces making separation seem unthinkable, were moving apart as if bound for the distance from which they began.

In a way the forces that drew the countries together—economic and cultural integration—were the forces that were pushing them apart. On being so close Canadians began to regret the overwhelming American influence and the dwarfing of their own identity. In addition there was a growing sense of disillusionment with the partner they had chosen. It was easy, in the period 1940-1960, to embrace the United States. In those decades, the United States was the greatest country in the world, the most powerful economically, the most powerful militarily, the strongest morally. The incentives for Canadians to merge were irresistible. The country next door was the best.

Before 1940, when Great Britain was dominant and the United States less significant, Ottawa had maintained the British connection. In the elections of 1891 and 1911, Canadians had rejected closer union with the United States. Prime Minister Wilfrid Laurier found then that "the best and most effective way to maintain friendship with our American neighbours is to be absolutely independent of them."

In the years after 1960, the decline of the United States began and simultaneously the decline in the Canada-U.S. relationship began. The wounds suffered in American pride in the sixties and seventies were grievous—Vietnam, racial riots, assassinations, Watergate, economic decline, Soviet advances. Canadians and their prime ministers weren't so sure they wanted to associate so closely with a falling giant. The incentive to look elsewhere climbed and it wasn't surprising that having moved away from Britain, which was once number one, and looking to move away from the United States, whose number one status was being threatened, the Canadian government now chose the new emerging world economic leader—Japan. Japan became Canada's second largest trading partner in 1972, replacing Great Britain, and in the following decade Canadian trade with Japan tripled, Ottawa seeking not just a trading relationship but an economic partnership. In addition the Canadian government began reaching out to the newly industrialized countries—Venezuela, Brazil, Saudi Arabia, South Korea, Algeria.

Canadian officials preferred to call the third option developments not a move away from the United States but a move toward other countries. American officials viewing the trend preferred another description of Canadians—fair-weather friends.

Ronald Reagan came to power with a policy designated to bring back the great days of the old partnership. He had been looking in the fall of 1979 for a fresh idea with which to kick off his run for the Republican nomination. He needed something that would put wings on a platform that was essentially a collection of 1950s bromides. What he found was the idea of a North American Accord, an agreement that would provide for a new blend of cooperation on the continent, leading to a greater sharing of its resources for the mutual benefit of Canada, the United States, and Mexico.

It was a difficult vision to criticize. In western Europe the countries had come together first economically in a common market, and later politically in a European parliament, and they were realizing the advantages of closer cooperation. In North America a different story was being written and Reagan's idea for addressing the situation seemed timely.

But what would happen to North American Accord, what would happen to the good intentions, what would happen yet again in the relationship of the president and the prime minister, would only serve to suggest that the trend in the Canada-U.S. relationship was not going to be easily overturned.

On the campaign trail, Americans greeted the Reagan proposal with indifference. Rarely a serious concern of Americans through history, Canadian relations, though troubled, bored his audiences and soon Reagan dropped the accord plan from his speeches, leaving it quietly in the platform books.

In Ottawa, the government discourteously dismissed the accord plan as an attempted energy grab, compelling Reagan to deny he had such intentions.

Eventually, by the time Reagan won the election, the accord was viewed only as an informal concept meaning closer cooperation. To foster it, Reagan wanted a series of meetings with Trudeau at regular intervals, beginning with an unprecedented visit to Canada before his inauguration. But even this minor manifestation of good will was foiled, Trudeau already having committed himself to a world trip on the dates Reagan wished to see him.

Trudeau harboured early suspicions about Reagan's capabilities. Early in the former California governor's campaign for the nomination, the prime minister remarked privately that he found it difficult to understand how the Americans could be serious about making Reagan president. But reflecting the early inclination of most presidents and prime ministers, Trudeau was initially prepared to show good faith and was quickly given the opportunity.

When Reagan came to Ottawa in March of 1981, it was the first visit by a president to Canada in nine years, the longest absence since the 1920s and in itself a sign of deteriorating relations. Strangely however, the supposedly well intentioned Reagan chose the week before the visit to lay a miserable foundation for it. The east-coast fisheries treaty, dropped by the Senate Foreign Relations Committee in the Carter years, still wallowed in the capital, Canadian diplomats hopeful that Reagan, with the help of a new Republican majority in the Senate, would resurrect it. But on the day before his trip, discerning that the pact had no chance with the legislators, Reagan officially withdrew it from consideration. Weeks earlier, weeks later, the move might have made more political sense. Also on the visit's eve the State Department sent a letter to Ottawa protesting Trudeau's National Energy Plan. It was so scalding in tone that upon finding out the details, Secretary of State Alexander Haig apologetically retracted it. At the same time, the White House retreated on its support for the Law of the Sea Treaty, an agreement governing the world's seabeds which was years in the making and which Canada, having high stakes, strongly supported.

The atmosphere created was not exactly a new accord one and Reagan found out as much on the gray, snow-sprinkled day he arrived. Out of respect, and many times out of admiration as well, Canadians virtually always provided United States presidents with warm if not wonderful receptions. Harding, Roosevelt, Truman, Eisenhower, and Kennedy all went away delighted with their Canadian welcomes. One of Johnson's appearances and Nixons's visit met with protests amid the applause but the demonstrators were not yelling about Canada-U.S. relations. They were denouncing the presidents on a multilateral issue—the Vietnam war.

Reagan faced a different situation. No war or multilateral issue of immediate alarm drove hundreds of Canadian protesters to Parliament Hill. The motivating factor was bilateral relations, most specifically the environmental problem of acid rain. While thousands of supporters turned out for earlier presidents, President Reagan found virtually none. Those in attendance who were not demonstrating against him were quiet. His reception, though not poor in comparison to how American presidents are sometimes received in other countries, was an embarrassment by Canadian standards, the worst a president had ever been given on Canadian soil.

When Reagan spoke, the cries of anger from those carrying placards were so disrespectful and disruptive that Prime Minister Trudeau, visibly irritated, decided that as good host he must retaliate. The day before the visit, attacked by the Opposition over the Reagan fish treaty decision, the prime minister had responded in a conciliatory vein. "This Government is putting importance on maintaining good relations with the United States." Now, with Reagan relieved to have made it to the conclusion of his remarks, Trudeau grabbed the microphone and admonished the noise-makers. "Hey guys, when I go to the United States I'm not met with these kinds of signs. You know, the Americans have some beefs against us too but they receive us politely. So how about a great cheer for President Reagan?" There was no cheer, only some polite applause overpowered for the most part by jeers.

For the remainder of the visit, the prime minister maintained an outward posture of respect for the fortieth president, leading Reagan to pronounce, "I like him." But Trudeau was discovering through his talks with the seventy-year-old president that some of his suspicions about the man's ability were accurate. When Reagan expounded his views on the Middle East, in one session, he seemed to sound so simplistic that his American colleagues were embarrassed. Canadians present practically dropped their jaws in amazement. A superb script reader who had the ability on television to appeal to the lowest common denominator, like most top ranked TV programs, Reagan possessed a wonderfully pleasant style and personality. But many Canadians considered him the most uninformed and shallow man to occupy the Oval Office in decades. Ralph Nader's description of Reagan—"he owns more horses than books"—was deemed harshly appropriate. Top Washington observers who weren't sure about his depth soon had their worries confirmed. David Broder was startled by the ignorance displayed by Reagan in some press conferences. James Reston, who had seen so many presidents close up, was appalled. The fear was that Trudeau would not have the patience to tolerate the new president.

Aside from the chasm separating the two leaders in mental fire-power, there was a stark difference in the direction they wished to move their own countries. The United States had always espoused the free enterprise ideology to a greater degree than Canada, which had socialist NDP provincial governments, and Liberal federal govern-ments which chose to dicker with the economy more than American administrations. But the Reagan election of 1980 and the Trudeau re-election the same year polarized the neighbouring countries. Propounding a 30 percent reduction in taxation in his first term, Reagan sought nothing less than a conservative fiscal revolution, moving income in great bulk from the public to the private sector. In contrast, Trudeau, in an interventionist mode, was seeking to reinvigorate nationalism and protection for the Canadian economy with NEP and with a plan to strengthen the Foreign Investment Review Agency.

Reagan and Trudeau clashed on philosophies for third world development, the president favouring free enterprise to great doses of foreign aid. On the Soviet Union, Reagan, an unmitigated cold warrior, opened his dialogue with the Kremlin leaders labelling them liars and cheaters while Trudeau paraded his more progressive view in response to the declaration of marshal law in Poland. Possibly thinking of what the White House might do in a similar situation with the shoe on the other foot, Trudeau, who once declared the equivalent of marshal law in Quebec, asserted that the Soviets were acting with restraint.

Perhaps there had never been as many differences between a president and a prime minister. On acid rain, the hot bilateral issue from the Canadian standpoint, Reagan was hardly riveted, reporters wondering shortly before his Canadian visit whether he had ever heard of it and a spokesman replying that he wasn't sure. With comments like, "if environmentalists had their way we'd all be living in rabbits' holes and birds' nests," Reagan left no mystery to his pro-business bias. He made the remarkable comment during the campaign that trees caused more pollution than automobiles. The line quickly became a subject of ridicule. On passing beautiful forests, reporters on his campaign bus would chastise the foliage for being so menacing to society. Campaigning at a college in California, Reagan was met by a banner students had strung across a beautiful oak: "Chop Me Down Before I Kill Again" it said. For his ceremonial tree plant in Ottawa, reporters asked White House officials if the species would be of a non-polluting variety.

But the issue constituting the major source of aggravation in bilateral relations as the 1980s opened was the National Energy Plan. American big business got to Reagan and its clamour over being discriminated against in the Canadian market was heard. Usually throughout the bilateral history, it was the small power country, Canada, fighting the actions of the big power, the United States, on such items as fish and tariffs—issues that to most Washington politicians and Americans were generally inconsequential. Less often, much less often, as in the case of the National Energy Program, the small power country would make a stroke bold and daring enough to capture attention in the big power capital. Canada, as William Fulbright asserted, wasn't really powerful enough to be unfriendly but occasionally it tried and then it was the presidents who were outraged by the impudence. Grant was ready to "wipe out" Canadian commerce after John A. Macdonald's authorities arrested American fishermen. Kennedy heaped scorn on Diefenbaker for having the gall to talk back. Johnson battered Pearson for speaking out against Vietnam.

The National Energy Program was as philosophically abhorrent to Reagan as it was philosophically compatible to Trudeau. Seeking to have the plan modified or eliminated, the Reagan White House opened a vituperative rhetorical campaign from the State Department, the office of United States Trade Representative Bill Brock and the ambassador to Canada, Paul Robinson. Ottawa refused to flinch under the pressure, its effort led by Allan Gotlieb, the new ambassador to Washington, who in the space of a few months earned the reputation as one of the toughest and best diplomats Canada ever sent to the American capital. When the New York *Times* ran a business column suggesting that Canada be allowed to "freeze in the dark" because of its ill-advised treatment of American oil companies Gotlieb fired off a response making the *Times* column look like it was written in a mental vacuum. Gotlieb's outspoken wife Sondra was finding many Americans in a mental vacuum on the subject of Canada. "For some reason a glaze passes over people's faces when you say Canada," she told the *Times*. "Maybe we should invade South Dakota or something." Gotlieb served as undersecretary of state for External Affairs and his experience and astuteness contrasted that of the ambassador Reagan chose for Canada. Robinson was one of the least qualified Canadian ambassadors in decades. A Chicago businessman with a strong anti-Soviet bent, he was given the posting following his work as an Illinois fund-raiser for Reagan. Possessing neither diplomatic experience nor a sound knowledge of Canada, he was quick to demonstrate his shortcomings. He spoke of the prospects of a Canadian political party that no longer existed, he wrongly listed Yugoslavia and Albania as being under Soviet domination, he lectured Canadian newspaper editors commanding that they run more anti-Soviet stories on their front pages, he denounced Canadian frugality on arms spending and, clearly stepping out of bounds, he ventured into the realm of Canadian domestic policy, complaining that Canada was spending too much on social services.

But Robinson, who entered his post warning of bilateral storm clouds on the horizon, was only reflecting the new climate of Canada-U.S. relations. He was doing little more than the Reagan White House wished him to do. By the summer of 1982, the president and the prime minister, after only a year and a half, had given up on each other. Reagan's good intentions had collided head-on with the reality of the next-to-impossible situation: two dramatically different leaders taking their countries in dramatically different directions. Trudeau's patience with Reagan, impressive at first, evaporated. In a meeting prior to the Ottawa economic summit in 1981, he didn't, as some reports suggested, truculently lecture Reagan but he came close, making a pointed, unyielding affirmation of his energy policy which left Reagan irritated. Then, with the president looking on, he gratuitously told the media that he, not Reagan, would be running the summit agenda and that Reagan would have ample opportunity to have his say when Washington held the summit. At a NATO meeting the following year, the prime minister, departing from his norm of avoiding public criticism of the presidents, lashed out at Reagan's high interest rates and hawkish foreign policy which presumptuously allowed that serious arms reduction talks with the Soviets would be predicated on good Soviet behaviour. Then Trudeau threw a personal insult into the mix. While he and other leaders posed for photographs, an American journalist shouted a question at Reagan who had gained, by this time, a reputation for knowing very little about international affairs. Hearing the question, Trudeau pointed at Secretary of State Alexander Haig and advised the reporter: "Ask Al."

The little war was on. In the Canadian-U.S. lexicon all fights were little ones, barely noticed by the United States media and, because of the great assumption of the bilateral relationship, hardly worried about by the average citizen. The great assumption was that because the countries needed one another so much, because they had so much in common, all disputes between them would be necessarily short-lived and the wonderful friendship would be necessarily restored.

By 1982, with the accord idea a flop, with the president and the prime minister on the rocks, with the governments of the two countries on divergent paths, with the Canada-U.S. *modus vivendi* having become blisters as usual, the great assumption was in worse trouble than at any time since before the war. The drift toward animosity that began in the early 1960s was accelerating and Canada now had two exploratory tools it did not have in those days. One was a new constitution, imbuing a stronger sense of national pride and independence. The other was the third option. The latter had begun with mincing steps in the 1970s and by the end of the decade Canada was still as economically dependent upon the United States as it had ever been. But by the summer of 1982, with MacGuigan speaking of "intense stresses" in the relationship, the third option—though not used frequently by name for fear of offending the Americans—had suddenly taken on a new, meaningful life. The realization was clear that if Canada was to make a significant break from the United States, if it was to fashion a truly different society from the American one, it first had to take steps to diminish its overwhelming economic dependency on the United States. A renewed third option, the National Energy Program being one of its cornerstones, was a major step. For Americans who cared enough to listen—and there still weren't many by 1982 ("We're thought to be boring," declared Gotlieb)—it was a warning that Canada was seriously willing to look elsewhere. It was a warning that the great assumption could no longer be accorded blind faith.

NOTES

CHAPTER ONE

1. Description of Camp David scene compiled from interviews with Charles Ritchie, Rufus Smith, Dick O'Hagan, Dean Rusk, A. E. Ritchie, and others. Also from *Mike: The Memoirs of the Right Honourable Lester B. Pearson* (Toronto: University of Toronto Press, 1973), and an article by Charles Ritchie in *Maclean's* magazine, January 1974.
2. Interview by author with Dick O'Hagan.
3. Memorandum from Dick O'Hagan to Lester Pearson, April 19, 1965.
4. Interview by author with A. E. Ritchie.
5. Memorandum to Lyndon Johnson from McGeorge Bundy, May 1, 1964.
6. Curtis speech at seminar on Canada-U.S. relations, Harvard University, April 27, 1982.
7. Interview by author with Dean Rusk.
8. From the diaries of Hamilton Fish, Library of Congress, Washington, D.C.
9. From the diaries of Arnold Heeney, Public Archives of Canada, Ottawa.
10. Interview by author with Dean Rusk.
11. Ibid.
12. Interview by author with Charlotte Gobeil.
13. Ibid.
14. Interview by author with Ivan Head.

CHAPTER TWO

1. Fish diaries.
2. Ibid.
3. John A. Macdonald papers, Public Archives of Canada, Ottawa.
4. Ibid.
5. James S. Young, *The Washington Community: 1800-1828* (New York: Harcourt, Brace, and Jovanovich, 1968).
6. Macdonald papers.
7. Bruce Hutchison, *The Struggle for the Border* (New York: Longmans, 1955), p. 390.
8. Donald Creighton, *John A. Macdonald: The Old Chieftain* (Toronto: Macmillan, 1955), pp. 70-102.
9. Macdonald Papers.
10. Fish diaries.

CHAPTER THREE

1. All Brown quotations are from his letters in Volume 9 of his papers in the Public Archives of Canada, Ottawa.
2. Fish diaries.
3. Letters of Thomas Bayard, Library of Congress, Washington, D.C.
4. James Morton Callahan, *American Foreign Policy in Canadian Relations* (New York: Macmillan, 1937), p. 412.

CHAPTER FOUR

1. Compiled from Chicago and New York newspaper accounts, October 1899.
2. The *Globe*, November 15, 1897.
3. Minto papers, letter from Laurier to Minto, Vol. 7, p. 39, August 21, 1899.
4. Compiled from Toronto, Chicago, and New York newspaper accounts, October 1899.
5. Franklin D. Roosevelt quotations are from his letters, Library of Congress, Washington, D.C.
6. Mackenzie King quotations are from his diaries, Public Archives of Canada, Ottawa.

CHAPTER FIVE

1. Henry F. Pringle, *The Life and Times of William Howard Taft* (Farrar and Rinehart, 1939), pp. 47, 123, 124, 963.
2. Message from Taft to House of Representatives, January 26, 1911, Library of Congress, Washington, D.C.
3. Correspondence to and from the president and his staff from the Taft papers, Library of Congress, Washington, D.C.
4. Compiled from New York and Washington newspaper accounts, September 1911.
5. Ibid.

CHAPTER SIX

1. *Robert Laird Borden: His Memoirs*, Vol. I & II (Toronto: Macmillan of Canada, 1938).
2. The best account of background events in Canada that led to independent foreign policy may be found in: John S. Galbraith, *The Establishment of Canadian Diplomatic Status at Washington* (Berkeley: University of California Press, 1951).
3. From the papers of Woodrow Wilson, Library of Congress, Washington, D.C.
4. Ralph Allen, *Ordeal By Fire* (New York: Doubleday, 1961), pp. 188-191.
5. From the diary of Robert Borden. Public Archives of Canada, Ottawa.
6. *The Cabinet Diaries of Josephus Daniels* (Lincoln: University of Nebraska Press, 1963), pp. 557-58.
7. King diaries.

CHAPTER SEVEN

1. Andrew Sinclair, *The Available Man* (New York: Macmillan, 1965), p. 283.
2. *The New York Times Magazine*, January 15, 1928.
3. *The Memoirs of Herbert Hoover* (New York: Macmillan, 1952).
4. Ibid.
5. Compiled from Vancouver, New York, and Washington newspaper reports.

CHAPTER EIGHT

1. Hoover papers, Herbert Hoover Library, West Branch, Iowa.
2. Hoover papers, MacNider memorandum to Assistant Secretary of State William R. Castle Jr., October 14, 1930.
3. Hoover papers, memorandum to Under Secretary of State William Phillips from subordinate on strategy to be employed in Bennett visit.

CHAPTER NINE

1. All Mackenzie King quotations in this chapter are from his diaries and correspondence unless otherwise indicated.
2. Roosevelt's experiences at Campobello compiled from: Frank Friedel, *Franklin D. Roosevelt: The Ordeal* (Boston: Little, Brown and Company, 1954), pp. 92-105; Finis Farr, *FDR* (New York: Arlington House, 1972), pp. 42, 126-133; and several newspaper and magazine accounts.
3. Roosevelt quotations in this chapter are from his correspondence in the Roosevelt Library, Hyde Park, New York, unless otherwise indicated.
4. Roosevelt papers, Roosevelt Library, Hyde Park, New York.
5. King diaries.
6. Roosevelt papers.
7. Interview by author with Jack Pickersgill.
8. Interview by author with Paul Martin.
9. Interview by author with James Reston.
10. King diaries.
11. Ibid.
12. Ibid.
13. Roosevelt papers.
14. King diaries.

CHAPTER TEN

1. Harry Truman Library, Independence, Missouri.
2. King diaries.
3. Lester B. Pearson, *Mike: The Memoirs of the Right Honourable Lester B. Pearson*, Vol. I (Toronto: University of Toronto Press, 1973), p. 240.
4. Ibid.

5. Ibid.
6. King diaries.
7. Reston interview.
8. Interviews by author with Simon Reisman, J. L. Granatstein, Jack Pickersgill, A. E. Ritchie. Also from State Department correspondence and the King diaries.
9. Pickersgill interview.
10. King diaries.
11. John W. Holmes, *The Shaping of Peace: Canada and the Search for World Order*, Vol. 2 (Toronto: University of Toronto Press, 1982), p. 145.
12. Quotations and description of meeting from notes taken by Truman adviser David Bell who was in attendance. Papers from Harry Truman Library.

CHAPTER ELEVEN

1. Martin interview.
2. Lester B. Pearson, *Mike*, Vol II, p. 69.
3. Ibid.
4. Pickersgill interview.
5. Eisenhower Library, Abiline, Kansas.
6. Interview by author with Eugene Griffin.
7. From the diaries of Arnold Heeney.
8. Eisenhower Library.

CHAPTER TWELVE

1. Theodore C. Sorensen, *Kennedy* (New York: Harper and Row, 1965), pp. 58, 59.
2. Heeney diaries.
3. From the president's papers, Kennedy Library, Boston, Ma.
4. Interview by author with Dean Rusk.
5. Kennedy Library.
6. Interview by author with Rufus Smith.
7. Ibid.
8. Rusk interview.
9. Kennedy Library.
10. Ibid.
11. Ibid.

12. Interview by author with Stu Macleod.
13. Rusk interview.
14. Benjamin C. Bradlee, *Conversations with Kennedy* (New York: W. W. Norton and Company, 1975).
15. Interview by author with Charles Ritchie.
16. J. L. Granatstein, *A Man of Influence* (Ottawa: Deneau, 1981), p. 353.
17. Peter Stursberg, *Diefenbaker: 1962-1967 Leadership Lost* (Toronto: University of Toronto Press, 1976), p. 17.
18. Rusk interview.
19. Peter C. Newman, *Renegade in Power* (Toronto: McClelland and Stewart, 1963), p. 337.
20. Rusk interview.
21. Charles Ritchie inverview.
22. Rusk interview.
23. Interview by author with Benjamin Bradlee.
24. Interview by author with Peter Trueman.
25. From transcript of interview with Hugh Sidey in oral history, Kennedy Library.

CHAPTER THIRTEEN

1. Charles Ritchie interview.
2. Lester B. Pearson, *Mike*, Vol III, p. 100.
3. Ibid.
4. Johnson Library, Austin, Texas.
5. Story of visit to ranch compiled from interviews with Paul Martin, Dean Rusk, Dick O'Hagan, Charles Ritchie, and Pearson memoirs.
6. Martin interview.
7. Roger Frank Swanson, *Canadian-American Summit Diplomacy, 1923-1973: Selected Speeches and Documents* (Toronto: McClelland and Stewart, 1975), p. 241.
8. Martin interview.
9. Johnson Library.
10. Rusk interview.
11. Charles Ritchie interview.
12. Ibid.
13. A. E. Ritchie interview.
14. Ibid.
15. Rufus Smith interview.
16. Pickersgill interview.

17. Pearson papers, Public Archives of Canada, Ottawa.
18. Rufus Smith interview.

CHAPTER FOURTEEN

1. Interview by author with Ivan Head.
2. Nixon memoranda obtained through U.S. Freedom of Information Act, U.S. State Department.
3. Henry Kissinger, *White House Years* (New York: Little, Brown and Company, 1979), p. 383.
4. Interview by author with Mitchell Sharp.
5. Rufus Smith interview.
6. Memoranda obtained through U.S. Freedom of Information Act, U.S. State Department.
7. Interview by author with Simon Reisman.
8. Sharp interview.
9. Story of Nixon's and Kissinger's evenings in Ottawa compiled from interviews with Ivan Head, A. E. Ritchie, Charlotte Gobeil, Rufus Smith, and others.
10. Kissinger, *White House Years*, p. 383.
11. Reisman interview.
12. Interview by author with Don Jamieson.
13. Smith interview.
14. John Hay, "Still Sleeping with an Elephant," *Maclean's* magazine (January 26, 1981).
15. Ibid.
16. Head interview.

CHAPTER FIFTEEN

1. Head interview.
2. Jamieson interview.
3. State dinner atmospherics from Val Sears in the Toronto *Star*, February 23, 1977.
4. Interview by author with Claiborne Pell.

INDEX

Abbott, John, 52
Anti-ballistic Missile system (ABMs), 238-39, 240, 242
Acheson, Dean, 109, 155, 172
Acid rain, 275-76, 282
Ackley, Gardner, 231
Adams, Henry, 51
Adams, Sherman, 172
Afghanistan, 272
Agnew, Spiro, 257
Alabama claims, 12, 23, 26
Alaska boundary dispute, 52, 54-65, 83, 85
Alexander, Governor-General, 158
Allingham, Chesley, 117
Alsop, Joseph, 232-33
Alverstone, Lord, 62-64
Amchitka, 242
Annexation, 12, 22-25, 37, 40, 72-81, 86
Appleton, Henry, 77
Arctic sovereignty, 243
Armistice Day, 153
Armour, Norman, 117, 120-21
Arthur, Chester, 38-39, 94
Articles of the Confederation, American, 240
Assimilation of French in Quebec, 139-40

Associated Press, 10, 106
Atherton, Ray, 151, 156
Attlee, Lord Clement Richard, 148, 150, 151, 153
Atomic energy, 149-51, 153-54. *See also* Nuclear weapons
Austin, Jack, 257
Auto pact, 219-22, 227, 239
Aylesworth, A. B., 62-63

Bain, George, 3-5, 205
Baker, Newton, 86
Ball, George, 197, 203, 223-24
Bank Act, 232
Bay of Pigs. *See* Cuba
Bayard, Thomas, 40-41, 83
Belafonte, Harry, 263
Bell, David, 165
Bennett, E. H., 115
Bennett, R. B.: admiration for Hoover, 16, 101-07; contempt for FDR, 108-12, 120
Benson, Edgar, 243-44
Bering Sea dispute, 49, 54, 86
Berlin Wall, 239
Bill C-58, 276
Blaine, James G.: annexation desire, 38, 46; presidential nomination, 39;

reaction to Cleveland's embargo, 43; secretary of state under Harrison, 46-49

Bluenose, 117, 261

BOMARC missiles, 208

Borden, Laura, 83, 86

Borden, Robert: contempt for presidents, 16; friend of Teddy Roosevelt, 65; prime minister, 80, 82-83, 85-89; reciprocity, 73, 76; unveiling of portrait, 158

Bostock, Hewitt, 100

Boston *Post*, 182

Boundaries (Canada-U.S.), 25

Boutwell, George, 27

Bowell, Mackenzie, 52

Bradlee, Ben, 208-09, 210, 260

Britain: *Alabama* claims, 12, 23, 26; control of Canadian foreign policy, 13, 15-16, 24-32; end of control, 13, 34; meetings between leaders of and U.S. presidents, 5; military contributions to NATO, 9; preparation for WW I, 130-34; withdrawal of Canadian fishing privileges, 25

British Columbia, 124

British Commonwealth Air Training Plan, 139-40

Brock, Bill, 283

Broder, David, 215, 281

Brooklyn *Citizen*, 44-45

Brooks, Arthur, 99

Brown, Anne, 34

Brown, George, 33-36

Brown, Jerry, 273

Bryan, William Jennings, 56, 87

Bryce, James, 66, 76, 85

Brzezinski, Zbigniew (Big Z), 272

Byrd, Harry, 167

Brynes (American secretary of state), 150

Buffalo *Evening News*, 64

Bundy, McGeorge, 6-7, 197, 203, 205, 211, 226

Burns, General (Canadian; Suez crisis), 173

Butterworth, Walton, 198, 203, 205, 207, 232

Cadieux, Marcel (Canadian ambassador to U.S. under Trudeau), 252, 256

Calder, John, 116

Cambodia, 255-56

Camp, Dalton, 201

Camp David, 1-5, 16, 226-27

Campobello International Park, 229-30

Campobello, New Brunswick, 8, 114-17, 229

Canadian constitution, 285

Canadian embassy, establishment of, 141

Canadian Legation, establishment of, 88-92

Canadian Mercantile Bank, 231-32

Candian Press, 4, 194

Caron, Adolphe, 44

Carter, Amy, 263

Carter, Jimmy, 15, 241, 262-76

Carter, Rosalynn, 265

Castle, William, 104-05

Chamberlain, Joseph, 41-42

Chapple, Joe, 98

Chevrier, Lionel, 165

Chicago *Tribune*, 175

China, People's Republic of, 193, 217, 232, 246

Christie, Ambassador (Canadian), 133

Christopher, Warren, 271

Churchill, Winston, 130, 131-34, 138, 143

Citibank of New York, 231-32

Clark, James Beauchamp, 72-73, 80

Clark, Joe, 273-75

Clark, Lewis, 154

Clarkson, Stephen, 240

Clemenceau, Georges, 83

Cleveland, Grover, 12, 37, 39-42, 43-46

"Code of Conduct," 225

Cold War, 174

Columbia River Treaty, 180, 218-19

Connally, John, 220-21, 247-48, 249, 273

Coolidge, Calvin, 13, 90-92, 100

Conscription, 143-44

Corby case, 152

Cortines, Adolfo Ruiz, 171

Costle, Douglas, 276

Crerar, Thomas Alexander, 142

Cuba, 186-88, 195-96, 198-201

Council of Economic Advisers, 231

Curtin, John, 119

Curtis, Kenneth, 7-8

Dafoe, J. W., 62
Daniels, Joe, 89
David J. Adams, 39-40
Davis, Norman, 117
Declaration on Atomic Energy, 154
de Gaulle, Charles, 5, 201, 217, 240, 241
De Grey, Lord, 30-31
Democratic Review, 24
Dennett, Tyler, 61
Diefenbaker, John: contempt for Kennedy, 16, 18-19; damaging press release, 6, 203-06, 236; prime minister during Eisenhower administration, 11, 175-80; prime minister during Kennedy administration, 11, 18, 181-210, 283; Nixon contribution to memorial fund, 257
Dillon, Douglas, 224
Diplomacy in the Nuclear Age, 212
Douglas, Tommy, 199-200, 204, 207, 239
Drapeau, Jean, 234
Dufferin, Governor-General, 37
Dulles, John Foster, 15, 170-72
Dunn, James, 86
Dupuy, Pierre, 234

Early warning systems, 156
East-coast fisheries treaty, 269-71, 280-81
Economic independence, 245, 252
Eden, Anthony, 173-74
Edmonds, J. Duncan, 274
Ehrlichman, John, 256
Eisenhower, Dwight: friendship with Diefenbaker, 18, 175-80; ignorance about Canada, 9, 11, 15; president, 166-80, 182, 250; Prime Minister St. Laurent, 16, 166-75; return of the Republican party, 14-15; WW II, 138
Edward (king of England), 126
Eisenhower, Mamie, 169
Elizabeth (queen of England), 176
Embargo Canada bill (1888), 43-46
Enders, Tom, 268
Environmental Protection Agency, 276
Espionage, 151, 152-54
Evans, John, 265
Evans-Novak column, 4
Evarts, William, 38
Expo '67, 233

External Affairs, Department of, 85

Fassett, Senator (Republican), 43
Fenians, 28
Fielding, W. S., 70, 79, 89
Fisheries jurisdiction disputes, 22, 25-32, 38-42, 54, 86, 283. *See also* East-coast fishing treaty
Foreign Investment Review Agency (FIRA), 245-46, 255, 276, 282
Fish, Hamilton, 23-32, 34-35
Fisher, Douglas, 204
Ford, Gerald, 241, 257-61
Foster, John J., 78
Free trade agreement, 12-13, 16
Free Trade treaty attempt, 35-36
Frost, Leslie, 165
Fulbright, William, 239, 240, 283

Galbraith, John Kenneth, 215
Galt, Alexander, 83-84
Gandhi, Indira, 238
Garfield, James, 38
Geddes, Auckland, 90
George, Lloyd, 83, 86-87
George VI (king of England), 119, 129-30
Gertrude Thébaud, 117
Gettysburg Address, 177
Gillies, Jim, 274
Gladstone, William E., 22-32
Glazebrook, George, 15, 172
Globe and Mail, 2-3, 205
Gobeil, Charlotte, 20-21, 254, 259
Goldwater, Barry, 218
Good Neighbor policy, 128
Gordon, Walter, 231
Gotlieb, Allan, 283, 285
Gotlieb, Sondra, 283
Goulet, Robert, 240
Gouzenko, Igor, 151
Grant, Ulysses S.: *Alabama* claims, 12, 23, 26; desire to annex Canada, 22-25, 36; fisheries jurisdiction issue, 22, 25-32, 283; free trade treaty attempt, 35-36
Great Britain. *See* Britain
Great Depression, 104-05
Green, Howard, 177-78, 184-88, 194, 200
Grey, Governor-General, 64-65, 67, 70

Griffin, Eugene (Ottawa correspondent for Chicago *Tribune*), 175
Group of Seven, 141-42

Haig, Alexander, 280, 284
Haldeman, Bob, 19-20, 253-54, 256
Halibut Treaty, 90
Hamilton, Alvin, 207
Hammarskjold, Dag, 171, 173
Hammond, John Hays, 75
Hanson, R. B., 142
Harding, Florence, 93, 98-99
Harding, Warren G., 13-14, 89, 93-100, 250
Hartness, Douglas, 193-94, 204-05
Harriman, Averell, 232
Harrington Lake, 11-12, 234
Harrison, Benjamin, 46-49
Harvard University, 118, 119, 123, 215
Hay, John, 55-56, 59-64, 84
Hayes, Rutherford B., 12, 37-38
Head, Ivan, 241-57 passim, 263, 272
Heeney, Arnold, 6, 15, 170-79 passim, 182-87, 230
Henry, William, 37-38
Hepburn, Mitch, 111
Herridge, William, 107-09
Herter, Christian, 180
Hickerson, Jack, 161
Hilles, Charles, 76, 77-78
Hitler, Adolf, 131, 134
Hiroshima, 149-50
Holmes, Oliver Wendell, 62
Hoover, Herbert, 13, 16, 92, 95-98, 102-107
Hoster, William, 77
Hughes, Charles, 90
Hull, Cordell, 120, 128. 144
Humphrey, Hubert, 224
Huntington, L. S., 83
Hyde Park Agreement, 136, 149, 159

Ickes, Harold, 122
Immigration into Canada, 66-67
Import surcharge, 243-45, 247
Industry and Humanity, 122, 124
International Commission of Control and Supervision in Vietnam, 256
International Joint Commission, 85
International Monetary Fund, 147
Iran, 272, 274-75

Jackson, A. Y., 141-42
Jamieson, Don, 238, 255, 262-64, 266, 267, 272
Japan, 10, 66, 124, 244, 252, 278
Javits, Jacob, 271
Jefferson, Thomas, 197
Jetté, Sir Louis, 62-63
Johnson, Andrew, 24-25
Johnson, Lady Bird, 1, 216, 217, 220
Johnson, Lyndon Baines, 1-5, 11-12, 219-35, 238, 283
Jordon, Hamilton, 265
Juliana (princess of the Netherlands), 136-37

Katz, Julius, 257
Kaysen, Carl, 196
Keenleyside, H. L., 131, 132
Kennedy, Caroline, 198
Kennedy, Edward, 270, 273
Kennedy, Jacqueline, 189, 259
Kennedy, John: attitude toward Diefenbaker, 18-19; mispronunciation of Diefenbaker's name, 11, 18, 184; president, 181-211, 212-16, 250, 283; treatment by Diefenbaker, 16, 167; upset of Diefenbaker government, 6, 203-06
Kennedy, Robert, 200-01, 213
Khrushchev, Nikita, 199-200
King, J. H., 96
King, Tom, 91
King, William Lyon Mackenzie: contempt for free-trade package, 16; Japanese immigration issue, 66-67; prime minister, 91-92, 93-100, 101, 117-46, 147-62; special relationship with FDR, 8-9, 14, 113, 117-46; special relationship with Truman, 14, 147-62
Kipling, Rudyard, 79
Kissinger, Henry, 20-21, 241-42, 250, 252-56, 259
Knox, Philander, 73-74, 78, 127
Korean Commission, 160-61
Korean war, 163-64
Krock, Arthur, 6

La Follette, Robert, 77
Laird, Melvin, 239
Lank, Norman, 114, 117

Lansdowne, Governor-General, 45
Lansing, Robert, 86, 89
Lapointe, Ernest, 90
Laurier, Wilfrid: contempt for presidents, 16; creation of Department of External Affairs, 85; free-trade fetish, 37; prime minister, 16, 51-67, 68-81; reciprocity, 48, 68-81
Law of the Sea Treaty, 280
Lawrence, Bill, 215
Leacock, Stephen, 78-79
League of Nations, 87-88, 125
Lee, Arthur Hamilton, 58
LeHand, Marguerite (Missy), 127-28, 130
Levesque, René, 263-64
Lewis, David, 248
Lincoln, Abraham, 24, 55, 117
Lincoln, Mrs. (Kennedy's secretary), 209
Lippmann, Walter, 2, 168
Lodge, Cabot, 171
Lodge, Henry Cabot, 41, 60, 62
London *Express*, 64
London *Morning Post*, 58
London *Saturday Review*, 62
Low, Maurice, 58
Lynch, Charles, 193, 207, 208

MacArthur, Douglas, 163
McCarthy era, 175
MacDonald, Bruce, 3
Macdonald, James A., 69-70
Macdonald, John A.: anti-annexation, 38-40; contempt for U.S. presidents, 16; fisheries jurisdiction settlement, 22, 25-32, 283; prime minister, 22-32, 33-50; reaction to Cleveland's embargo, 43-44; tariff reaction, 47-50
McDougall, William, 177
MacEachen, Allan, 258, 261
McGhee, George, 203
McGovern, George, 265
MacGuigan, Mark, 271, 285
Mackasey, Bryce, 261
Mackenzie, Alexander, 32-39, 84-85
Mackenzie, Arch, 4
Mackenzie, Ken, 215-16
McKinley, William, 16, 47, 51-57, 84
Maclean's magazine, 275

Macleish, Archibald, 134-35
Macleod, Stu, 197
Macmillan, Harold, 200, 202
McNamara, Robert, 208, 222, 229
MacNider, Handford, 105-07
Maffre, John, 209
Malcolm, James, 103
Manifest Destiny philosophy, 23-25
Marchand, Jean, 20
Marion, Ohio *Star*, 94
Mariscal, Don Ignacio, 56
Marshall Plan, 149
Martin, Paul: anti-American attitude, 17-18; King-Roosevelt relationship, 123; Lyndon Johnson, 222, 233; Organization of American States, 194; United Nations, 171, 220-21; USSR, 220-21, 232; Vietnam, 223
Massey, Vincent, 90-92, 103, 109, 156
Means, Gaston, 99
Meighen, Arthur, 89
Merchant, Livingstone, 6, 9, 187-207 passim, 230
Minto, Governor-General, 54, 56
Missing-memo affair, 191-92, 197, 208-10, 215
Mitchell, John, 256
Monroe Doctrine, 125
Montreal *Gazette*, 112
Montreal *Standard*, 87
Montreal *Star*, 79, 203, 205, 209
Morrison, Harold, 194
Moyers, Bill, 218
Moynihan, Senator, 273
"The Muckers," 182
Muskie, Ed, 276

Nader, Ralph, 281
Nagasaki, 149-50
National Energy Program (NEP), 276, 280, 282-85
NATO: Canadian military contributions to, 9; Martin, Paul, 171; nuclear weapons for Allies, 6-7, 202-03; Trudeau threat to withdraw, 243, 284; USSR, 220-21
Nehru, Prime Minister (of India), 174
New Deal (Roosevelt), 110-12
New Deal, Mini (Bennett), 112
Newfoundland, 138, 232
"New Frontier," 183

Newsweek magazine, 206-07, 208
New York *Herald*, 27
New Moon, 114
New York *Star*, 33
New York *Times*, 6, 42, 70, 115-16, 123, 168-69, 215
Nixon, Richard: April summit speech, 251-52; Canadian trade importance, 10, 244-45; Diefenbaker memorial fund, 257; end of Canada-U.S. special relationship, 19-21, 213, 245, 252, 258-59; name for Trudeau, 12, 256-57; president, 236-57; vice-president, 180
Nobel Peace Prize, 196
NORAD, 200-01, 203
Norman, Herbert, 175
Norris, Congressman, 73
Norstad, Lauris, 202
North America Accord, 279, 285
North American Air Defense Command, 178
Noyes, Frank, 106
Nuclear weapons issue, 193, 198, 201-06, 214, 237, 243

Ochs, Adolph, 115
Ogdensburg pact, 149
O'Hagan, Dick, 3, 4-5, 215, 219, 253
Onassis, Jacqueline Kennedy, 259. *See also* Kennedy, Jacqueline
O'Neill, Tip, 264, 265
Operation Rolling Thunder, 1, 223-24
Organization of American States (OAS), 18-19, 187-91, 194
Organization of Petroleum Exporting Countries (OPEC), 237, 255
Osborn, Charles, 79
O'Sullivan, John, 24
Ottawa *Citizen*, 208
Oxford University, 229

Panama Canal, 10, 94
Panama Canal Treaty, 267
Paris Peace Conference, 10, 16, 83, 86
Pearson, Lester (Mike): anti-American attitude of Canadians, 17; atomic energy concerns, 153, 202-04, 207; Canadian ambassador to U.S., 139-57 passim; Cuba, 199; Hyannis, 210, 214-16; Kennedy eulogy, 212-13;

Nobel Peace Prize, 196; prime minister, 1-5, 9, 11-12, 15, 16, 210-35, 283; speech writer, 110-11
Pearson, Maryon, 220
Peffer, William, 58
Pell, Claiborne, 270
Pelletier, Gérard, 250
Pentagon, 155-56, 201, 239
Pepper, Charles, 76, 77
Pericles, 219
Perkins, Frances, 122
Permanent Joint Board on Defense, 133-34, 144
Phillips, Bruce, 4
Phillips, William, 103, 111, 121
Pickersgill, Jack: anti-American attitude of prime ministers, 17; as aide to Mackenzie King, 123; Korean commission, 161; as aide to St. Laurent, 165, 171, 172; attitude toward Butterworth, 207; Soviet air rights, 232
Pierrepont, Moffat J., 133, 138
Poland, 282
Porter, William, 260
Portillo, Lopez, 263, 264
Power, Charles G. (Chubby), 142
Powers, David, 215
Presidents. *See* specific names
Prime Ministers. *See* specific names

Quebec, separatist government, 263-65, 266
Quebec conferences, 141-43, 150
Queen's University, 127

Ralston, J. L., 132
Reader's Digest, 276
Reagan, Ronald, 15, 241, 278-85
RCAF, 185
Reciprocity, 37, 48, 68-81
Reedy, George, 1
Reisman, Simon, 160, 247-48, 255
Republican party, 14-15
Reston, James, 123, 157, 168, 281
Richard, S. R., 76
Ritchie, Albert Edgar (Ed), 5, 189, 229, 232-33, 241, 253
Ritchie, Charles, 2, 19, 198, 207, 212-29 passim
Roberts, John, 276

Robertson, Norman, 151-52, 175, 200, 207
Robinson, Basil, 183
Robinson, Paul, 283-84
Rockefeller, James, 232
Rogers, William, 241, 256
Roosevelt, Eleanor, 14, 115, 119, 128
Roosevelt, Elliott, 116, 126
Roosevelt, Franklin Delano: Campobello, 8, 69, 114-17, 229-30; pledge of American military support, 73, 127, 250; president, 108-12, 113-46; special relationship with Canada, 8-9, 14
Roosevelt, James, 123
Roosevelt, Theodore: Alaska boundary dispute, 52, 58-65; Canadian attitude toward, 17; Canadian representation, 84; desire for annexation, 12, 75-76; Japanese immigration, 66; reciprocity under Taft, 71-72; president, 51, 69, 82; trip to Panama, 10, 94; WW I, 86
Root, Elihu, 65-66
Ross, G. W., 55-56
Rostow, Walt, 188, 191, 229, 233. *See also* Missing-memo affair
Royal Canadian Navy, 185
Rush-Bagot Agreement (1817), 54
Rusk, Dean: anti-American attitude of Canadians, 17-18, 19; mispronunciation of Diefenbaker's name, 11; secretary of state, 183-205 passim; 221-33

Sackville-West, Sir Lionel, 41, 46, 85
Saint John *Telegraph-Journal*, 117
St. Laurent, Louis: Korean Commission, 160-61; prime minister during Eisenhower, 16, 166-75; prime minister during Truman, 10-11, 162-65; St. Lawrence Seaway, 16
St. Lawrence Seaway, 16, 92, 102-08, 118, 164-65, 181-82, 242
Salinger, Pierre, 209
Salisbury, Lord, 56
San Francisco *Chronicle*, 30
Schlesinger, Arthur, Jr., 186-87
Schmidt, Helmut, 259
Seaborn, Blair, 223
Segretti, Donald, 46

Sequoia, 153, 261, 265
Sevigny, Pierre, 199-200, 202
Sharp, Mitchell, 231, 241-56 passim
Sidey, Hugh, 209-10, 265
Sifton, Clifford, 53, 62
Simpson, Wallis, 126
Sinclair, Gordon, 250
Sirica, John, 256
Skowcroft, Brent, 261
Skybolt, 202-03
Sky Shield exercise, 178
Smalley, George, 59
Smith, Adam, 104
Smith, Bob, 21
Smith, Rufus, 188, 191, 231, 233, 244-55 passim
Smoot-Hawley tariff act, 120, 144
Sorenson, Theodore, 191, 197
Southam News, 193, 205, 207
Soviet Union. *See* USSR
"Special relationship," 19-21, 213, 245, 252, 258-59
Stalin, Joseph, 143
Stalwarts, 38
Stanfield, Robert, 245
Statute of Westminster (1931), 149
Stephen, George, 48
Stettinius, Edward, 146
Stewart, John, 78
Stimson, Henry, 105, 107, 134
Strickler, Frank, 256
Suez crisis (1956), 172-74

Taft, Annie, 68-69
Taft, Charles, 68
Taft, Horace, 71, 77, 80
Taft, William Howard: annexation fear, 72-81; free-trade agreement, 12-13, 16; Mexico/Panama Canal visits, 94; reciprocity, 37, 68-81
Taylor, Elizabeth, 263, 265-66
Taylor, Kenneth, 275
Teapot Dome scandal, 96
Temple University, 224, 238
Thant, U, 10
Third option, 255, 276, 278, 285
Third world development, philosophy of, 282
Thompson, John, 41, 52
Thompson, Robert, 204
Thomson, Will, 64

Thornton, Sir Edward, 23, 85
Time magazine, 209, 265, 276
Tito, Marshall, 16
Toledo Blade, 217
Toronto Globe, 34, 70, 91
Toronto Star, 191, 240
Toronto World, 64
Towe, Peter, 268, 270, 272, 273
Trail smelter case, 108, 111
Treaty of 1818, 39
Treaty of 1854, 39, 120
Treaty of 1871, 39
Treaty of Washington, 31-32, 33, 39, 83
Trudeau, Justin, 254
Trudeau, Margaret, 263, 266
Trudeau, Pierre: attitude toward U.S., 16; definition of Canada-U.S. relationship, 5; prime minister, 11, 12, 236-57, 257-61, 262-76, 279-85
Trueman, Peter, 203, 205, 209-10, 215
Truman, Bess, 155
Truman, Harry: president, 147-65, relationship with Mackenzie King, 14, 16, 146, 147-62; visit by Louis St. Laurent, 10-11, 162-65
Truman, Margaret, 159
Tupper, Charles, 27, 40-41, 48, 52, 56, 83
Turner, George, 60
Tweedsmuir, Governor-General, 123, 127
Twenty-ninth parallel, 235

UCLA, 274
United Nations: Atomic Energy declaration on, 153-54; Canada's role, 147, 149, 219; Cyprus peace-keeping mission, 224-25; member additions, 170-71; naming of, 141; USSR refusal to pay dues, 220-21
United Nations Conference, 147, 151

USSR, 9, 195-96, 198-200, 220-21, 282
U.S.S. Henderson, 94
U.S. Tariff Commission, 167-68

Vaccaro, Tony, 10
Valenti, Jack, 2, 228
Vance, Cyrus, 266, 272
Vancouver Daily Province, 63-64
Vancouver Sun, 96, 99
Vietnam, 1-2, 16, 220-37, 249, 253-56

Wales, Prince of (1920), 96
Wall Street Journal, 3
War of 1812, 148
War Measures Act, 257
Washington, George, 27, 94, 117
Washington Post, 44, 45, 209, 260
Washington Star, 106, 215
Washington treaty. See Treaty of Washington
Watergate, 237, 250, 255, 257-58
Webb, James, 164
Welles, Sumner, 130
West Germany, 9, 227
Wheat, 193
Whelan, Eugene, 267-68
White, Henry, 61
Wilkie, Wendell, 133
William and Mary College, 162
Wilson, Harold, 220
Wilson, William, 11
Wilson, Woodrow: interest in Canada, 13, 218; to Paris Peace Conference, 10, 16, 87-88, 94; president, 86, 89
Woodsworth, J. S., 112
World War I, 86-89
World War II, 130-36, 138
Wrong, Hume, 105, 106

Zablocki, Clement, 12, 265